<u>Part 1</u>

An Endless Quest

Chapter 1

The Quest Begins

As a boy I left my father, ran off to other lands, Tried hard to become a tiger —didn't even make it to cat! If you ask what kind of man I am now, Just the same old Eizo I've always been.

Ryokan, (1758-1831)

Moving slowly across the dojo floor, I walked toward the east wall, which was lined with makiwara (punching posts). A squeak, hardly noticeable, arose from the floor. The floor was very old, although not as old as I, and was in constant need of repair. To replace it, however, would be unthinkable. My teacher, Doctor Tsuyoshi Chitose, grandson of Sokon "Bushi" Matsumura and the founder of the Chito-ryu style of karate, had practiced on this floor. On this very floor he had taught, trained, and demonstrated his art. This floor and the wood which comprised it were historical and could not be replaced. It would be repaired again and again for decades to come. I stepped in front of the post, which was less than five feet tall, the top eight inches wrapped in straw. I slid my left foot forward and settled into a seisan dachi (stance). My right fist shot forward a split second later, striking the straw. The post bent backward under the impact. My fist slammed into the straw again and again. I changed my stance; my right foot shifted forward and I began punching with my left hand. Over the years the makiwara and I had become old friends. I had developed the ability to punch, strike and kick it without conscious effort.

As I continued to punch the makiwara, I reminisced about the many years that had passed – five decades – since I had become aware of the existence of an art known as karate. Gradually my thoughts focused on a time forty-eight years ago when I first started my search for a karate teacher. This quest for a qualified karate teacher ultimately led to my maiden voyage to Japan.

JAPAN

The large transport ship that had been a temporary home to over five thousand soldiers had stopped moving. The drone of the large engines and the constant slap of the waves against the sides of the ship ceased. Several others and I slipped from our hammocks and made our way upward to the deck of the great ship. We had dropped anchor off the coast of Japan near Sasabo Bay. The old Japanese naval port of Sasabo is located on the western side of Kyushu, the southern most main Japanese island.

There was great excitement on the upper deck. It was very dark and little could be seen from the deck of the ship as we stared into the darkness. I leaned against the ship's railings; I could see nothing as I peered into the darkness. Then, slowly, I began to make out a couple of very faint lights off of the port side. The lights looked fragile and very far away. "That's Japan!" a sailor yelled to us. "The ship is going to dock early in the morning." Then he returned to his business of checking electrical boxes on the side of the ship.

As promised, early the next morning two tugboats came alongside our troop ship, the USS John Pope, and escorted us to one of the large piers. An Army band, playing military march music, was lined up on the pier. They looked very trim and proper standing there dressed in their Class A uniforms, which were adorned with white trim. A large crowd had also gathered on the pier, most were military personnel, some were dressed in army OD (olive drab) and others were wearing navy uniforms. A few people dressed in civilian clothes were scattered among the military personnel. Several Japanese dancing girls with white powdered faces wearing brightly colored, beautiful kimonos were positioned to the left of the band. They were performing a dance to welcome us. Corporal James Dody, a soldier who had served two previous tours in Korea and Japan, told me they were professional entertainers called "Geishas".

"Ain't they sweet?" Dody said, as he elbowed me.

I did not find them at all attractive, with their powdered faces. They looked ghostly and a little scary to me. Within a few short weeks however, my outlook about Japanese womanhood would undergo a drastic change.

We remained at the Sasabo base for two days for in-processing. On the morning of the third day, everyone except Corporal Dody loaded onboard the small Japanese trains for the trip to our assigned units. Corporal Dody had done what he usually did best. He got drunk at the base beer hall and then he got into an argument with an army major while loading onto the buses that were to take us to the train station. While we were loading onto the train, Corporal Dody was sitting in the Sasabo base brig – minus his corporal stripes.

All airborne soldiers (paratroopers) were assigned to the 187th Airborne Regimental Combat Team (ARCT), and were commonly referred to as "Rakkasans." I was told that the Japanese word "Rakkasan" meant "umbrella coming upside down." The 187th ARCT had units at various locations throughout Kyushu. The Q.M.P.M. Company (Quartermaster Parachute Maintenance) was assigned to the Kokura area in Northern Kyushu. The 1st Battalion and the Regimental Artillery Battery were stationed at the city of Kumamoto on the western side of the island. The Regimental Headquarters Company, 2nd and 3rd Battalions and other support units were stationed in the city of Beppu, which was located on the eastern side of the island.

Our crowded train slowly snaked its way across the island, twisting and turning as we sped past mountains, some tree-covered, some barren. Looking out the windows I saw many waterlogged valleys, which were broken into small squares and rectangles by rice fields. To an eighteen-year-old boy from the mountains of West Virginia, it was as if I were on another planet. The long ship ride across the Pacific and my arrival in Japan had caused a thought to enter my mind; I might never see my home again.

The author when he first arrived in Japan (1953).

Our train finally arrived at an old train station in downtown Beppu just as the skies started to darken and it began to rain. To our good fortune, the area alongside the tracks was covered and offered us some protection from the blowing rain. We formed three long lines as we off-loaded the train. A manifest was checked by a very tall Master Sergeant. After the officer in charge was assured that everyone was present and accounted for, we loaded onto several buses for the short trip to our new home. The large cumbersome army buses slowly negotiated their way through narrow, pedestrian-clogged streets. Gradually the buses worked their way up the hill that led to our new home, Camp Chickamauga.

As the bus turned, slowed, then regained its speed, I thought about the events

The main gate at Camp Chickamauga.

of the past few months which had led me here to Beppu City, Japan. I had, through personal choice elected to be here. It was as if some unseen force had drawn me to this spot. I knew that my life was about to undergo a dramatic change. Would the change be for better or for worse? I had no way of knowing. My future was in the hands of fate.

Our drivers had been ordered to take us to the post gymnasium upon our arrival at the camp. There, we were to be in-processed. The post gymnasium was organized like a miniature reception center. Several tables were set up at the far end of the gym. Large signs listing the letters of the alphabet were attached to the front of the tables. I strode toward the first table, which had a large sign with an equally large "A", "B", "C" and "D" painted on it. My orders were checked – it was verified that I was to be assigned to the headquarters company of the 2nd Battalion.

"Take a seat," the sergeant said to me, as he pointed to his left. "Over by the wall."

As I sat, waiting to be processed, a public address system made a squawking sound as it came on.

"Attention! Attention! All incoming personnel who can play any musical instrument, please report to the large desk by the gymnasium's main entrance." A few soldiers, myself included, immediately headed toward the desk. We were greeted by a Staff Sergeant named Giblin, who was seated behind the desk.

"Put your name, serial number and grade on this clipboard," he said. Then he handed the clipboard to the man at the front of the small line. After each of us had completed the required information, he proceeded to inform us about the advantages of being in the band over being in a field organization.

"Brigadier General Roy E. Lindquist has just taken over as our new regimental commander. He is very dissatisfied with the present condition of the regimental band," Sgt. Giblin informed us. "Several band members whose tour of duty had expired have been rotated back to state-side without being replaced. The General wants immediate recruitment of new band members to replace those who have left. Band duty beats the hell out of battalion duty," he continued. "But don't think that it's going to be a bed of roses – 'cause it ain't."

We were informed that the members of the band functioned as the regimental anti-tank platoon each time the unit went to Korea. Those of us who had signed our names all agreed that we wanted to try out for a position with the band.

The five of us, along with our duffle bags and AWOL bags, were transported in a pickup truck to the Regimental Headquarters' anti-tank platoon, a.k.a. "the band". We were issued linens and assigned to a bunk. The band was designated a sub-unit of the Regimental Headquarters and Headquarters Company. I was

The author at Camp Chikamauga, Japan (1953).

assigned to a bottom bunk in a small room located on the south side of the old Japanese barracks that housed Headquarters Company.

"You are all scheduled to audition at 1300 hours tomorrow," Sgt. Giblin informed us. "First formation is at 0700. Breakfast is between 0530 and 0630 hrs. If you do not want breakfast you can sleep in, but do not miss first formation." I looked at my watch; it was now 2310 hours (11:10 PM). It had been a long, tiring day. I lay down on my bunk and immediately fell into a deep sleep.

The next morning after breakfast, I sat on my bunk and read the information packet I had been given about Beppu City the previous night at the theater. It read:

> Beppu is a vacation resort, much like Miami, Florida. Because of the volcanic nature of the Japanese islands, hot springs are located throughout the area. There are also areas on the local beaches where the sands are very hot. Japanese tourists travel from all over to visit Beppu for the therapeutic effect of the warm sands. With the ocean and a large bay situated to its east, the western side of Beppu is up against a 1,575-meter mountain called Mori Yama. Beppu itself is located on the lower slopes of this mountain, on a small flat area, just before the land drops into the ocean. South of Beppu, one of the few good roads in the area curves around the bay and leads to the city of Oita. Oita is several miles away, with two- and three-story buildings of grey stone. To the east of Oita, a small peninsula sticks out into the bay like a thumb. A rough gravel airstrip is located on this little piece of land surrounded on three sides by water. This small airstrip had been Japan's largest kamikaze base during the final days of World War Two. Many of the kamikazes that flew missions against the U. S. fleet during the battle of Okinawa flew from here.

At 1100 hours the five of us were taken to supply and issued the instrument of our choice. I was issued one Conn trumpet, one trumpet case, one music stand, two mouth pieces, a wa-wa mute, cleaning oil, various pieces of sheet music, a small marching band music book, a music carrier to attach to the trumpet and a training manual for the 3.5-inch anti-tank rocket launcher, more commonly known as a bazooka.

"You guys only get to keep this stuff if you pass your audition," Sgt. Giblin informed us. By 16:30 hours that afternoon four of us had successfully passed our entrance exam and had been admitted to the band.

Band practice started at 08:30 the next morning. We practiced until 11:30 hours and went to lunch. At 1300 hours we started practicing again until 16:30.

This was our permanent schedule unless we had special practice at night because we needed to get ready for some special event.

"You new guys should spend a few nights practicing on your own," Sgt. Giblin informed us. "The Chief (Warrant Officer Bell – the band leader) wants you to knock off some of the rust. We were told that the band was scheduled to participate in a special ceremony within a couple of weeks, and we were expected to be ready for it.

Even with the additional practice sessions in the evenings, I still had some free time available to travel downtown and see Beppu City. After practice on Wednesday I headed to downtown Beppu again to check things out and to get the lay of the land. As I walked along the road that led to the city, I observed a nice home on the left side of the road surrounded by a large concrete block wall. A sign in front printed in large English letters read, "Hock Shop Charlie's". I later learned that this was the place to go when you were short of money prior to payday. Charlie would hock anything – no questions asked.

By the end of my first week at Camp Chickamauga I had made three trips into Beppu City during the evening hours. I spoke to no one during my first two trips.

The main street in Beppu City (1953). This photo, taken by the author, is looking West. Three blocks up the street on the left is the Hanago Bar and Grill.

On my third trip I observed a lone, old Japanese gentleman, stooped with age, shuffling towards me. I uttered a weak, "Konnichi wa."

"Konnichi wa!" the Japanese man said, as he smiled, bowed, and continued on his way.

I was pleasantly surprised to find that many of the local Japanese could speak some English. On my fourth trip to Beppu, I spoke to a woman whom I had overheard using some English.

"Do you speak English?" I inquired.

"I little speak," came her reply.

"Do you know where I can find a karate school?" I inquired.

She raised a hand to her face as if to hide the look of shock that appeared on her face. "Karate bad!" she said, then quickly turned and scurried away.

Overall, I discovered that the local population was very friendly. They were totally different from what I had expected. After seeing many American World War II films when I was a youngster in Clarksburg, West Virginia, I expected most of the people would be 'monsters'. What I found was a very kind, soft-spoken people with a great sense of humor. They were people who worked hard, were honest, had great dignity and who were extremely fond of children. I attempted to memorize some basic Japanese phrases so I could

Author early 1954

communicate with them. I made many mistakes which left them laughing. Most were always kind enough to correct and teach me. They really appreciated it when I attempted to talk to them in their language.

Upon entering the barracks one afternoon I observed a Japanese man sitting on one of the footlockers, spit shining a pair of jump boots. Corporal Hall, a tall, lanky Texan from Dallas who had been in Japan for several months, introduced him to me.

"Bill, this is Rocky, our houseboy. You owe him five dollars, script (military money used overseas), so pay up. Rocky cleans our room, shines our shoes, washes our underwear and makes our beds. Every platoon member pays him five dollars a month, which puts him at the top of the wage scale in the Beppu area."

I fumbled with my wallet, located a five-dollar script and handed it to Rocky. He jumped to his feet, bowed, then introduced himself to me.

"Kuwata Kenji desu." he said.

Rocky was twenty-four years old, married, with two children. In addition to his duties as the platoon houseboy he also served as the platoon advisor, father confessor, and general all-round wise soothsayer.

During my second week at Camp Chickamauga I observed several posters that advertised a judo demonstration. The demonstration was going to be held at the Post Service Club and was scheduled for Saturday evening at 7:00 PM. I looked forward to attending the demonstration. I arrived early at the service club on Saturday and found it packed. The large overstuffed chairs and sofas had been removed from the center of the floor and placed against the walls of the main room. Several straw mats now covered the center of the floor. Five Japanese men, wearing loose fitting white clothes, strode into the center of the room, bowed to the crowd, then to each other. One of the older Japanese, who was rather stocky and had a large gap between his front teeth, seemed to be in charge. A handsome, shorter, much younger, Japanese with a crew cut, explained the demonstration as it progressed. His English, though it was not proper grammatically, was understandable.

The demonstration started with falls and rolls onto the mats. As the men fell, jumped, and flipped onto the mats they made loud slapping sounds with their hands. The judo men then stood, formed into groups of two, and faced one another. They tugged, pulled and pushed each other. Suddenly, without warning, one of them would be thrown head over heels, slamming hard onto the mats.

The demonstration lasted approximately thirty minutes, after which the majority of the crowd immediately left. The remaining soldiers mingled with the

Japanese judo men who answered their questions. Two of the demonstrators spoke understandable English.

Within five minutes many of the soldiers who had remained after the demonstration to ask questions began to slowly drift away. Finally I had my opportunity to speak to the commentator. As I approached him, he bowed. Surprisingly, without thinking, I found myself automatically returning his bow. I introduced myself and learned that his name was Hidika Ito. He was twenty-four years old.

"You like to take judo?" he inquired.

"I am not interested in judo, but I am interested in karate," I said. "I would like to find the best karate teacher I can find and study karate."

"Number one karate teacher live on other side of island in the village of Kikuchi near city of Kumamoto." Mr. Ito said. "His name, Chitose."

"I would like to meet him," I said. "Do you know him?"

"Yes! But I think it do no good you see him. He very few karate student has."

Talking to Ito-san, even for a few minutes, was very beneficial. I obtained the address of Mr. Chitose and directions on how to locate him – if I could get to Kumamoto.

The judo men at the demonstration were all Beppu City police officers. I surmised that one purpose of the demonstration was to inform the soldiers at Camp Chickamauga, in a subtle way, not to mess with the local police. I was positive that those who had not attended the demonstration would get a blow-by-blow description from those who had. I was also confident that the abilities of the demonstrators would become more formidable with each telling.

● ●

Chapter 2

Meeting Chitose Sensei

The only way to avoid being miserable is not to have enough leisure time to wonder whether you are happy or not.

George Bernard Shaw

An announcement was finally made about the special event for which the band had been practicing. We were to travel by train to Camp Wood, which was located on the western side of Kyushu Island, in Kumamoto City. The train ride was a slow, long and tiring one. The band members, instruments and all, rode the small Japanese train across the width of the island. The train was very dilapidated and crowded, conditions which one of the older band members informed me were normal. There wasn't room for everyone at the station to get inside the train. Many people were forced to wait for a later one. Two members were chosen to ride in the baggage car with the instruments. Corporal Toney and I were the lucky ones. The train made numerous stops as it wound its way across the island. Several crates were loaded into the baggage car at one stop; tentacles hung out of one of the boxes. "Octopus," Corporal Toney said.

Upon our arrival in Kumamoto we were bussed to Camp Wood. When we got to camp we were assigned to temporary barracks. We immediately dressed in our Class A uniforms with blue neck scarves, white belts over our Ike jackets and white shoe laces, laced in a box or ladder lace, on our highly polished Cochran jump boots.

I asked one of the local sergeants who had been assigned to assist us if he knew where Kikuchi was.

"I think it's about twelve miles north of Kumamoto," he informed me.

"Formation!" First Sergeant Munro yelled loudly. We ran out of the barracks, fell into formation and marched to the parade grounds six blocks away. Upon arriving at the parade ground we took our place directly across from the reviewing stand. Corporal Redwine raised his baton, then brought it down sharply. Within seconds we were playing "Stars and Stripes Forever". The troops started marching onto the parade field and lining up in company formations.

General Lindquist, Major General Thompson, United States Marine Corp's and a General from the newly formed Japanese Self Defense force were on the reviewing stand. As the last unit brought its formation up into line with the many other gathered units, Corporal Redwine raised his baton above his head and brought it down sharply. The band immediately stopped playing. A second later, he raised his baton again and brought it down slowly – the band played "Kime Giro", the Japanese National Anthem, as the troops presented arms. Upon the completion of "Kime Giro", we paused a second and then started playing the "Star Spangled Banner". Short speeches were made by the three Generals. Mutual cooperation, the communist menace, and how this was a great time to be in the service of your country was the content of the speeches. General Lindquist said, "Commanders take charge of your units!" Immediately, shouts could be heard from every direction. "Battalion!", "Company!", "Platoon!", "Forward march." The troops of the 187th moved into company-sized formations as they marched past the reviewing stand with great precision.

When the ceremonies ended we returned to our barracks, packed our instruments, and ate supper at the local mess hall. Buses returned us to the Kumamoto train station for our return trip to Beppu.

The band in Parade Formation. Corporal Redwine is the Drum Major.

At Camp Wood. The author is 2nd row from the top, 4th from the left (looking to his left).

The return trip from Kumamoto to Beppu did not seem to take as long as the trip over. This gave me confidence that I could, with a little luck and my Japanese language translation book, make the trip back to Kumamoto to locate Mr. Chitose, the karate instructor.

Two weeks passed before I had the opportunity to travel to Kumamoto. Good fortune followed me. I was able to locate Mr. Chitose with the assistance of a very cooperative taxi cab driver and the expenditure of three thousand six hundred yen. The first thing I noticed about Mr. Chitose was his demeanor – that of a nobleman – and his piercing, dark eyes. He wore his jet-black hair combed straight back. He had a little moustache reminiscent of Charlie Chaplin's. It was obvious that he was a very intelligent individual; he seemed to understand most of what I was trying to tell him. He had a good grasp of English even though he could only speak a little of it. I was pleasantly surprised by his kind demeanor toward me even though our conversation was a short one.

"You Camp Woodo boy?" he asked.

"No! I am from Camp Chickamauga in Beppu," I answered. "I would like to become your student and study karate."

He gazed at me for a full minute; his dark eyes seemed to burn right through me – body and soul.

"No karate teachi, Nihon jin teachi owney."

He bowed, turned and walked away. I was very disappointed. Our short conversation did, however, tweak my curiosity. I was surprised that he did not teach karate and wondered about this art he taught called "Nihon Jin". Maybe it was better than karate.

I made three additional trips to Kumamoto and Kikuchi over the next few weeks. During one trip, I was unable to locate Mr. Chitose. However, the two trips when I was able to locate him also ended in failure. Mr. Chitose continued to give me the same answer – "No!" He did take more time to converse with me on my last trip. His answer to my request nonetheless remained the same, "No!" As I rose to leave, he shook my hand. He had never done that before. His hand felt rather leathery, almost as if he was wearing a glove – I could feel the strength in it.

After my return from Kumamoto, the following week went by very quickly. Friday after breakfast, the unit marched to Chapman Field, which was adjacent to the main gate. Chapman Field functioned as the post football field, track, and parade grounds. Training with the 3.5-inch anti-tank rocket launcher took up the entire morning. There was not much to a 3.5 – an open tube with a trigger grip, a sight and an electrical firing mechanism. That afternoon was spent on our basic soldier skills, map reading, first aid, and vehicle identification.

Corporal Howard Staff, a saxophone player from Monroe, Louisiana, was one of the four soldiers who joined the unit the same day I did. Because of this, Howard and I had gravitated to each other and become good friends. Howard had met a Japanese girl, Kazuko, and was now going steady. While I was attempting to find myself a karate teacher, Howard was doing other things.

"Kazuko and I are going to the post dance Saturday night," he told me. "She has a girlfriend named Junko who would like to go, except she does not have a date. Do me a favor and take her girlfriend."

"OK," I replied in great doubt.

I met Junko the next evening. One look and my heart almost stopped. She was a beautiful eighteen-year-old girl, approximately five feet tall with dark brown eyes and long black hair that she wore in a Veronica Lake (a famous movie star of the 1940s) peek-a-boo hairstyle. For the first time since I had left Clarksburg I no longer felt lonely – I felt at home.

The dance ended at 11:00 PM and Howard and I walked the girls home. Conveniently both girls lived in the same building. Kazuko's mother and father owned the building.

Meeting Chitose Sensei

Kazuko's family lived on the first floor. Her mother operated a small tailor shop in the front room. Her father was a Spanish merchant. He had come to Japan on business, met her mother, fallen in love, and stayed. His last name was Castro, but upon becoming a Japanese citizen he adopted his wife's family name, Kitayama.

Junko's parents rented the second floor from Mr. and Mrs. Kitayama. Junko, her mother, father, and little brother lived there. Hiroshi, her father, worked in the city of Oita at a small factory. Kaiko, her mother, stayed at home to care for her four-year-old son, Jiro. Junko's mother always treated me nicely, her father, however, was very reserved. A few months after I started dating Junko, I learned that during the war her father had served as an officer in the Japanese Army. He was not fond of the fact that his daughter was dating someone who, a few years earlier, had been the enemy. His manner toward me, while reserved and distant, was always very correct. He never failed to greet me when I arrived at his home to pick up his daughter.

Being a member of the regimental band had its advantages. One of the biggest was that the band was not required to go to the field for FTX's (Field Training Exercises) as often as the line units in the Battalions. We didn't go as often, but we were still required to occasionally participate in field training. Most FTX's lasted for two weeks; ours was scheduled for only one week.

Reverting to the status of Regimental anti-tank platoon, we were scheduled to participate in an FTX on Mount Mori. We were issued the 3.5-inch launchers from the arms room, received our field gear, and then boarded the two waiting ? ton trucks for the trip to Mori Yama. The trucks rocked back and forth in the ruts that lined the road as they climbed the side of the mountain toward the training area. When the trucks left the Beppu area it was warm, but the air was gradually getting colder and damper as our altitude increased.

The skies began to darken on our second day at Mount Mori. A light drizzle started, which blanketed the entire mountain. The rain slowly increased in intensity, soaking everyone and everything on the mountain. By the afternoon of the third day, nothing was dry. No one had dry clothes, the equipment was soaked, and the best of the tents had long since started leaking. We worked, trained, slept, and then worked some more in the rain. Since the unit's cook tent was just large enough for the cooks and their stoves, we ate outside in the rain, trying to shield our food from the downpour with our ponchos (military field rain coat). On Thursday, as I ate my dinner, I watched my waterlogged mashed potatoes slowly wash over the side of my mess kit because of the heavy rain. To honestly know how true 'wet and cold' felt a person needed to be an infantryman at least once.

On Friday, we had C-rations for breakfast and lunch. After lunch, we loaded the mud-covered equipment into the trucks for the trip back to Camp Chickamauga and Beppu. When the equipment had been loaded, the trucks started forward slowly, their wheels spinning and throwing mud in all directions as they attempted to gain traction. Our truck lurched suddenly as the wheels gripped solid earth through the mud. The trucks were carefully maneuvered down the narrow, winding, mountain road that would lead us back to Camp Chickamauga, our barracks, and the comfort of a good dry bed.

Everyone was exhausted, wet, hungry, and cold. No one spoke as the trucks, their automatic transmissions shifting back and forth, plowed their way through the mud. The canvas roof of our truck had a large rip in the center and water came careening through, drenching everyone. In spite of the rain, however, several of us dozed off. Suddenly, the truck hit a large hole, causing it to rock more violently than before and waking everyone on board.

Our small convoy was now on the eastern slope of Mori Yama. The lights of Beppu could be seen in the distance through the rain. Our truck negotiated its way around another of the many curves. Finally, we arrived at the main gate of the camp. The trucks were waved through the gate by a military policeman. A minute later, our truck stopped in front of our barracks.

"Listen up!" Staff Sergeant Reese yelled. "Everyone into the barracks, dry off, and get to the mess hall as soon as possible. The mess will remain open until 2200 hrs (10:00PM). After you eat, report back here. We will then off-load and clean the equipment."

• •

Chapter 3

The Big Surprise

When you are unable to find your teacher, do not be surprised if your teacher finds you.

Unknown

After a week of hard work on Mount Mori, Saturday was an off day for the platoon. The morning sky, a beautiful blue, was almost clear of clouds except for one large white puff that looked like cotton. After eating breakfast, I returned to the barracks, lay down on my bunk, and quickly drifted off to sleep.

Corporal Medina, the C.Q. (Charge of Quarters), came into the squad bay looking for me.

"Bill!" he said shaking me, "Wake up. Are you in some kind of trouble man?"

"Not that I know of," I told him, as I fought back the sleep that had overtaken me.

"Well, you must be. There are a couple of gook cops in the orderly room asking about you, and they want to see you."

I woke up immediately, wondering what I had done and what type of trouble I must be in. I checked my watch – it was 8:20 AM.

With great apprehension and a certain amount of fear, I walked into the orderly room. Two Japanese police officers, one short and stocky, the other tall and thin, bowed as I entered the orderly room. I automatically returned their bow.

The stockier police officer took off his hat. His hair was cut in a crew cut. He looked familiar; after he spoke to me in his broken English, I recognized him. It was Hidika Ito, the young police officer I had met some weeks before at the judo demonstration.

The old Beppu City Police Headquarters.

"Chitose Sensei is at the Beppu Police Station, and would like to speak to you," he said.

Still half asleep, I could only mutter, "Why?"

"I do not know reason. I did not think idea good to ask," Ito responded.

Officer Ito told me that he thought that it would be a good idea for me to come to the police station at ten o'clock.

"Will you come?" he asked.

"Yes, I will come," I replied.

Both officers saluted, turned sharply and left the building. From the orderly room window, I saw them enter a small Japanese police car being driven by a third officer.

I returned to my squad room, showered, shaved, dressed in civilian clothes, and headed to the main gate. I walked to the rickshaw stand located outside the main gate. After hiring one, I climbed inside for the ride downtown.

The driver beeped his horn at several pedestrians who started to walk in front of his vehicle. Soon, we were nearing the eastern end of Nagare Kawa Street, which was the main thoroughfare to and from Camp Chickamauga. The GI's often referred to it as "Broadway". Nagare Kawa Street ran dead into Mochigahama Street. If you turn to the right, or south, on Mochigahama Street it will eventually lead you to the Beppu-Oita highway. If you turn left, it will take you north, toward Takazaki Yama (Monkey Mountain). A few blocks north

Mary Shigamoto, who was like a big sister to me during my early training in Japan.

of Nagare Kawa Street is where the Beppu Police Headquarters is located. My rickshaw finally arrived in front of a large, two story, dirty stone building. The main entrance, which was located on the northeast corner, was designed in a round, turret-style of architecture.

"Shichijugo yen," (75 Yen) my driver said as he held out his hand. I gave him a one hundred yen note, then waved him away. I turned, and with apprehension, walked toward the building and entered. Two police officers standing behind a large desk were engaged in conversation. They looked at me curiously. The tall, younger one bowed; he was the officer who had been with Officer Ito in the orderly room. He pointed down a hallway to his right then continued his conversation with the other officer.

I walked down the narrow hall, which led to another structure that was attached to the main building. An old, wooden shoe rack was located by the door. I removed my shoes, placed them in the rack, and entered. In the room were several people, stretching and exercising. In the far corner of the room, I saw Officer Ito in his white uniform with a black belt around his waist. Upon seeing me, he stopped training and walked toward where I was standing.

"Ah!" he said in mock surprise, "I see you here. Prease follow me."

We walked back down the hall toward the police department. He opened a door on his right, which led to an office. The office was small and had a tiny desk and three chairs, two of which were occupied. Mr. Chitose was seated in one, in the other sat a very kind looking woman.

"Dometrich-san, I think you know Chitose Sensei. I like you meet Shigamoto-san," Ito said, and then he left the room.

Mr. Chitose stood, bowed, and extended his hand. I bowed and extended my hand to him. The Japanese lady, stood, extended her hand, and introduced herself.

"I am very pleased to meet you, Mr. Dometrich," she said, in excellent English. "My name is Mary Shigamoto."

Mary explained that she had been born and raised in Dayton, Ohio. She had traveled to Japan to meet and visit with many of her relatives on September 21, 1941. The attack on Pearl Harbor came as a surprise and she was stranded in Japan. She fell in love with and married a Japanese National. The United States Army hired her as a translator at Camp Chickamauga and Camp Wood. In her spare time, she taught English to Japanese businessmen and members of the Beppu Police Department.

The Big Surprise

"Chitose Sensei would like for you to observe a karate class," she said in a soft voice. "After watching a class if you still wish to join, I will help you with your application."

"Mr. Chitose has turned me down on several occasions," I said, "Why am I being accepted now."

"I do not know the answer, and to ask Chitose Sensei would be very impolite. We may never know why, just be thankful that he has reconsidered. Everyone calls him Chitose Sensei – I suggest that you start doing the same."

Mary spoke with Chitose Sensei for a few minutes; he stood, bowed to both of us, then left the room.

"Ito-san will escort you to the training hall where you may observe a class. After the class is over, if you still wish to join, I will help you with your application." Mary called down the hall for Ito. He came and escorted me into the training area.

There were seventeen Japanese lined up in two rows.

"Seiza."

They sat on the floor on their heels. Chitose Sensei sat in front of the class. A stocky Japanese man in the front row gave the commands. He was the man with the gap between his teeth that had been in charge of the judo demonstration.

"Mokuso." They all sat in meditation for a couple of minutes.

"Mokuso yame," quietly they opened their eyes.

"Shomen ni, rei!" They bowed to the front wall, which had a small Japanese flag mounted on it.

Chitose Sensei turned to face the class.

"Sensei ni, rei!" The class bowed to Chitose Sensei. Everyone jumped to their feet and began swinging their arms, squatting down, doing push-ups in a divebomber fashion, and stretching.

The students, standing in two lines, started punching in unison as the stocky man counted, "Ichi, Ni, San, Shi." After he completed a ten count, the person at the far right of the front row continued the count. After the last person in the second row had completed their count, the instructor yelled something unintelligible to me. The count started again with a person in the front row. Several hundred punches later, the students started kicking. "Ichi, Ni, San, Shi," the

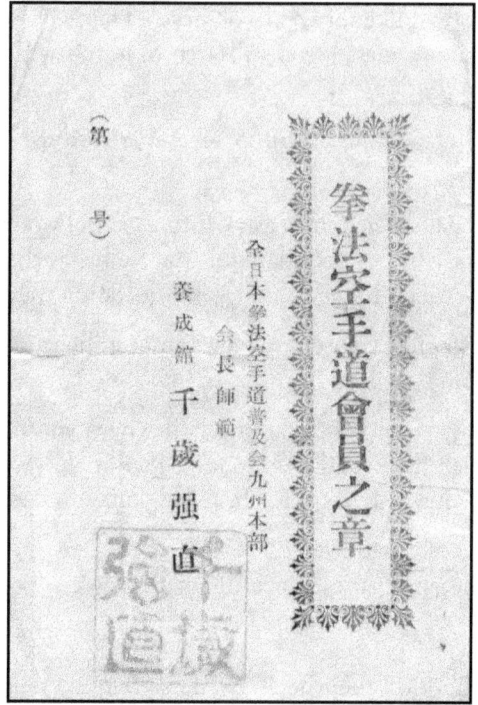

My early 1953 membership card.

count continued. Within a very short time the students' uniforms were covered with perspiration, and shortly after that, their bodies and the floor of the dojo were both covered with sweat as well.

The students stepped back and blocked downward. They started moving forward as they punched, blocked and kicked. Their eyes looked straight ahead, unblinking; they were focusing their entire being on each technique. I was impressed. I knew then and there, without a doubt, that this art, the art of karate, was what I wanted to devote the rest of my life to. An hour and a half later the class was finished. They bowed to the front wall with its small Japanese flag and then to Chitose Sensei.

Class was over. Ito walked in my direction.

"What you think of crass?" he asked, standing there in his karate uniform, dripping with sweat.

"Why didn't you tell me about the dojo, and that you practiced karate when I spoke to you at the service club?" I asked incredulously.

The Big Surprise

"You never ask about dojo," he said with a smile. "You ask about number one teacher and I tell you. On this island of Kyushu we are very conservative, more so than our karate brothers in Tokyo and Okinawa. I have heard that some members of your air force bomber crews are practicing judo and karate at the Kodokan Judo Institute in Tokyo. Some American G.I. on Okinawa have been granted rimitted access to a few dojo there," Ito explained to me. "I sent you to the number one karate teacher on Kyushu Island. Our dojo will only accept you with Chitose Sensei's approval. On Kyushu, karate is still considered a very deadly art. We must be very careful who we teach, at least in the beginning with students we not know. Chitose Sensei, for some reason, say we give you chance. Now have chance. You want join, OK yes or you want to join, OK no?"

"I want to join, yes." I replied.

He motioned for me to follow him to the office.

"I no think you last," he said with a grin, as I followed him down the hall.

After the application form was completed with Mary's help, I asked Mary if there was a training fee.

"Yes, there is a fee," she answered. "But I am not sure that you can afford it."

My face must have showed concern. She looked at me and laughed.

"It will be five hundred yen a month (approximately one dollar and thirty four cents) for your dojo membership fee," she said with a twinkle in her eye. "You will also be required to pay an additional fee of one thousand yen as a training fee for Chitose Sensei."

"Is there a store where I can purchase a uniform?"

"Do you know of the Hanago Bar and Grill?" she asked. "There is a small shop on the side street, next to the grill which is just a few doors west of Nagare Kawa Street."

"Thanks for your help," I said. After bowing, I left the office.

I walked back into the training area. Chitose Sensei came over to me – Ito tagging behind – he smiled, shook my hand, looked into my eyes, and spoke to me for two minutes in Japanese. I did not understand one word that he said. "Chitose Sensei say because he live Kikuchi, Kumamoto Ken, you live Beppu, he no here all time. Shirahama Sensei, other sensei, me, Ito, to teach. When we teach, teach come from Chitose Sensei. You no forget. We all Chitose student. You now Chitose student. I help you karate learn. You hard practice all time."

"Inform Chitose Sensei that I will do my best."

Yamaguchi and Chitose 1954.

"He think that already." Ito said. "Nobody come him three time before, only you. Tuesday night, you first class do."

There was nothing more to say. I thanked them again; they bowed, turned, and strode away. I walked to the door, slipped on my shoes, and stepped into the busy streets of Beppu.

Locating the uniform shop was not as easy as I thought it would be. I stopped at several stores, received additional instructions, and finally located the shop. The owner made it known to me, through the use of sign language and his broken English, that he had no karate uniforms in my size.

"Two week, me have," he repeated over and over.

"Judo-gi good size," he said, as he continued to thrust a heavy judo uniform over the counter at me.

"Ikura desu ka?" (How much?) I inquired.

"One thousand eight hundred yen," ($5.00) he stated.

With no other prospects of obtaining a uniform before class on Tuesday night, I purchased the heavy uniform. With uniform under my arm, I left the shop and headed up Main Street back toward Camp Chickamauga.

Chapter 4

The First Class

. . . journey of a thousand miles begins with the first step.

Ancient Chinese Saying

Sunday was another fantastic day. The temperature was a little warmer than Saturday. The sky was peppered with great puffs of white as the clouds drifted lazily overhead in a sea of blue.

Howard, Kazuko, Junko and I rented some bicycles. We rode around the city sightseeing. We had a terrific time. After peddling around in south Beppu for a couple of hours, we rode north to the base of Takazaki Yama (Monkey Mountain). "Next time go bicycle, we go up Takazaki Yama and do whole day," Kazuko said. Everyone agreed that this sounded like a good idea.

Two hours later, we returned the bicycles and walked downtown. We stopped for a good meal, then started back up the hill to the girls' home.

"Bill-san, you like come Buddhist church and me Wednesday night?" Junko asked.

It was very obvious as I looked into Junko's eyes that this meant a great deal to her. "Sure, I would love to go." I replied.

After dropping the girls off, Howard and I stopped at the American Bar for a couple of beers, then headed back to Camp Chickamauga.

Sunday went by quickly; however, the next two days seemed to move in slow motion. My first karate class, scheduled for Tuesday, was constantly on my mind. Now that I had been accepted as a student of the local dojo with Chitose Sensei's blessings, I had some misgivings and worried that I might not be capable of doing well.

Tuesday night finally arrived; I dressed in sports clothes, packed the heavy judo-gi into an AWOL bag, and prepared for my trip to the dojo. My stomach had a bad case of butterflies. I had plenty of time before the class was scheduled to start and decided to walk to the dojo, hoping it would help me settle my jitters.

I flashed my military I.D. to the Military Policeman at the gate and walked out onto the main street. Turning left, I walked down the street to the center of Beppu.

The sights, sounds and smells of Japan fascinated me. They were like nothing I had ever experienced. The many voices I could not understand, the sounds blending as they greeted one another, conversing and bargaining at the little shops. The putt-putt of the small motor-powered rickshaws weaving in and out of traffic with their bells' "ringie, ringie" filled my ears. I felt wonderful and alive – I became lost in my thoughts, forgetting my apprehension about my first karate class.

Without thinking, I automatically turned north onto Mochigahama Street. I was within sight of my destination – the large grey stone structure that lay ahead of me.

Several people, their uniforms wet with sweat, were already practicing. Ito-san was nowhere to be seen. I removed my shoes, placed them with the others by the door, and entered. A tall, young Japanese man walked toward me.

"Sato Tatsuo desu," he said as he bowed.

"Bill Dometrich," I replied, returning his bow.

He motioned for me to follow him to the dressing room, which was small and rather plain looking and had large wooden pegs in one wall. Several pegs had judo-gi hanging from them. As I changed into my uniform, Ito-san walked into the dressing room and informed me that my training uniform pants were on backwards.

"Bill-san, I happy see you here. Why you Judo-gi buy, why no karate-gi?"

I explained that the merchant had no karate-gi available in my size.

After making the necessary change with the gi pants, Ito-san instructed me on the proper way to tie my belt.

"Now you member, I show dojo," Ito said.

I followed him to a door leading from the dojo onto the street.

The First Class

"This door use, come dojo," he said. "No use police room door."

I followed him down a hall. He opened a door and pointed. "Benjo," (toilet) he said. I stared at the small porcelain ring, which was sunk into the floor and experienced yet another smell of Japan.

Sensei Ichiro Shirahama

Ito and I walked from the dressing room onto the training area. Standing there in the middle of the floor was the imposing figure of Sensei Ichiro Shirahama.

Sensei Shirahama was thirty-eight years old. He had a large, stocky build and looked to me like a living Buddha with hair. He hardly ever smiled but when he did he displayed a gap between his front teeth which looked big enough for a small car to drive through. I thought he was a police officer but I was mistaken. He lived with his wife, Michiko, at 7-9 Akiba-Cho where they operated the Niagi Pharmacy. I learned that he was ranked Go-dan in both Judo and Karate. He practiced karate and was very good, but his first love was Judo.

A young black belt yelled; everyone started to line up. Ito walked me to a spot in the second row and motioned for me to stand there. Quickly, he walked to the front and took his position. At the very front of the class stood Shirahama Sensei.

"Seiza." Everyone sat down on their heels. I followed their example. Suddenly I felt a sharp pain in my feet which had never been in this position before.

"Mokuso." A tall, young black belt with long hair and glasses instructed. Eyes became partially closed. No one moved, no one spoke, all was quiet. My feet were really hurting now. I wondered how long we were going to remain in this position. An eternity later, I heard the command.

"Mokuso Yame." Everyone's eyes opened fully.

"Shomen ni, rei." Everyone bowed to the wall that held the small Japanese flag.

Shirahama Sensei turned and faced the class. "Sensei ni, rei." We bowed to him.

The class jumped to its feet. We started stretching, as we followed along with the young, bespectacled black belt leading the exercises. His name was Kakudo Murakami. He was twenty-one years old, a Ni-dan (2nd degree black belt) and a college student.

Shirahama Sensei was a very good karate sensei and an excellent judo sensei.

Murakami quickly and silently switched from one exercise to the next. It was "monkey see, monkey do." I followed along to the best of my ability. Thanks to my youth and daily military P.T. training, I was in excellent physical condition. A few minutes into the class, Murakami's legs slid outward and he did a full split. He turned his toes up toward the ceiling, then slowly turned his head from side to side, placing his ears on the floor. I knew then that I was in trouble.

Upon observing many of the other members of the class it was obvious that they were having as much trouble as I was. Even Ito was having some difficulty in doing a full split. Shirahama Sensei stood at the back of the class doing his own exercises as he watched us.

Shirahama Sensei yelled. The class jumped to its feet and everyone started punching as each student took turns counting, "Ichi! Ni! San!" After we practiced punching for approximately ten minutes, front kicking was next. "Ichi. Ni. San." When it was my turn to count, I yelled as loudly as I could, "One! Two! Three!"

"Kihon!" Shirahama Sensei yelled. I glanced around to see what was next and followed along. My limited training at Fort Campbell was paying off. At least I would not be totally lost in the class.

Everyone stepped into a forward stance and leg blocked. Just then I felt a foot kick my ankle. I almost lost my balance and fell. "Stance bad," I heard in broken English. As the class progressed, "Block bad," followed by "Balance bad." "Punch bad," Ito-san said over, and over, and over again, none too gently. I was now sweating profusely. The students moved almost as though they were a single person performing basic techniques under the direction of Shirahama Sensei. The class punched, blocked and kicked as we moved forward and backward across the floor.

"Yame." The class returned to the natural stance, hachi dachi.

"Kata!" Shirahama shouted.

Ito came over, took my arm and motioned for me and another student, a young Japanese who was also wearing a white belt, to be seated by the side of the training area.

"Seisan!"

The students remaining on the floor bowed, circled their left and right hands overhead, then brought them down in front of their stomachs. The left foot of the students slapped the inside of their right thigh as they assumed a stance which looked as though they were riding a horse.

"Hajime!"

The entire class in unison slid their left feet forward, as their left arms made an outside motion at chest level. Their right fists shot forward in a punch, slashing through the stillness of the dojo as their wet uniforms cracked against their bodies. They blocked and breathed in through their noses as if sniffing the air then expelled the air through their barely open mouths. I noticed that the timing for breathing in and out had the same duration. Other kata were practiced; when these kata were completed, the class started to practice basic sparring. I remained seated with the other white belt and watched intently. I wondered how long it would be before the two of us would learn the kata and be able to participate with the class.

"Yame." The class stopped. Ito motioned for the young Japanese white belt and me to line up.

"Seiza." We sat down once again on our heels.

"Mokuso."

"Mokuso yame."

"Shomen ni, rei."

"Sensei ni, rei."

Ito told the other white belt and me to remain after class for some additional instruction in some of the finer points concerning the stances. "Zenshin Kotai,

My first karate uniform was a judo-gi. It is obvious from this photograph that after one lesson I had no idea how to tie my belt properly.

first kata," Ito told me. "I do kata, you see, you do."

The kata consisted of four punches, four blocks, and two kicks. We both learned the movements very quickly. I had trouble, however, with the side kicks. Doing the kata well would take some time.

I hired a rickshaw to carry me to Camp Chickamauga as I left the dojo. My first class had worn me out. Upon arriving at my barracks, I showered and immediately fell asleep.

Chapter 5

The Lesson

The way of seeking after the truth is a way without end, a travel to Infinity. It is long and far. However enthusiastic one's faith may be, the actual evidence will not appear immediately.

President Nikkyo Niwano, Rissho Kosei-Kai Buddhist Sect

Upon arriving at Junko's home a little after 6:00 PM, she and her family were waiting for me. All of us were to attend a service at the Buddhist Temple. Junko was dressed in a flowered, pink kimono – she looked beautiful. Mr. Arakawa, Junko's father, was wearing an old 1930s western designed, double-breasted, dark brown suit. Her mother and little brother were also wearing kimono. Her father, as usual, was not very friendly toward me, but he was very correct.

We walked in silence to the Buddhist Temple, which was only a few blocks from their home. The Temple was small and plain; it had been designed with simplicity in mind, yet it was very beautiful. Junko's home was a few blocks from the main gate of Camp Chickamauga. My total walking time to her home, and then the temple, had been less than ten minutes.

Junko explained the basic beliefs of her religion to me as we walked to the temple.

"There are many types of Buddhism," she said. "Our Buddhism is known as the Rissho Kosei-Kai. The members of the Rissho Kosei-Kai believe in true Buddhism and try to practice Buddhist teachings sincerely. They feel that they are all fellow disciples of Lord Sakayamuni. The Rissho Kosei-Kai is based upon service, which is the lubricant of society. Service to one another and the world produces kindness in the human mind and happiness in the world. When all people have this spirit, true peace will come to the world. These are not my words," she said, "but the words of one of our leaders, Niwano Nikkyo Roshi."

Camp Wood group.

Their priest resided at the temple, she explained. In this way, he could always be available to serve the people. This was one of the most important teachings of the Rissho Kosei-Kai, one of universal service to all mankind. When we entered the temple, I was surprised to see that the temple had seats exactly like an American church. People were starting to arrive. A few younger people were present but the majority, however, were adults.

An older man wearing glasses and a western style suit, who I would guess to be 55 years old, entered the room. He spoke to several people, then walked up to Mr. Arakawa and engaged him in conversation. He looked at me and spoke to Junko.

"I welcome you to our humble temple. May your visit here help lead you to enlightenment," Junko translated. He bowed, then turned and walked toward the front of the room, occasionally stopping to speak with a member of the congregation. The entire service was a little over an hour. Upon completion of the service the priest told Junko that he would be honored to have me stay.

He wanted to know if I had any questions. I had two, which he answered to my satisfaction. Junko informed him that I had started taking karate the day before.

The Lesson

The priest asked Junko to explain to me that what he was about to tell me was very important.

"Karate is a Budo, and Budo can be a very wonderful thing or a very terrible thing. It is all in your perception and in your heart. Budo must be used for good and never for evil. You should always be very careful. Use it wisely and with great restraint."

The priest looked at me with a smile on his face. He turned to Junko and spoke again.

"The way of seeking the truth, be it religion, or budo, is a way without end. Do not dwell upon the goal, but enjoy the path, for true seeking is a travel to infinity – an endless quest."

I bowed and thanked him for his advice. The family and I walked from the temple – it was dark. To my surprise, I actually enjoyed attending temple services with Junko and her family. It was as if I had, in some small way, become a part of their family through my attendance at their temple.

We came to an intersection, turned left, and strolled down the street toward their home. As we approached an alley, we spotted a Pachinko Parlor on the corner – it was open. Junko's father gave her permission to play the machines for a while. Pachinko is the Japanese version of a pinball machine. Instead of lying horizontally, like a western pinball machine, the pachinko machine is vertical. Small steel balls are shot to the top by levers, where they bounce on numerous pegs, as they fall to the bottom of the machine. During the early 1950s, the Japanese, as a nation, were addicted to the game. Approximately a quarter of the Japanese gross national profit passed through these establishments annually.

The steel balls cost 5 yen each. I purchased 500 steel balls from a little old lady in a booth where the balls were sold. An hour later, we both decided to call it a night. We cashed in the remaining balls, we had almost 200, and left. Walking hand in hand, we headed toward Junko's home.

I arrived at the dojo at 5:50 PM on Thursday. Neither Shirahama Sensei nor Ito-san was to be seen. The class was going to be taught by Sensei Isshu Sakaguchi. Sakaguchi Sensei, at five feet eight inches tall, was a little taller than Ito.

The class was called to attention, we bowed, warmed up, and soon everyone was sweating profusely.

"Kihon!" Sakaguchi shouted

The class immediately began working on basic techniques. Sakaguchi walked among the students making corrections. He stopped beside me, kicked my leg roughly, and checked my stance as he said something in a low, growling voice that I did not understand. After a grueling twenty minutes of basics, we started working the kata, Zenshin Kotai. The additional time Ito had spent with me after class on Tuesday helped me greatly with the kata that, while not complicated, was very challenging to a new student.

After a few minutes, Sakaguchi told the class to perform Shihohai. The idea of the first two kata seemed to be to perfect the side kick which was common to both. The new Japanese student and I made it through Zenshin Kotai, but sat out the more complex kata, Shihohai. After Shihohai, several more advanced kata were practiced. Sakaguchi told the students to practice three-step sparring (sanbon kumite). My partner was the new white belt. We were shown what to do and practiced to the best of our ability, which was almost non-existent, back and forth across the floor. Our sanbon kumite consisted of punching and blocking, making mistake after mistake, while not maintaining good balance. Sakaguchi motioned for everyone to leave the center of the floor and to sit around the walls of the dojo.

The advanced students were to participate in kumite (freestyle sparring) training. Sakaguchi pointed to two brown belt students who stood. Neither looked as if he understood Sakaguchi Sensei, or knew exactly what he wanted them to do. They donned a type of heavy armor similar to what is depicted on pictures or statues of samurai warriors; other students gathered around to assist. Students who practiced were required to wear the armor, which was called "bogu". Chitose Sensei's rules mandated that students wear bogu when sparring – no one was to violate these rules when sparring. The bogu was very complex, old and uncomfortable looking. It consisted of leg guards which covered the shins and instep, a large groin protector, which was worn outside the karate uniform, two arm guards, similar to the leg guards but smaller, a large chest protector that hung down past the groin, a large mask with bars on it, and two gloves that resembled boxing gloves with the ends of the fingers cut out.

The two brown belts stood in the middle of the dojo floor. They looked like two knights from the middle ages.

"Hajime!" (Begin!) They proceeded to move around the center of the floor as each student attempted to attack or counter attack the other. It quickly became obvious that Sakaguchi was becoming disgusted by their lack of ability and spirit. He stopped the match. Slowly looking around the room, he chose two black belts, and ordered them to don the bogu. One student was a sho-dan (1st degree

The Lesson

Practicing Niseishi Sho Kata.

black belt), the other, a ni-dan (2nd degree black belt). With the help of other students they put on the cumbersome equipment. Within minutes they stood facing each other in the center of the floor.

"Hajime!" Sakaguchi yelled.

Both men attempted various attacks against each other. None of their techniques were effective. They were only marginally more successful than the brown belts. The match was stopped and both students were told to leave the floor.

Sakaguchi turned and stared at another black belt, Inokuma, and motioned for him to move into the training area without the armor. Sakaguchi stood directly across from Inokuma.

"Hajime!" Sakaguchi commanded.

They started moving around the center of the dojo, circling each other. Suddenly Sakaguchi's foot shot forward and stopped just short of Inokuma's body. The kick was followed immediately by a lighting fast punch to Inokuma's nose, which stopped a fraction of an inch short of contact. Inokuma blocked most of the techniques that followed; a few would certainly have made contact if they had not been pulled. A lighting fast kick seemed to come from nowhere as Inokuma's foot snapped up and around in a perfect round kick which struck

Sakaguchi in the face. He went down hard onto the floor. Shaking his head, Sakaguchi regained his footing and staggered to his feet. Almost immediately upon regaining his feet, Sakaguchi's right hand shot forward with a vicious punch that connected full force on Inokuma's face. Inokuma's head snapped back as his body started to sag; he was out cold as he slumped toward the floor. As Inokuma fell, Sakaguchi's right foot flew forward and caught Inokuma with an exceptionally powerful front thrust kick in the stomach, slamming him into the wall. Sakaguchi looked around the room; his eyes settled on me, my blood ran cold. He looked away, and then told a couple of students to check on Inokuma. It was a full two minutes before they were able to get him on his feet. Two students helped him as we lined up in preparation for ending the class.

Sakaguchi Sensei changed clothes quickly after class was over and left the dojo immediately. Mary Shigamoto had been alerted that there had been a problem in the dojo. She ran from the office to assist Inokuma, who had a broken nose and possibly broken ribs.

As I practiced with the band on Friday, I spent a great deal of time contemplating the wisdom of wanting to study karate and evaluating my decision to do so. It was then that I understood the shocked reaction of the Japanese woman I had stopped on the streets of Beppu when I inquired about karate.

I knew immediately that something was up when I arrived at the dojo Saturday morning. I may have been new, but there was a feeling of tension in the air that could be felt by all. The dojo was crowded. Students stretched and practiced basics or kata if enough space could be found amid the multitudes. Inokuma was standing in a corner with his karate-gi (karate uniform) top off. He had a large patch over his nose and tape wrapped around his midsection. He had two black eyes, which made him look like a raccoon. He would have looked comical, if I had not witnessed him getting the injuries. I could only guess at the amount of pain he must be in.

Shirahama Sensei and Ito-san were already there in their karate-gis. I bowed in greeting to them as I walked toward the dressing room. As I entered the dressing room, Sakaguchi passed me on his way out. I bowed to him, he did not acknowledge me but looked at me coldly, and continued out the door to the training area. I changed into my heavy judo-gi and walked to the training area. Shirahama Sensei bowed the class in and then Ito-san took charge of the warm-up exercises.

The class was typical of my first two classes that week. Bow in, warm up, stretch, kata, three-step sparring, and sparring with bogu. Today, however, we went outside and I learned how to strike a makiwara (straw covered karate strik-

―― *The Lesson* ――

ing post).

When we came back inside the dojo, students prepared for the free-sparring segment of the class, which was about to begin. White belts and lower ranking students never participated in this part of the training. We were to observe and learn. Shirahama Sensei motioned for Sakaguchi to step forward. He asked Sakaguchi if he wanted to spar with or without the bogu.

"Without!" he answered contemptuously.

"Ito-san!" Shirahama bellowed. A sudden stillness came over the building.

Ito moved to an area across from Sakaguchi.

Both men bowed, first to Shirahama Sensei and then to each other. Ito was short with a stocky build; Sakaguchi, tall and lanky, stood opposite, looking down at him.

"Hajime!" Shirahama Sensei said.

Both men moved around the floor, as each tried to gain an advantage over the other. Sakaguchi's fist snapped forward, Ito parried it with his forward hand. Next, Sakaguchi's foot shot forward in a powerful front thrust kick; Ito slid away and to his right as he slapped the kick away. Sakaguchi slid forward and executed a lightning fast reverse punch to Ito's face. Ito parried the punch with his left

Talk before training.

A very young Masami "Mas" Tsuruoka, who was the terror of Southern Japan in kumite during the early 1950s.

hand and simultaneously punched Sakaguchi in his solar plexus. Sakaguchi's head dropped and his chin fell forward into Ito's second punch. At the very moment his second punch landed, Ito round kicked; the kick caught Sakaguchi's left hand, which had opened when he was hit in the solar plexus, and broke it. Without slowing down or stopping, moving like a well-oiled machine, Ito spun one hundred and eighty degrees and did a perfect back kick with his left foot. The kick lifted Sakaguchi off of the floor and slammed him into the same wall that Inokuma had smashed into two days earlier. It took a lot of work to revive Sakaguchi. Two students carried him from the floor. Shirahama Sensei ordered everyone to sit in seiza; he looked solemnly at the Class and began to speak.

"Karate can be either a terrible art, or it can be a wonderful art. The decision belongs to each of us who study it. Karate should be studied only for self-perfection and self-protection. It should never be used to hurt, maim, or kill, except under dire circumstances. It is not a toy that can be played with and shown off to one's friends. The movements of karate are lethal – one slip can cause serious injury or death. Since beginners lack control, they practice only basic techniques, kata and three step sparring. Black belts are expected to have control, not only of their technique, but also of their temper. Because of this control, they are allowed to spar in class. Whenever a black belt injures someone, it will be for one of several reasons:

First: The black belt lacks control and if this is true, he should not be a black belt;

Second: The black belt intended to hurt the other person, as a boost to his ego, in an attempt to impress others;

Third: When ordered, and only then, by their sensei to teach a lesson to those who constantly violate numbers one and two;

Fourth: A student violated Chitose Sensei's rules and failed to wear bogu for protection.

Sakaguchi caused a serious injury to Inokuma during Thursday's class. I had asked him to teach the class because Ito and I were away on business. Sakaguchi not only violated Chitose Sensei's rule about the bogu, but when he was struck by accident, he was embarrassed. His ego was hurt. He felt that he had to hurt Inokuma-san to prove a point. This morning I ordered Ito, who did not wish to do so, to put Sakaguchi in his proper place. I am not proud to have done such a thing, but I felt that it was necessary. We must not forget the saying of Funakoshi Sensei: 'Karate begins with courtesy and ends with courtesy.' "

I had been amazed at the ease with which Ito had disposed of Sakaguchi. It was common knowledge that Sakaguchi liked to spar and that, occasionally, he drank a little too much sake. He had the reputation of being a very good fighter. Ito-san hardly ever sparred; he was known for his kata.

During my first week of karate training, I had gained two valuable insights. The first, that basics and kata practice are of primary importance to my karate training, and second, not to do anything which would get any of the senior students mad at me.

After class, I approached Ito-san and spoke with him about his kumite.

"That was amazing!" I said in my youthful enthusiasm. "I bet you must be the best fighter on the island."

"No, not really." he answered. "Shirahama Sensei is excellent and much better than I am. There are many others," he said humbly.

"Who is the best fighter on the island?" I asked.

"There are many good karate fighters on Kyushu. The strongest fighter I have ever sparred with is about my age and lives in Kumamoto; his name is Mas Tsuruoka."

Ito continued, "Never forget, karate-do is not about fighting, it is about self-protection and, more importantly, self-perfection."

• •

Chapter 6

The Secret of Karate

It is too clear and so it is hard to see. A dunce once searched for a fire, with a lighted lantern. Had he known what fire was, He could have cooked his rice much sooner.

The Gateless Gate

The months flew by and several had passed since I had joined the dojo. The strange rituals and words associated with karate training and the dojo were now second nature to me. The karate-gi I had ordered arrived at the little store in Beppu during my fifth week of training. The judo-gi that I had been training in was always very sweat-filled and heavy. Upon wearing the lighter karate-gi, I found that the heavy sweat-laden judo-gi had helped me in the development of my punches. My punches seemed to be a little faster than those of the Japanese boy who had started his karate training the day I had.

After the initial shock of my second and third classes, I fell into the dojo routine with great abandon. The classes soon settled into a predictable routine. I quickly realized that many of the techniques I had been taught at Fort Campbell were a great deal different from what I was now being taught. As my days in Japan turned into weeks, and the weeks into months, my training improved rapidly because of the excellent instruction I was receiving.

Junko was in her last year of high school. This fact limited our dating chances mostly to Saturday afternoon and Sunday. Her father was very strict about her dating on school nights when she had lessons.

During the week, I spent most of my spare time at the dojo. I did this for two reasons – the first was that I had fallen in love with the art of karate, and the second, but equally important reason was that I, like most soldiers, had little money to do anything else.

On one of my trips to the dojo, Mary Shigamoto spoke to me about a few of Doctor Chitose's accomplishments. She told me that Chitose Sensei held rank in karate, judo, kendo, iaido, Okinawan kobudo, and kyudo. Karate, however, was his first martial art and his first love. It had become the primary reason for his being.

The dojo also held Judo and Kendo classes on a regularly scheduled basis. These classes were the primary classes; all karate training had been scheduled around them. When I was not taking classes, working with the band, dating Junko, or practicing karate at the post gymnasium, I tried to schedule some additional practice time at the Beppu dojo. I enjoyed dojo practice much more than my solitary practice at the army post. At the dojo, I could occasionally find a ranking karate-ka to assist me.

When I was unable to get to the Beppu dojo for training or practice, I would practice at the post gymnasium. The regimental boxing team practiced there nightly. I would usually find an empty corner and practice alone. While I practiced my basics and kata I drew many inquisitive looks from the boxers. After a few practice sessions, however, they became used to my presence. Jake Morrison, one of the better regimental boxers, would occasionally come over and ask me questions. He could not understand kata training. I did not admit it to him, but to some degree, neither did I. Since my first karate class I had learned three kata to the point of approval: Zenshin Kotai, Shihohai and Niseishi Sho and Dai, with the Kaisetsu, which is an explanation of how the various kata movements

The back street which led to the rear gate of Camp Chickamauga.

such as moving, blocking, striking, punching and kicking may be utilized in various self defense situations. Each succeeding kata became a little easier as I became more proficient in the preceding kata. I was now attempting to learn my most challenging kata, Seisan.

Three months earlier I had been practicing after class when Chitose Sensei and Ito-san approached me. Ito informed me that Chitose Sensei wanted to see me perform the three kata that I knew and a few basic techniques.

Chitose Sensei said, "You now green belt." Ito told me, "You pay Shigamoto-san 1,800 Yen ($5.00) for belt." I paid Mary, but she had no green belt to give me.

The Japanese economy, which was still recovering from the devastation of World War II, was in poor shape. Most students could not afford new belts as they advanced in rank. Some yon-kyu wore a freshly dyed green belt; others continued to wear their white belts. The majority of the belts worn by the green, brown and black belts were their original white belts, which had been dyed after each promotion. Mary Shigamoto asked me if I would purchase some boxes of dye at the Post Exchange. I bought the boxes of dye and gave them to her. This enabled her to not only dye my white belt to green, but also to dye the belts of several other students.

After three months as a yon-kyu I was rapidly gaining confidence in my ability – confidence that had been lacking when I first started training.

Saturday morning I awoke feeling full of energy. I showered, shaved, and attempted to find some clean civilian clothes to wear to the dojo; unfortunately, all of my civies needed cleaning. A family emergency made it necessary for Rocky, our houseboy, to take two weeks off. He was not due back until Monday. I quickly dressed in my Class A uniform. The barracks door slammed as I strode through it and headed across Camp Chickamauga toward the rear gate. I had discovered that leaving through the rear gate cut off several blocks of travel to the dojo. The streets which connected the rear gate to downtown Beppu were narrow and twisting, making me think of the Burma Road. I walked within sight of the large Beppu Buddha, a major tourist attraction.

Upon my arrival at the dojo, I placed my shoes in the familiar, rickety, old shoe rack. Some students had already arrived and were engaged in individual practice. Chitose Sensei was already present. Both he and Shirahama Sensei were wearing judo-gi and occupied one corner. They were moving back and forth on some tatami mats. They grasped each other's uniforms and moved around the mats. Shirahama attempted to throw the much smaller and older Chitose. A second later, Shirahama's feet left the mat as Chitose Sensei threw him down with a perfect hip throw. It was obvious that they were enjoying themselves. A third black belt, Sensei Masato Aso, a sixth dan in judo, stood to one side of the mat and was coaching them. He had trained at the Kodokan Judo Institute in Tokyo. A few weeks earlier I had the opportunity to visit his home at 2-10 Asami 1-Chome with Ito-san and Shirahama Sensei.

The karate class was due to start in a few minutes. The judo-ka bowed and left their mats. Chitose Sensei walked from the mat to the dressing room where he changed into a lighter karate-gi top.

"Retsu o tsukuru," (Line up.) Ito said. "Seiza."

"Mokuso."

"Mokuso yame."

"Shomen ni, rei." We bowed to the little Japanese flag on the wall. Chitose Sensei spun on his knees and faced the class.

"Sensei ni, rei."

"Tachiagaru." (Stand up.)

Kakudo Murakami, the tall boy with the horn-rimmed glasses, was in charge of the calisthenics. We punched, kicked, and stretched and then we punched, kicked and stretched some more. After ten minutes our uniforms were starting to soak through with perspiration. Chitose Sensei stood with Shirahama Sensei in the corner near Mary Shigamoto's office talking and observing us as we participated in the exercises. Once the warm-up exercises were completed Murakami stood at attention, faced Chitose Sensei and Shirahama Sensei and bowed.

"Hidari seisan dachi. Chudan soto uke," Chitose Sensei said. (Left seisan stance, outside chest block).

We proceeded to punch, block, and kick as the two senior Sensei took turns managing the class. I would occasionally catch a glimpse of Chitose Sensei as he practiced along with us. As everyone else stepped across the floor, he seemed to glide across it.

"Seisan kata." Chitose Sensei said.

A few of the newer students retreated from the floor as the remainder staggered the lines so our front kicks would not hit the students in front of us.

"Hajime!"

Students practicing Seisan kata.

My left foot slid forward; I chest blocked as I breathed quietly. I inhaled and exhaled rhythmically in a one-two in, and, a one-two out count. I reverse punched, then breathed again as I performed an outside chest block. My right foot slid forward, I reverse punched again, another chest block while breathing lightly, and on it went, as we stepped, slid, blocked, punched and kicked our way through the kata.

"Moichido!" (Do it again!) came the order.

After doing the kata Seisan two more times we were told to leave the floor and sit against the wall.

Murakami, Ito and Inokuma moved into the center of the training area.

"Seisan!" Shirahama Sensei said.

In perfect unison, they moved together as each step, block, punch, and kick, had perfect timing. The thrust of their front kicks caused the floor to tremble. They slid back, their hands open, pulling their hands back to their hips, then made a counter-clockwise twist.

"Yame!" Shirahama Sensei commanded as they completed the last movement of the kata.

Chitose Sensei spoke to Shirahama, then walked to the center of the training area.

"Seisan," he said, almost in a whisper. Chitose Sensei's left foot stepped into

Broken nose from Wally Slocki.

an uchi hachi stance and his arms made a circle above his head. His hands – one in a fist and the other open – came to rest in front of his midsection.

His left foot slid forward into a left seisan stance. He breathed ever so lightly through his nose and exhaled almost silently through his lips, which were barely open. He locked in his stance as his hip made a vibrating motion. His right hand exploded forward as he reverse punched. The entire dojo floor vibrated, much more than when the three young black belts had done the kata together. I was amazed at the amount of power Chitose Sensei could generate in relation to his body size. His punch was faster and had generated more power than any punch I had ever seen. I wondered how it was possible for a man no bigger than he was to develop this power. I was convinced that Chitose Sensei must have some secret training method.

The class ended. I asked Ito-san if he would walk with me to where Chitose Sensei and Shirahama Sensei were standing. I asked Ito to ask Chitose Sensei to explain the real secret of karate to me. After looking me over for a couple of seconds, Chitose Sensei answered my question with one word, "Kata."

I looked at Chitose Sensei, very slowly my gaze shifted toward Shirahama

Sensei, finally I looked at Ito, then back to Chitose Sensei. I could hardly believe what I had heard.

"Arigato gozaimasu," (Thank you.) I said, and bowed. I should have known better, I thought. I walked away thinking, "These Japanese know the real secret of karate, but they will never share it with an American."

After leaving the dojo, I headed south toward Nagare Kawa Street. That evening Junko and I had a date to go to a movie. As I was crossing the street in front of the Hanago Bar and Grill, I heard a voice some distance behind me, shouting my name.

"Bill! Corporal Dometrich!"

I glanced over my shoulder and saw Corporal Don Matthews gaining on me from half a block away.

"Bill, where are you headed?" he asked as he caught up with me.

I explained that I was headed back to the camp to get ready for my date with Junko later that evening.

"You have time for a couple of beers?" he said in a pleading, 'Don't let me drink

Group wtih Soke and Taira Shinken.

alone, buddy,' tone of voice.

"OK, I'll have one, but then I have to get back to camp."

Several bars, beers, and hours later, I had forgotten about my date with Junko. Somewhere between bars, we had hired our own three-piece Japanese band. One member played an accordion, one played a banjo and the third played the harmonica and tambourine. They had a list of American and Japanese songs encased in a sheet of plastic.

"Start with #1 song and play them all," Don and I told them. "When you get to the end, start over again." Each song cost 100 yen. We gave them 5,000 yen and we were off. As we staggered from bar to bar, they followed us like baby ducks behind their mother. By three o'clock in the morning, I was in very bad shape. Don packed me into a small cab and took me back to camp. I spent all day Sunday in the latrine with the dry heaves. At first formation Monday, I was ordered back to bed by SFC Munro; I stayed in bed until Friday. On Friday afternoon I was feeling better and was once again on my feet. I was told to report to the orderly room, the First Sergeant wanted to see me. Immediately upon my arrival in the orderly room I received a very professional butt chewing from Sergeant Munro who took my pass privileges away for one week.

● ●

Chapter 7

Failure

What seems nasty, painful, or evil, can become a source of beauty, joy and strength, if faced with an open mind. Every moment is a golden one, for him who has the vision to recognize it as such.

Henry Miller

My one-week restriction to the post because of my excessive drinking had been a Godsend for me. The week gave me a chance to get my stomach straightened out and to overcome the tremendous headache I had as a result of my stupid drinking binge.

I asked Howard to speak to Kazuko and have her inform Junko that I was very sorry about missing our date. Junko was very upset, and rightly so. When she heard of how sick I had been, however, she forgave me. Her father gave her permission to visit me at the army post on Wednesday evening. We went to the post theater and saw the film, "Red Beret," starring Alan Ladd. The film was about the training of an American, Alan Ladd, as a member of a British paratrooper regiment during World War II.

By Saturday I was finally able to return to my normal eating habits. After breakfast I stopped in the orderly room to see if my pass privileges had been reinstated. I hoped that Sergeant Munro had remembered to put my pass back in the pass box. Corporal Underwood, the platoon's "Charge of Quarters" (C.Q.) for the weekend, looked in the box. My pass was there. Attached to the pass was a note:

1. Don't drink;

2. If you do drink, don't get drunk;

3. If you violate number two, you will go to the stockade.

Have a nice day,
SFC William Munro

Master Sergeant William Munro

Failure

The very thought of drinking any type of alcoholic beverage made me feel ill. I had learned my lesson the hard way, and certainly had no intention of drinking. I gladly took the pass, walked back to the squad area, and dressed in my civilian clothes, which Rocky had cleaned and pressed for me. Flashing my pass at the M.P. at the gate, I walked off post to the rickshaw stand where I hired a rickshaw for my trip to the dojo.

Upon arriving at the dojo the first person I saw was Mary Shigamoto.

"Where have you been Bill; have you been sick?" she inquired. "You do not look well."

"Something like that," I answered sheepishly.

I walked down the hall to the dressing room, changed into my karate-gi and got ready for class. I put my watch in the pocket of my slacks and put them in a neat pile by the wall. There were no lockers at the dojo; none were needed because nothing was ever stolen. Anything of value found lying loose – money, watches, rings – were always returned to the owner, or turned over to Mary, who would return them to the owner. Traditional martial artists never took anything that did not belong to them. The Japanese were the most honest people I had ever known. To think about stealing, even if they knew they would never be caught, was unheard of.

The Japanese feel that what another person thinks of you is of little importance. What you think of yourself is of the utmost importance. You may fool others, but you cannot fool yourself; only you know what you really are.

Walking past Mary's office as I headed to the training hall, she yelled out the door to me.

"Bill, take it easy today!"

The dojo was starting to get crowded. Many of the students were arriving, changing, and warming up. I could feel the soreness throughout my body as I started stretching. I had learned a valuable lesson as a result of my drinking binge two weeks before. No one could be an alcoholic and excel at karate – or any other athletic endeavor. People who think they can indulge their vices are fooling themselves.

Ito-san entered the dojo, nodded in recognition to several of us, and ordered the students to line up.

"Seiza."

"Mokuso." We sat, backs straight, heads erect, looking down at the floor through partially closed eyes.

"Mokuso yame."

"Rei." We bowed to the shomen, then to the instructor.

We jumped to our feet. Ito started running and he motioned for the class to follow him. He ran toward the door of the dojo, then into the street. Barefoot, we ran up Mochigahama Street for the familiar trip toward Takazaka Yama. We turned left and cut across a field. After three quarters of a mile we turned and retraced our steps back to the dojo. I was starting to feel nauseated; my stomach was churning. Upon returning to the inside of the dojo, Shirahama Sensei took charge of the class. After lining up we started doing hundreds of punches and kicks. Each student counted ten, then the student to the right would count, until Shirahama Sensei felt we should move on to other training.

There was no doubt about it; I was going to be sick. I asked to leave the floor and made my way to the benjo. Just as I entered, I heaved my breakfast down the toilet. Several minutes later, I returned to class. In a very short time I had to sit down again. I stayed seated on the floor for the remainder of the class.

"You look very sick Bill-san," Mary said. "Perhaps you not practice so hard until you feel better."

I told Mary about my drinking binge with Don Matthews. "You are too young to drink!" she scolded me. "If you are serious about karate training like you say you are, you will not drink at all, or only in moderation."

Ito-san walked into the office and informed me that I was expected to test the following Saturday.

"Next week? This is rather short notice!" I exclaimed. Ito, who had been listening to the conversation between Mary and me, spoke to me very sternly.

"You no get stinko (slang for drunk) and come class last week, you know we do test. Next Saturday you test. Shigamoto-san help fill paper out."

Ito turned and left. Mary reached into her desk for a test application and completed it for me. I paid her the 1,000 Yen, which was just about all of the money I had left. My wild weekend of drinking with Don had left me almost completely broke.

I attended Tuesday and Thursday classes at the dojo. On both nights I showed up early and left late. Sunday afternoon, Wednesday and Friday evenings I did additional training at the post gymnasium. I practiced basics, kata, and reviewed my three step sparring, which is nearly impossible to practice without a partner.

Jake Morrison and the members of the regimental boxing team were also train-

Failure

ing at the gym daily preparing for the Defense Department's Far East boxing matches.

"Did you break up with your girl?" Jake Morrison asked me on Wednesday when I was at the gym training.

"No, I didn't," I said. "Why would you ask something like that?"

"You've been spending an awful lot of time at the gym lately." I told Jake about my upcoming test and the need for extra practice. Being on the boxing team helped Jake understand my dilemma.

Saturday I was up early, as was my custom. I showered, shaved, dressed, and made my way to the mess hall for a quick, light breakfast. I returned to the barracks, picked up my karate-gi, and headed for the rickshaw stand by the main gate. With payday only two days away I had little money left. I decided to splurge and spend a quarter of it on a rickshaw for my trip to the dojo. I needed to conserve my energy for the test. Rocky had cleaned and pressed my karate-gi for the test. There was no doubt about it – I was ready.

Thirteen students tested, myself included. Only nine passed the test – I was not one of them. To say that I was disappointed would be an understatement. Immediately after the test, I dressed, put my gi back into my AWOL bag, left the dojo and started walking back to camp.

The barracks was empty except for Rocky who was sitting on a footlocker spit-shining a pair of jump boots.

Without speaking, I slid my AWOL bag under my bunk, lay down and closed my eyes. I felt totally devastated.

"Bill-san, you pass?" Rocky asked.

I looked at him for a moment. "No!"

"Too bad, you catchi next time."

"There may not be a next time," I said, feeling sorry for myself. "I'm getting tired of karate training, I may quit."

"You no quit, you real roose face, if quit," he said as he put down the shoe he had been shining, stood, walked over to my bunk and looked down at me.

"Most number one karate thing, practice," he said as he struggled to find the proper words to express his feelings.

"I worked hard for that belt. I thought they liked me."

"You no catchi belt cause they rike you. You catchi belt cause you good," he said with his serious, 'the world's troubles are on my shoulders,' look.

Later that night as I tossed and turned trying to go to sleep, I could hear Ito-san's voice over and over telling me I would quit. I realized that Rocky was right. I had joined the Army and traveled half way around the world to seek karate training. I would not quit, but I would never test again until I was positive that I was really ready to pass – any test.

I picked up the tempo of my training after failing my san-kyu test. The thought of quitting never again entered my mind. Instead, I discovered from somewhere deep inside myself a renewed determination. I now had one reason for my existence, and only one, to train in karate as often and as hard as I could.

The sweat was soaking through my karate-gi although the heat in the post gymnasium was turned down. I practised my kata. I stepped, blocked, punched, kicked, and struck out with my arms and legs as the sweat ran down my body in rivulets.

I bowed and assumed a preparatory stance prior to practicing the kata, Seisan, for the thirty-sixth time that day. My left foot slid forward, I blocked, then punched as I worked my way through the kata. I did another outside chest block, my right foot slid forward, my left hand punched. For the first time, the sound and feeling of the movements as I continued the kata, were a natural high for me. I had never felt like this before. I was still practicing Seisan when the NCO (Non-Commissioned Officer) in charge of the gymnasium informed me that it was 5:45 PM.

"I close at 6:00 PM on Sundays," he said. "It's time to call it a day."

• •

Chapter 8

Rohai-Niseishi

If you understand "it", all things are One; If you do not, they are different and separate, If you do not understand "it", all things are One; If you do, they are different and separate.

Zen Monk, Mumon (Wu-men) (1184 - 1260)

When his busy schedule allowed, Chitose Sensei would travel by train to Beppu approximately three times a month. On rare occasions, he would show up more often. Everyone felt fortunate to have him in attendance to teach the Saturday class. Several times he would spend the night in Beppu and teach a second class on Sunday for those who were fortunate enough to attend. When he did stay over in Beppu he would hold classes in Judo and Kendo in addition to karate. A few times Chitose Sensei arrived on Thursday and stayed through Sunday. The additional two days gave the judo, kendo, and karate students in Beppu access not only to his technical knowledge, but also to his unique insight and wisdom in the various martial arts.

On numerous occasions, the band was required to travel to Kumamoto and Camp Wood to participate in training or in formal military ceremonies. There usually was some free time during these trips to Kumamoto that allowed me the time I needed to train with Chitose Sensei, Ishikawa Sensei, and others from the western side of the island. Training in the Kumamoto area was held in an old, small, rather run-down building that was used as a dojo, not far from the army base. Training there was much more formal than the training in Beppu. My impression was that this formality existed because Chitose Sensei lived in the area.

Chitose Sensei, who I learned was a medical doctor, was a very demanding teacher. He was very tough on his students during class but, at the same time, he was very kind to everyone after the classes were over. I began to look upon

Chitose Sensei less as a karate sensei, and more as a father. When I first met him, my impression was that he was a rather aloof person. As I got to know him better, I found that he was a very warm person, who was extremely sure of himself.

One Saturday, after a very rigorous class at the Beppu dojo, Chitose Sensei asked me if I would like to accompany him to downtown Beppu to go shopping. I was flattered by his offer and accepted at once – this was to be the first of many such shopping trips.

Sensei and I left the dojo and strolled downtown. After a few blocks we turned right onto Nagare Street and entered the main business district with its busy shops. Leaving Nagare Kawa Street a few blocks later, we turned left onto one of the primary side streets that was covered by a glass roof. (Covered streets are very common in Japan.) The streets were crowded with weekend shoppers. We walked among the crowd; Chitose Sensei stopped occasionally to enter a small store to make a purchase. As we navigated our way through the throng, I would occasionally be bumped by or bump into a passing pedestrian. This caused me to become aware of a very strange phenomenon while walking with Sensei. While I was being bumped, Chitose Sensei was never bumped, jostled or even touched. His movements through the crowd reminded me of a fish that I had seen swimming in a pond. Chitose Sensei unconsciously moved around people as he walked, looked into store windows, or tried to engage me in conversation that I had trouble understanding. Since that day, I observed this phenomenon on several occasions and I eventually asked Sensei how he did this.

"Do what?" he asked in response. He had been unaware that anything was happening and was at a loss to explain it.

On Sunday, I walked to the dojo for a special class. I left Camp Chickamauga through the back gate. The streets, as usual, were crowded. A large group of little girls wearing sailor suit dresses were at the Beppu Buddha taking a tour. At 12:45 PM, I arrived at the dojo. Chitose Sensei was in a corner training several black belts. I removed my shoes, turned and bowed to them. They paid me no notice.

"It makes no difference whether your instructor returns your bow or not," Ito had explained to me many months before. "The bow is for your benefit, not his."

I bowed again, just for good measure, before I walked into the dressing room. I hurriedly changed into my karate-gi. I felt great – full of energy. I started to stretch and warm up in anticipation of a hard training session.

"Seiretsu." (Line up.)

The students and instructors lined up in rows. We knelt in seiza. Our eyes closed, we sat in silence for a couple of minutes, opened our eyes, then bowed to the wall holding the little Japanese flag. Chitose Sensei spun around to face us.

"Sensei ni, rei." We bowed to him. "Osu," we said in unison.

The class sprang to its feet immediately and we started doing stretching and warm up exercises. Predictably, we did the usual hundreds of kicks, punches, blocks, and strikes. We began perspiring and our karate-gi became soaked with perspiration. Twenty minutes later it was kihon (basics) time.

Shirahama Sensei and every one of the black belts were frantic about basics because Chitose Sensei was; their obsession was understandable. Chitose Sensei had instilled this fanaticism in everyone who had been fortunate enough to become his student.

The class stepped forward into Seisan dachi. Chitose Sensei walked among the students, making small corrections and explaining the finer points of the stance: leg muscle tension, the balance points of the bottom of the foot and the proper method of punching and directing the energy forward. Ito-san checked me and was there to advise me as Chitose Sensei would explain some of the finer points about a technique.

We started punching and kicking as we moved forward and then backward. The entire class was now sweating profusely. The training floor was wet and getting slippery.

"This is not a retirement home!" Shirahama Sensei yelled in Japanese. I had heard that statement so often that I knew it by heart, it needed no translation. Several more passes were made back and forth across the training area. We did several repetitions of seisan dachi, combined with blocks, punches, strikes and kicks.

"Mawashi geri!" Chitose Sensei said, just loud enough to be heard. The mawashi geri is a kick that strikes the target horizontally. The ball of the kicking foot is snapped into the opponent's kidneys, chest, throat, or temple/face area, with great power. The leg swings at a ninety-degree angle as the foot strikes the opponent while the supporting leg is bent. Many of the most experienced instructors can perform the kick without pivoting on their supporting leg, however, only the most gifted karate students could do it right after the first few times.

"Knee up!" Shirahama Sensei would shout.

I was usually a little slower responding to commands than other members of the class because of the language problem. Most of the commands I had become aware of but there was always one or two I was unsure of. I would watch the Japanese students, see what they did, and follow along. Occasionally this would earn me a knock for responding slowly to the command.

Chitose Sensei and Shirahama Sensei stayed behind in the dojo as the class went outside for makiwara practice. The number of makiwara was limited and the students would line up three or four deep behind them. I was third in line and I patiently waited for my turn. The second student completed his set of punches and kicks. I moved forward to face the straw post and placed my left hand against the straw to measure my distance. I slammed my right fist into the straw-covered post again and again. Next, I moved a little farther from the post and practiced several side kicks against it. I felt a sharp pain in my buttocks.

The author with Robert Smith.

"Knee up," Ito said from behind me.

Automatically my foot raised a full four inches. I glanced around looking for Ito. He was already two makiwara away with a shinai in his hand checking another student. I backed away from the makiwara and the student behind me stepped forward and began to punch. Each student took three turns at the makiwara. The class jogged back into the dojo after makiwara training.

It was kata time. A quick snap of the hands to the left and a right shuto (knife hand strike), followed immediately by a left nukite (spear hand thrust) to the opponent's throat.

"Go!" (Five!) Shirahama Sensei said as Chitose Sensei and he continued to make corrections. We were nearing the end of the Potsai kata.

"Nijusan!" (Twenty-three.) The students rotated their left feet ninety degrees to the left.

The kata Niseishi Sho flows as the class performs it.

"Nijushi!" (Twenty-four.) We stepped to the right and performed a Sagurite-no-kamai (open sweep hand position).

Another yell from Shirahama and we moved our right feet ninety degrees to the right.

"Yame." (Finish).

We stepped back into musubi dachi, the natural stance, and bowed. We stood there, our uniforms wet; Chitose Sensei spoke to us and told us to make our uniforms neater. We were able to rest for approximately one minute before beginning another kata. Students who had been seated were ordered to stand and join the class.

"Niseishi Dai!" Chitose Sensei said. "Niseishi Dai!" the students yelled.

The students assumed the uchi hachi dachi stance in unison as their right hand, made into a fist, was covered by the left hand. Upon the command of "Hajime!" the students double-chest blocked as they breathed in through their nose, and out through partially closed lips, rhythmically. Niseishi was practiced several times as Chitose Sensei made corrections. After the completion of Niseishi kata training, the class formed in groups of two and began practicing Niseishi Kaisetsu. Kaisetsu are the self-defense movements within a kata.

The end of class neared and Chitose Sensei was going to demonstrate Potsai kata. The students cleared the center of the training area as Chitose Sensei moved into it.

"Potsai," Chitose said and he sank into uchi hachi dachi. As he demonstrated the kata, his uniform snapped loudly each time his hands and arms moved to perform Shuto (knife hand) and nukite (spear hand) techniques. The kata became a thing of beauty and raw power.

When demonstrated by the other black belts Potsai was always extremely well done, however, it was just a kata. Seeing Chitose Sensei demonstrate a kata, on the other hand, was almost like a religious experience.

Finally, the class was over. We were ordered to line up and Chitose Sensei made some comments about our practice. He mentioned specific areas where he felt that we as a class needed improvement. After the final seiza and meditation we bowed and the class was dismissed. A few students retreated to the dressing room where they removed their wet karate uniforms. Many of the students, enthused by Chitose Sensei's performance of Potsai, continued to practice.

As I was preparing to leave the floor, Ito informed me that Chitose Sensei would like to see me do a kata. I had, during the many months I had been training, learned the movements to all of the kata, including Potsai. The majority of my time however, was spent practicing the kata Seisan. Chitose Sensei, Shirahama Sensei, Ito-san, and a group of students, stood around waiting for me to do my kata. "My Seisan is getting better," I thought, "I should have no trouble demonstrating it."

"Rohai Sho," Chitose Sensei said.

Caught by surprise, I hesitated for a moment, bowed, stepped into uchi hachi dachi, and started the kata. I dropped down on one knee into an iaigoshi dachi, blocking downward, then sprang up and did a double side punch (morote yoko tsuki). I worked my way through the kata, gaining confidence as I went along. I front kicked, stepped forward into a kosa dachi, did a juji uke to the side, and an X block to my right side. Instead of stepping back with my left leg and punching to my right, I stepped back and performed a haito uchi strike with my left hand. I snapped my hips and faced to my left as I did a shuto strike, and completed the kata. Suddenly I realized that I had made a major mistake. I had started one kata and finished with another. Chitose Sensei, Shirahama Sensei, Ito, and the rest stood there with big grins on their faces.

"Atarashii kata (new kata), Rohai-Niseishi." Chitose Sensei said to everyone present, while smiling at me. "Moichido!" (One more time!)

On my second attempt to do the kata, I made no mistakes.

"Gould bouy," Chitose Sensei said, as he patted me on the shoulder and smiled.

"Chitose Sensei is scheduled to return to Kumamoto City later this evening," Ito told me. "We stay and train, would you rike stay, train?" Ito asked.

I remained at the dojo with a few others. We trained an additional hour and forty-five minutes. With Ito-san translating Chitose Sensei's comments, I learned a great deal that day and I came to realize why Chitose Sensei's last name meant, "the man of infinite wisdom."

Ito, a few others, and I visited a local bathhouse after we left the dojo. For over an hour we soaked in the steaming waters. Some small plastic cups appeared as a cold bottle of Asahi beer was passed around. I took a cup and attempted to sip the beer from it but had great difficulty. I drank a little; however, after my night out with Don Matthews, my taste for beer had not fully returned. I bowed to Ito upon leaving the bathhouse after an hour of soaking and we went our separate ways.

I took Rocky's words of wisdom seriously when he told me that I should relax and enjoy life and not do karate all the time. On Sunday of the following weekend, Howard, Kazuko, Junko, and I planned a trip to Takazaki Yama, the famous Monkey Mountain just to the north of Beppu. We had been anticipating the trip for some weeks.

Howard and I saw the girls standing in front of the Hanago Bar and Grill when we were still half a block away. Kazuko was wearing a green flowered American style dress; Junko was wearing a purple blouse and black slacks. Both looked radiant.

"Have you been waiting long?" Howard inquired.

"Not long," Kazuko answered as she flashed Howard a big grin.

I winked at Junko and asked her if she had missed me since I had been spending so much time on training.

"No miss," she replied with a shrug. "No miss pain in butt."

"Gee, thanks," I replied. "It's nice to know that you were concerned."

This made her laugh and the one eye peaking out from behind her hair twinkled with delight.

We entered the Hanago Bar and Grill and sat at a booth in one corner. Howard and the girls had the standard Japanese fare. I never learned to eat many vegetables and was leery of food I couldn't easily identify. As a result, my meal consisted of fried chicken and french fries. The fried chicken was delicious although the french fries, which were quartered like boiled potatoes, tasted as if they had been deep fried in fish grease.

After our meal, we walked to the bicycle rental shop, which was adjacent to the Beppu Buddha. Howard and I paid the four hundred yen for four old bicycles. We inspected all the bikes and located the best four. To our good fortune, we located one that was a little smaller than the rest – the ideal bike for Junko. The owner of the small shop, an old man, adjusted the seat of the smallest bicycle to its lowest position so Junko's feet could reach the pedals.

"Now that we have the bicycles, who knows the best way to Monkey Mountain?" I asked.

"Follow me," Junko replied.

We rode single file through the narrow side streets of Beppu as we wound our way northward.

The sun was coming out from behind the clouds, which were slowly dissipating. Motorized traffic was very light. As we rode north on the bay road, an occasional three-wheeled truck passed us. The pedestrians, however, were another matter. Large numbers were walking in both directions. We rang our little bicycle bells to warn them that we were behind them as we rode through the throng on

The Beppu Buddha.

our way to the mountain.

After a short ride we were in the countryside. The houses were thinning out and giving way to lush tropical vegetation. To our right was an unobstructed view of the bay. After pedaling for fifteen more minutes, we started up the mountain. The mountain had a gradual slope that was easy to ascend, even with the old one-speed bicycles. As we slowly advanced up the side of the mountain we became aware of chatter coming from the trees. Monkeys were becoming more and more numerous the higher we went up the mountain. The road gradually became steeper. We had to stop and push the bicycles up the mountain road on a few of the steepest grades. At last, the road leveled off. We climbed back onto our bicycles and began pedaling again. The girls were holding up very well and did not seem winded from the ride. Howard and I were starting to feel fatigued and a little saddle sore from the bicycle seats. Of course, being U.S. Paratroopers and heroes in our own minds, we would never let the girls know that they were hardier than we were.

Ahead of us lay a sharp curve. Upon rounding the curve we caught view of a small store on the left side of the road. Outside the store were several benches and, surprisingly, a brand new Coca Cola sign hanging in front. We agreed that this would make a good rest area. Howard and I painfully got off of the bicycles.

As we entered the store, we were warmly greeted by a little old lady in her seventies who had come out of a back room to wait on us. Kazuko and Junko did the ordering; Howard and I did the paying. We each had a cold Coca Cola and a candy bar. We went outside and sat on the benches to consume our snacks. As soon as we opened our drinks and candy, we were surrounded by monkeys. Some of them were very brave and came right up to us begging to be fed. Occasionally, a monkey would run up to us and try to swipe our candy bars from our hands.

Our return to Beppu was much easier since it was mostly down hill. After returning the bicycles, the four of us headed back to the Hanago Bar and Grill. Upstairs above the grill was the bar, which had a very large dance floor. The floor was crowded, as usual. Howard, Kazuko, Junko, and I had been dancing for about a half-hour when suddenly a commotion erupted in the center of the dance floor.

A pretty, young Japanese girl, using both hands, pushed her GI boyfriend, with whom she had been dancing, away from her. She had a look of anger on her face. I recognized the GI who was her boyfriend immediately. It was Antonio Cavello, an Italian national who had joined the U.S. Army. After serving in the Army for five years he would be eligible for American citizenship.

The Monkey's of Takazaki Yama.

"What's the matter me?! What's the matter you?! That's what's the matter me!" the little Japanese girl exclaimed. Despite her barely understandable English, she had a great Italian accent. Everyone in the bar roared with laughter. Tony, who was barely capable of speaking passable English himself, had taught his girlfriend English – and what a job he had done!

We left the Hanago and strolled up Nagare Kawa Street in the direction of Kazuko's and Junko's home. After a hug and a good night kiss, Howard and I headed back to the main gate of Camp Chickamauga thinking life couldn't possibly get any better than this.

● ●

Chapter 9

Zazen

After the bells had rung, and were silent, Flowers chimed, A pearl of fragrance.

Basho

My right fist slammed into the makiwara again and again. I had, through dedicated daily makiwara practice, become addicted to the little post wrapped in straw. Against advice, I over-practiced with my right hand and under practiced with my left hand. This improper practice on my part resulted in my right hand developing very rapidly while my left did not develop at all.

As I propelled my fist into the makiwara, I thought of the Rissho Kosei-Kai priest and his words of wisdom. The kind words he had imparted to me on my visit had been on my mind a great deal recently. "Do not dwell upon the goal, but enjoy the path. True seeking is an endless quest." I thought I understood what he meant, but I was not positive.

On Tuesday after class ended, I spoke with Ito-san about my visit to the small Buddhist temple with Junko and her parents. I told him what the priest had told me.

Ito said that as a small child he had been raised as a member of the Rissho Kosei-Kai. His family was still active members.

"The Rissho Kosei-Kai is a great religion for the masses," Ito told me.

"The very name, Rissho Kosei-Kai, tells the story of the organization. 'Rissho' means to establish the true law or teaching of the Lotus Sutra. 'Ko' means the relationship of many people working together in harmony. 'Sei' expresses ideals

Makiwara training on Kyushu Island.

of the attainment of Buddhahood and the completeness of your being. 'Kai' is a word meaning a group or family.

"I still attend the local temple with my family when I go home on vacation," he told me.

"As a young police officer, the Zen method of Buddhist training with its reliance upon self is better suited for me at this time of my life. There is no conflict between Zen and the Rissho Kosei-Kai, just as there should not be a conflict between the practice of judo, karate or kendo. We all search for the "Do" or way, and use various vehicles to assist us on our journey to become a better and more complete person. Just because people travel different paths to the same realization is no reason for conflict," Ito explained to me.

"I now follow the path of Zen, which I feel will enhance a deeper understanding within me of the true essence of the "Do". The final goal of the Rissho Kosei-Kai is to make Zen, karate, judo or kendo the same. Life-long training should

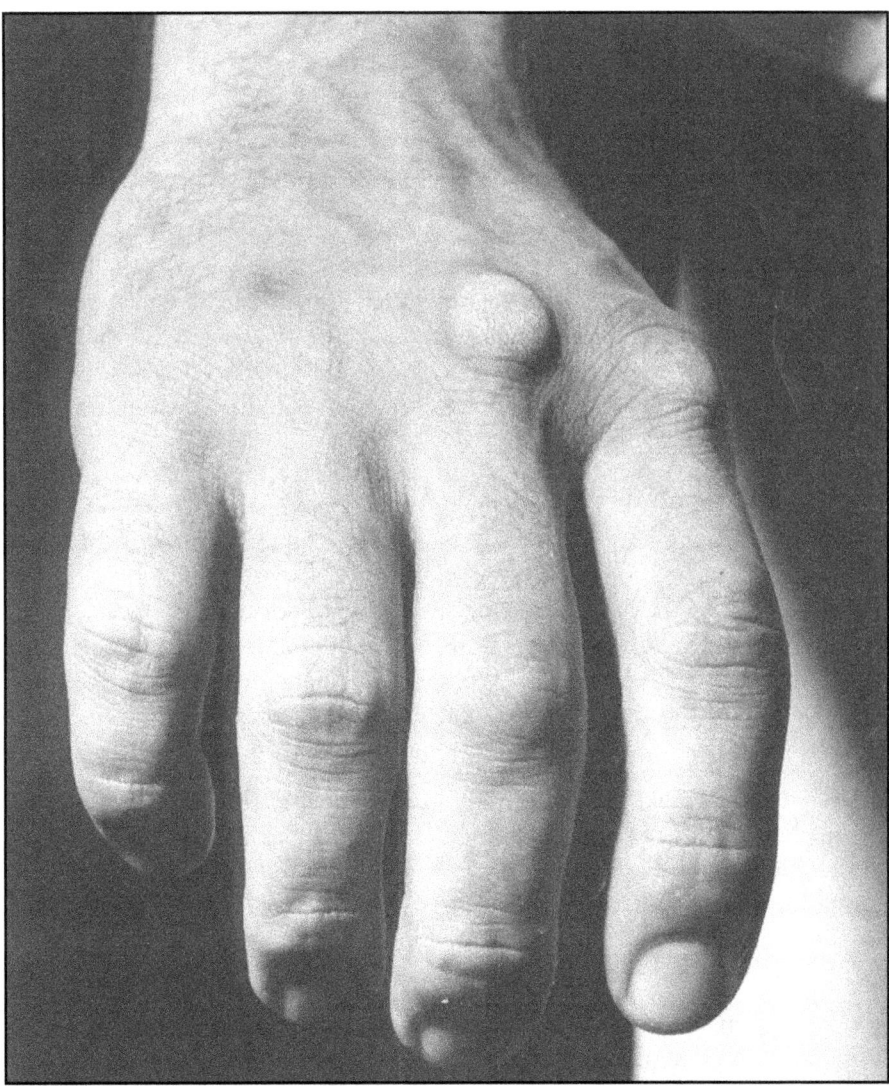

My hand in the early stages of development

lead to self-perfection. The major obstacle to attaining self-perfection is self-deception. My own study and practice of Zen is to overcome this self-deception. To seek only the physical aspects of the martial arts is to seek mere technical expertise. To follow the 'Do' (way), or 'Michi' (road) is the essence of training. The first step on the road to knowledge requires observing, listening, and doing. The first step on the road to wisdom is contemplation. In my training I listen, learn and practice. During Zen practice I meditate and contemplate. By application of both of these methods, I hope to go beyond mere physical technique in my job, my karate, and most importantly, my life. Zen teaches us to look at the present. It you seek to understand the past, look at the present, the eternal now. If you seek to know the future, look at the eternal now. This now, this present, is all that we truly have or ever will have."

"I would like to learn more about this thing you call Zen." I said.

"Learning the proper way to sit and breathe is the core of zen training as I understand it," he informed me. "I am still only a novice, but if you like I will try to help you get started. I belong to a small Zen temple here in Beppu city. The temple is open twenty-four hours a day and members may go there and meditate whenever they have the time. The priest holds three services a week. The next service is tomorrow night at 7:00 PM; if you would like to attend with me, I know that you would be welcome."

"I would like that very much."

The next evening at 6:15 PM, I met Ito-san at the main gate of Camp Chickamauga. The little Zen center was halfway between the camp and downtown, not far from the Beppu Buddha. We walked briskly down the street, passed Hock Shop Charlie's and turned left one block later. This street took us past the rear gate of Camp Chickamauga. We turned right and headed down the winding road toward the city. Two blocks later, we stopped in front of a small Zen temple, paused for a moment to remove our shoes and entered.

Roshi Gentai Sasaki, the priest, was introduced to me. He was about five feet, five inches tall and sixty-one years old. He stood almost rigidly erect. He had, during his youth, been a monk at the Unganzenji Temple in Kumamoto. I followed Ito from the small side room into the temple Zendo (meditation room). We arrived early so Ito could instruct me in how to sit and breath during meditation. Fifteen minutes later the formal meditation services began.

Ding . . . ding . . . ding . . . a small bell sounded. Everyone sat on their heels, in seiza, in absolute silence. I closed my eyes, but not completely, and sat erect glancing downward at a forty-five degree angle. The shoji (windows) had been closed, shutting out the fading evening light and bathing the room in a twilight haze.

In the distance I heard a dog barking, then the squeal of tires. I heard people talking as they walked down the street in front of the building. I heard the squeak of a board as someone in the room shifted their body. I heard distant breathing, it was my own breath; I heard a loud pounding, it was my own heart. How long had I been sitting here? My legs began to ache; my feet felt numb. I tried to move ever so slightly to ease the pain but a board squeaked; I stopped moving, the pain got worse.

KLAP! I jumped and hunched my shoulders as two large blocks of wood were struck together

Ding . . . ding . . . ding . . . A bell played upon my ears, it sounded like a soft high-pitched woman's voice. We stirred, we moved, we stood. To my surprise, Ito-san and several others also had trouble standing. We walked around the room in single file, hands upon our chests. Some of those present wore sandals, which they slipped on quickly. I had worn loafers that I quickly slipped my feet into as we prepared to leave the building.

Following the person in front of us, we walked outside into a small garden. The garden had a narrow path that twisted and turned past rocks, bushes and a tiny stream as we continued to walk in silence. Only the sound of gravel crunching under our feet broke the silence as we proceeded through the garden.

We filed back into the temple and knelt in seiza on the "tan" (mats) again.

Ding . . . ding . . . ding . . . more silence. The pain returned to my legs as I knelt on the mat. I heard a dog bark, this one sounded different. This was another dog, farther away than the first one had been. I became aware of my heartbeat and my breathing as these and other sounds blended into one.

Later, after we left the temple, Ito and I walked back up the hill to the rear gate of Camp Chickamauga.

"Do you understand?" he inquired.

"No," I responded.

"Someday you may. That is; if you don't quit," he stated.

I bowed and thanked him for inviting me to the temple. The feeling finally returned to my legs and ankles as I walked across the post to my barracks. I was intrigued by this thing called Zen although I was not at all sure what attracted people to it.

After class on Saturday, I hurried back to camp and went to the post library. I planned to spend the entire afternoon researching Buddhism and Zen. The librarian, a pleasant-looking, middle-aged woman with grey hair and glasses, assisted me in locating the books that I needed. I had several books stacked on the table in front of me. I opened the first book and started to read about Buddhism.

The Buddha, it said, was a man who lived approximately 500 years before Christ. He was a member of a royal family who saw the suffering of his subjects, and realized that he, their prince and leader, was powerless to help them overcome their suffering. He dedicated his life to searching for a method to help them overcome their suffering. Leaving his wife and son, he traveled into the wilderness where he meditated under a tree called the Bodhi tree, or Bo-tree. After many years of meditation, Buddha achieved complete enlightenment and understanding. After attaining enlightenment, he walked up and down the Ganges River for forty-nine years, sharing his knowledge freely with all. Buddha's first teaching was the "Four Noble Truths":

One - All mankind is subject to suffering.

Two - Suffering is caused by selfish desire.

Three - Selfish desire can be overcome.

Four - Selfishness can be overcome by following the "Noble Eight-fold Path".

I flipped to the back of the book and looked in the index for the "Eight-fold Path". I found it on page 176. Turning the pages rapidly in anticipation of what I was to find, I came to page 176. The Buddha's teaching is the realization within one's deepest consciousness of the oneness of all life. For the attainment of oneness, Buddha showed us the Eight-fold Path which consists of: Right Views, Right Thoughts, Right Conduct, Right Speech, Right Livelihood, Right Effort, Right Mindfulness and Right Meditation.

"Not bad," I thought. "Almost like the 'Ten Commandments.' "

The Zen form of Buddhism was derived from a particular incident in the life of the Buddha. After the Buddha became enlightened and reached Nirvana he realized that he had experienced a universal truth that was beyond words or letters. In an attempt to pass on this understanding, he developed the Four Noble Truths and the Eight-fold Path as guideposts to help his followers achieve that which he had achieved. According to the story, Buddha held up a flower one day at a sermon, looked at it, smelled it, rolled it in his fingers, but said nothing. A disciple, Mahakashyapa, looked at Buddha and smiled – he understood this silent sermon. This teaching of thought beyond words formed the basis for Zen.

Zen is considered a religion by many, but it is not considered a religion by those who practice it. Zen, if it is to be considered a religion, is a religion of tranquility. It neither appeals to the emotions nor to the intellect. The music of a Zendo (Zen center) is the wind in the trees or a babbling brook that may run beside the temple. It is an understanding beyond words, hence the meditation, which is beyond both words and the silence of the temples. Words are not reality – real-

Shirahama Sensei.

ity is reality. Seas are seas; trees are trees; mountains are mountains; nothing else need be said.

To my young, eighteen-year old mind, it all sounded very confusing. I continued to read and discovered that there were several types of Zen. The two major types were Soto and Rinzai. Soto practitioners face the wall and attempt to still their mind; the Rinzai practitioners face the center of the room and concentrate on something called a "Koan".

One of the most famous koans was, "Does a dog have a Buddha nature?" If you answer yes you will lose your Buddha nature, if you answer no, you will lose your Buddha nature. Now quick, what is the answer? There was another koan by an American Buddhist, "When you can see that 'A' is 'A', because 'A' is not 'A', you will have the answer."

I read through the books for over two and a half hours. I was still as confused, if not more so, as I had been before I opened the first book. It was all more than my young mind could comprehend. These first encounters with the Zen philosophy planted a seed that would continue to grow. Later in my adult life I would become a Zen monk. Little did the Roshi know what he had started.

Christmas Eve arrived. I went to the dojo and practiced harder than usual in an attempt to lose my loneliness in my practice. Later I walked from the floor exhausted, but still lonely. I left the dojo and made my way to a new bar that I had discovered a few days before. It was called the "Wander INN – Stagger OUT Musume Beer Hall." I took a booth towards the rear of the bar near the toilet and ordered a Kirin beer. I sat there in my loneliness and sipped the cold beer as I thought about home. Three beers later, I realized that my taste for beer had returned. These were the first complete bottles of beer I had consumed since my night out with Don Matthews and I enjoyed them.

Friday was Christmas. A small Christmas tree had been erected and decorated in the company dayroom. Christmas music played over the camp's many loud speakers but Christmas away from home still did not seem the same. I received a package from my parents and another one from my girlfriend, Wilma. I had mailed my Christmas packages late, so they probably would not arrive in West Virginia by Christmas. The letter that Wilma included with her gift had a strange question.

"Do you know a girl by the name of Barbara Ellen Webster? She is in my typing class; all she does is pester me about you."

I thought I remembered a girl by that name but I was not positive.

First formation on Monday, December 28th, was a little unusual. The platoon was marched to the chapel where dog tags and ID's were checked against a roster. We were then escorted inside. There were several Military Police stationed around the perimeter of the building. Standing at the front of the chapel was a major with a high and tight haircut wearing heavily starched fatigues and spit-shined jump boots. He motioned for us to be seated.

"You men of the regimental band/anti-tank platoon and other small units within the regiment are being asked to volunteer for a special mission. The mission may never happen. We are only preparing a list of volunteers in the event that it might. Second, if the mission does become a reality, there is a possibility that those of you who go could be seriously injured or killed.

"Why us?" Staff Sergeant Johnson asked.

"I'll tell you and I hope that I don't hurt your feelings," the young major said.

"The regiment has been tasked to supply some airborne soldiers for a mission with the air force. We don't want to utilize the regimental battalions, artillery, engineers or any other units, which would be necessary to respond to a combat situation. As you are aware, the 187th and the 1st Marine Division operate as the Defense Department's only rapid deployment unit in the Far East. We can go into combat without the anti-tank platoon; other units can furnish enough personnel to man the 3.5-inch anti-tank rocket launchers."

New Year's Eve beer party (1953-1954). The author is third from the right.

"In a nutshell, sir, it's because we aren't that damn important isn't it?" Corporal Corral both stated and asked.

"If you wish to put it that way, I would say you're right, Corporal," the major replied.

"What is the mission all about?" a voice called out.

"Because it may not be initiated, you do not need to know what the mission is at this time," the major answered. "If the mission becomes a reality, you will be informed of its nature when you have a need to know. At that time, if you wish to change your mind and refuse the mission, there will be no problem. For those who may be interested and want to volunteer, I will need to compile a roster with your names before you leave the building."

The meeting ended. Prior to leaving the Post Chapel, I placed my name on the list of volunteers for the mysterious mission, along with the majority of those present.

On Thursday the week before, Gib had invited me to attend the Regimental Engineering Company's New Year's Party being held at the Kit Kat Club (Sgt. Giblin had been a member of the engineering company prior to joining the band.). The Kit Kat was located on Mochigahama Street, a couple of blocks north of the dojo. It was unique because it was built on large wooden poles, which had been sunk into the bay.

The interior of the Kit Kat was large and laid out like a western saloon. The stage was at the far end of the room – on both sides was a balcony that looked down onto the dance floor situated between the tables and the stage.

A motorized rickshaw transported us downtown to the Kit Kat Club. The evening was cool but considering the time of year, the weather was not bad; it was actually a little warmer than usual. December had started off with a cold wave but on December 21st a warm air mass from the South Pacific came to the rescue.

The cafe was already crowded when we arrived. A popular, local Japanese bandleader nicknamed "The Fox" and his band were playing a slow song as the GIs and their girlfriends crowded onto the dance floor. A few members of the engineer company swapped war stories about Korea and combat in the Kumwha valley. Gib and I sat there listening intently.

Several of the soldiers pleaded for Gib to approach the bandleader, whom he knew, and ask permission for him to play with the band.

"Only if my little buddy, Bill, will consent to direct," Gib responded.

A few minutes later, Gib was playing and I was attempting to direct as the band played its rendition of an old favorite, "Blue Moon". One of Gib's friends yelled loudly, causing me to turn around as he took my picture.

Standing at the far left, I was to direct while Gib (fourth from the left) played.

While we were playing our second tune an argument broke out between two platoon leaders as to which platoon had the better jumpers. To settle the dispute, the dance floor was cleared and several empty tables were shoved onto the floor. The platoon leaders and their members climbed the steps to the balcony. The platoon leaders gave jump commands as the members of their platoons leaped from the balcony onto the tables. Table legs bent in all directions under the weight of the paratroopers crashing down on them.

"I think it's time we leave, partner," Gib said. We made our way to the door and headed south on Mochigahama Street. We were walking past the Beppu Police Station when two jeeps, with MPs in the front seats and their Japanese counterparts seated in the rear, left the station and headed north.

"Good timing," Gib said, smiling.

"What was that all about?" I asked.

"It's an annual ritual performed by the engineer company," he stated. "You know, sorta like the ball descending at Times Square on New Year's Eve."

It was 1:40 AM. We hired a rickshaw for the trip back to camp. Both of us were almost asleep as the rickshaw drove past Hock Shop Charlie's. Gib and I had visited Charlie on Wednesday to obtain the money necessary for the Kit Kat bash. Gib, half asleep, saluted Charlie's as the rickshaw drove by.

Sunday, Junko and I walked downtown to Beppu and went to a movie theater located up an alley across from the Hanago Bar and Grill. The movie was a Japanese love story about a wounded soldier returning to Japan after World War II. The film had English subtitles; at least I could follow along with the plot. The Japanese crowd consisted mostly of women who loved the movie. The film had one redeeming feature. The wounded Japanese soldier who had lost an arm in combat felt disgraced upon returning to Japan and had lost faith in himself. In an attempt to find some meaning in his life, he started studying karate. After months of hard work his karate training helped him regain his spirit and self esteem. The Japanese women were sobbing – there wasn't a dry eye in the house. The film proved useful as a recruiting tool for the local dojo. Approximately three weeks after the film was shown, two former Japanese soldiers, both of whom had lost an arm in the war, appeared at the dojo to join the karate class. Only one stayed. Within a short time he achieved green belt.

While Junko and I sat in the movie theater enjoying the film, the Military Police and their Japanese counter-parts were making history. They were raiding Hock Shop Charlie's on a Sunday for the first time ever. A soldier from the Engineer Company who had been arrested at the Kit Kat Club made a deal with

Chitose's Back Yard.

the MPs. "If you raid Hock Shop Charlie's, you'll be in for a big surprise," he told them. The Military Police and the Japanese Police conducted the raid. At Charlie's they found the usual military fare, field jackets, boots, Class A uniforms, field equipment, and other assorted military items. Only when they walked into Charlie's back yard did they get the big surprise. Parked there, in all of its glory, was a two and a half ton United States Army truck with 187 ABN RCT stenciled on its left bumper. On its right bumper in bold white letters was 3RD BND CO. Some fool had pawned an army truck and Charlie had been dumb enough to take it.

The MPs returned the truck to the motor pool. The driver was sentenced to six months in the Big Eight stockade. Gib and I had hocked our military overcoats, which were now lost. Don Matthews was out a pair of jump boots. Howard lost a Class A uniform and two other members of our unit lost their field jackets.

Everyone who had pawned equipment at Charlie's would be required to sign a statement of charges and reimburse the army for the lost items or purchase similar items to replace the items which had been confiscated by the Military Police. What a hell of a way to start off the New Year!

Chapter 10

Cherish the old while learning to understand the new; What is new, what is old, is simply a matter of time; Among myriad activities keep your mind clear. Who promises to attain the way and keep it true and well?

Shoto (Gichin Funakoshi)

A few days before the New Year, I learned of a special class that was scheduled for the last day of the year – Wednesday, December 31. The class was scheduled to begin at 11:00 PM. We were going to ring the old year out and ring the New Year in practicing kata. I learned that this old Ganjitsu custom had been the custom of many dojo throughout Japan for centuries.

"Shirahama Sensei wants to know if you will participate?" Ito inquired. Since I had nothing planned, I agreed that I would be there standing tall in my karate-gi.

On New Year's Eve the class started at 11:00 PM sharp. Almost all of the dojo members were present. This included many Judo and Kendo members. I had never seen the dojo as crowded as it was that night. We were packed in tight. A ranking Judo-ka was in charge of the warm up exercises. Instead of a practice session, it was organized more like a continuous demonstration. The Judo-ka worked out for a few minutes, then the Kendo-ka and finally it was our turn.

The first kata we did was Zenshin Kotai. We did it five times, bowed, and retreated from the floor. The Judo-ka, their mats at one end of the dojo, practiced break falls and throws. After a few minutes the Kendo people walked onto the floor to demonstrate. Soon it was our turn to demonstrate again.

"Hajime!" one of the visiting karate black belts from Kumamoto commanded.

Teaching in Pittsburg.

We did the kata "Shihohai Sho", then we did "Shihohai Dai". The Judo group returned to the center of the dojo. We continued to practice in this manner until an old clock, which hung opposite the Shomen, struck 12:00 o'clock midnight; the New Year had arrived. We continued practicing and demonstrating like this for another hour and then the Kendo group entered the training area – they were to be the last group to practice. The headgear of the Kendo armor was removed. All of the various groups - Judo, Kendo and Karate, lined up together by rank and sat in seiza. The Kendo shinai were placed on the floor beside the students and their instructors.

"Shomen ni, rei!" the ranking black belt Judo instructor said, as we faced the small flag with the red sun in the center.

A sake party was held to celebrate the end of the training and the beginning of the New Year. Lower ranking students, of which I was one, were to act as waiters. Everyone changed from their gis into civilian clothes.

My job, and that of other lower ranking students, was to assure that absolutely no ranking black belt's glass of sake or beer was ever empty. Several of us scurried around the dojo for three hours topping off the glasses. The party ended at 5:00 AM. The tables were dismantled, bottles put away, and the dojo floor cleaned.

Kangeiko

Ito thanked me and the other students who had acted as servers. "Do not forget to come to the dojo tomorrow night," Ito reminded me.

Thursday's class was dedicated to the practice of Seisan kata. We performed Seisan for an hour without stopping and then Shirahama Sensei spoke to us for a couple of minutes. Ito walked over to me and instructed me to raise and lower my hips at certain points in the kata.

"This make stronger," he said, as he demonstrated, thrusting his body upward and then lowering it as he walked me through the technique.

"Moichido," a voice said.

I followed along with the class. At the locations in the kata that Ito designated, I thrust my legs against the floor causing my hips to rise. I then dropped my center of gravity as my knees bent. Many movements in the kata took on a new meaning to me. Several small technical details were stressed during our practice of the kata. Each movement was explained in great detail. We received instruction in proper breathing techniques, which are performed at specific points within the kata. We were required to slide backward, lock in our stance, and block before unleashing punching and kicking techniques. Proper muscle tension was stressed throughout the training. I learned more about the kata Seisan that night than I had in many months of practice.

Fortunately, my paycheck had not been completely wiped out with the coming of the New Year. Gib knew of another pawnshop located in one of the back streets of Beppu where we could purchase some military items cheaper than we could at a surplus store. We made a trip to Toyotomi-san's Hock Shop and Used Store. The dilemma of our "confiscated" equipment was resolved. After class on Saturday, January 3rd, Ito-san asked me if I was going to attend a few of the Kangeiko (winter training) sessions. This training is always done during the coldest month of the year between the hours of 5:30 AM and 7:00 AM. Several members of the dojo had not missed a kangeiko since they had started their training many years before. Coincidentally, the weather had taken a turn for the worst on January 1st as the temperature plummeted.

I knew that I would be unable to make most of the classes because of my military duties and informed Ito of this fact.

"When does it start?" I asked.

"We start, yesterday morning," he said. "You miss it and today's class. Start next Saturday and come on Saturday and Sunday," he told me.

Saturday morning I got up very early, bundled up, left my warm barracks, hired a rickshaw for the ride to the dojo and asked myself, "Why am I doing this?"

For Beppu and Southern Japan, it was a very cold morning. We started class with our usual thousand punches and kicks, then stretched to the best of our ability in the cold dojo. We ran barefooted through the streets as we headed south away from the dojo. A thin karate-gi offers little protection against the elements in January, especially when it is wet with perspiration following a rigorous warm up session.

We turned left onto a small path that led to the public beach. During the spring, summer, and fall months, the beach was always crowded. Today, no one was on the beach except for twenty-seven white-clad karate-ka. Steam rose from our bodies and uniforms as we ran through the cold air that was pouring down onto southern Japan from Manchuria.

The students followed one another into the ocean until we were knee deep in the freezing cold water. We ran out of the water and farther down the beach. Hideo Matsumoto, a san-dan, had us form a circle; we assumed a shiko dachi stance and began to execute seiken cho tsuki (basic punches).

"Seisan dachi!" Shirahama Sensei yelled loudly. Everyone responded, and dropped into the stance, left leg forward.

"Jodan uke." Our arms arced upward as we performed the basic head block.

We moved up the beach blocking, punching, and kicking on each command. It was so cold that I had difficulty breathing. My chest felt heavy and I had a slight pain in my side.

"Mae geri!" one of the instructors yelled. First the right foot kicked, then the left foot, as we started back up the beach.

"Oi tsuki," I heard someone say. We were now lunge punching in unison up the beach.

"Gedan barai, gyaku tsuki." We proceeded to leg block, and then reverse punch, as we slid forward through the sand.

Steam no longer rose from our uniforms, which were wet and cold just like the people wearing them. There were no swimmers or colorful umbrellas on the beach. There were only the frozen, determined karate-ka practicing on the cold, barren stretch of sand.

We were not only developing our technical skill, but all aspects of our training as well – mental, physical and spiritual. We were also attempting to survive, or at least I was.

With Yamamoto and Adams.

Matsumoto Sensei was in the lead as we again started running up the beach toward the little path that led to the street. Bringing up the rear of the column to motivate any stragglers who might need it were Ito-san and Shirahama Sensei. We ran north toward the dojo, our wet karate-gi slapping against our bodies, as people on the street stared at us. I wondered what they thought of us. Did they admire our dedication and determination, or did they think we were more than a little crazy and foolish?!

The dojo was in sight. We ran to the north side of the building where the makiwara were located. We lined up behind the straw-covered posts. Each post had a metal can placed over the straw to keep it dry. We took turns punching – fifty punches with each hand. I tore the callus off of my right hand. Damn! I had worked so hard on building up that hand and now there was a big hole where my callus used to be. After the last group completed their required punches, we ran inside the dojo for kumite (sparring) practice.

The windows were open and the heat was off. We did have some protection from the wind although it was not much warmer inside the dojo than it had been when we were outside braving the elements. I quickly got a bandage for my hand and wrapped it so I wouldn't make it any worse. The bogu (armor) that we wore to spar in was very bulky. I suited up along with three others. We were called up two at a time. We moved forward toward the center of the training area. My opponent was Harada-san. Harada was a 1st degree black belt and had a lighting fast back fist strike and reverse punch. We bowed to Shirahama Sensei, the referee, then to each other.

"Hajime!" (Begin!)

Both Harada and I started moving around the contest area. Harada moved in fast as he executed a front kick. I slid away and blocked the kick; however, I did not see his punch. My head snapped back as his fist connected with my head protector, staggering me and loosening my headgear. Since my head protector was no longer tight, it started slipping around on my head and partially blocked my vision. Suddenly I felt a sharp pain in my ribs and immediately slumped to the floor. Because of the loose head protector, I had not seen Harada's technique – a strong side thrust kick. The impact penetrated through my chest protector as if it didn't even exist. I learned a valuable lesson that day – armor can never be a substitute for good technical skill. A punch, strike, or kick that is fully focused could cause serious injury to a person wearing bogu.

Upon returning to the barracks, I showered and went to bed, skipping lunch. I had difficulty sleeping or moving for a couple of days.

On Monday I reported to sick call.

"Your ribs are not broken or fractured," said the young doctor who wore captain's bars.

"You were lucky, they're just bruised. Take it easy for a while."

"A while" didn't last long – I was eager to get back in class. I missed class Tuesday night but by Thursday I was back in class. During January there were nine weekend kangeiko classes scheduled. I participated in five of them, including the last one on Sunday, the 31st of January.

• •

Chapter 11

San-kyu Test

One 'ouch' is worth a thousand 'be carefuls'.

Masami Tsuruoka

Timing, speed and proper stances, which allowed the body to function efficiently and enabled the power to be directed into the target, had become my main interest as I trained at the dojo. Relaxation, contraction of the appropriate muscles, proper hip rotation, leg thrust and vibration had by now become such a part of my training that I did not have to think about them. My body performed these movements without conscious effort. No longer did the higher ranks have to push me; I was now pushing myself, harder than they would. When my military duties allowed I trained three or four evenings a week at the post gymnasium. When I went to the dojo I usually got there early so I could have some individual practice prior to the class. As the tempo of my training increased I saw less and less of Junko. She had developed a friendship with a young Japanese college boy. Occasionally, however, we would still go out for a meal or movie with Kazuko and Howard.

The daily regimen I had established for myself consisted of one thousand punches and kicks and four hundred full squats. In addition, I did one hundred and fifty push-ups and a quarter mile run, barefoot, on a running track near the dojo that was covered with pea gravel. At first it nearly killed me, my feet were really sore, but over time they became quite tough. Finally I even developed calluses between my toes. I started running on the gravel track one day when I observed other students and instructors doing it.

My makiwara regimen consisted of approximately two hundred punches a day. Kata training was no longer a chore for me; I actually looked forward to practising them.

One day my left hand was kicked while sparring with a student. I was wearing the bogu but not the gloves, which were old, worn, and falling apart. The result was a dislocated left middle finger. Chitose Sensei came over to me, took my hand in his, and examined it.

"Dame, dame" (No good, no good.) he said as he rolled his fingers into a fist and showed me how to make a tight fist. After inspecting my hand for a moment, he jerked it suddenly and my finger was back in place.

The beginner's fist must be tight at all times. This is one of the first lessons of karate. Training on the makiwara was a valuable aid in making a strong, tight fist. I had been careless. Regardless of the sore finger, I felt that I was becoming more aware of the little things which used to seem unimportant, or had gone unnoticed by me during the early stages of my training. Quality of practice must take precedent over quantity of practice if I was to excel.

Several names were called off, including mine, during the first formation on Friday, March 12th.

"After chow, all men whose names have been called off are to report to the chapel at 08:00 hours for a briefing," SFC Munro informed us.

The unknown mission we had volunteered for months earlier had now become a reality. After we had first volunteered for the mission without a name, rumors abounded as to what it entailed. Everyone had their personal hunch, but none of us knew exactly what we would be required to do. It reminded me of an old Buddhist axiom.

"Those who say, don't know.

Those who know, don't say."

The C-119 Fairchild Packets flew in formation at 10,500 feet as we left Japanese air space on the first leg of our trip to the Philippines. Upon landing at Clark Field our aircraft were painted in the French tri-colors. Early the next morning our C-119s were joined by other C-119s of the 50th Troop Carrier Squadron as we flew west toward French Indochina. The equipment loaded on the aircraft was to be given to the French. The U.S. Army markings, which were stenciled in white, were painted over by hand, in olive drab, while the aircraft were in flight.

We landed at Gia Lam Airport, on the outskirts of Hanoi, at 3:45 PM. The U.S. Air Force pilots were replaced by 24 Americans who were private hires of Chennault's CAT Airline. CAT Airlines was an offshoot of the famous Flying

Tigers of World War II fame. The most famous of the CAT pilots was a giant, 250-pound legend named James B. McGovern. He had trouble fitting his large frame into a pilot's seat but he was a first class flier. McGovern and the other CAT pilots had been contracted to fly re-supply drops to the French Foreign Legion troops who were surrounded and fighting for their lives in Dien Bien Phu. His favorite bar when he was not flying was the "La Marseillaise" in Haiphong when he could get there. McGovern had a large black beard which earned him his nickname of "Earthquake". He looked like the cartoonist Al Capp's character "Earthquake Muldoon" in the "L'il Abner" comic strip. He was so famous among the other pilots and group of daredevils in Indochina at that time that they wrote a song about him.

"His three hundred pounds shake the earth when he walks,

He soars with the grace of a loon;

The legend makes claim that this beast from the East

Is known as Earthquake McGoon."

On our second day in Hanoi, several members of my unit and I had an opportunity to visit the Rue de Lattre. This was an area frequented by the French Foreign Legion enlisted troops when they were on R and R (rest and recupera-

Our planes in formation over the ocean.

tion). Much to my surprise, I soon discovered that a great many of the legionnaires were German. Most were in World War II and served in the Wermach and a few had even served in the Waffen SS. One of them, a short, youthful looking German named Rudi, later informed me he had been in the Waffen SS, Hitler Youth Division. He told me in his thickly accented English that they had a saying in the French Army in Indochina.

"The Legion is only as strong as its weakest German soldier." he informed me as he sat there with a big grin on his face. Everyone at our table had a good laugh at his statement.

The legionnaires invited us to walk with them to a local bar a few blocks away for a few drinks. The offer was greatly appreciated – and one which my fellow American soldiers felt should never be ignored or wasted.

Soldiers the world over share the same hardships and a common bond of brotherhood. Around the table sat twenty-one soldiers. French, Germans and Americans sat together as brothers. They were brothers because they were sol-

One of the U.S. Airforce C-119s over Dien Bien Phu. Notice the three diagonal stripes on the rutters and the French markings.

San-kyu Test

diers, but more importantly and binding, they were "paras". Communications were conducted in French, German, English and a little Japanese. A couple of words of this, four or five words of that, a little sign language, and communication was made. We drank, talked, told war stories and got inebriated.

For three days we stayed as guests at the Metropole Hotel in Hanoi. Howard Sochurek, another free spirit, and staff photographer for Life magazine was also staying there.

He had made his first combat parachute jump during October 1950 when he parachuted into North Korea with the 187th ARCT at Suchon. He joined the French at Dien Bien Phu in November 1953 when he parachuted in with some of their paratroopers. He had just returned to Hanoi after being evacuated from the beleaguered outpost on one of the few C-47 aircraft which were used to evacuate the wounded.

While we enlisted men or, enlisted swine, as we were sometimes jokingly called, were cementing friendships with our French Foreign Legion brothers, the American officers had a unique opportunity to visit the world-famous French officer's club, "La Roseraie."

On the morning of the fourth day we left Indochina, flew east to the Philippines, refuelled then headed north to Ashiya Air Force Base in Japan.

Upon arriving back in Japan on March 26, we were debriefed by our intelligence officers. "You are not to discuss this mission with anyone. Do you understand?" a rather large, mean-looking major asked us. A thirty years restriction has been placed on any discussion of this mission.

"All mission records have been destroyed. You are neither to affirm or deny," he continued. "Nothing concerning this mission will appear in your personnel files. For the record, you have been in Japan for the past two weeks and have never left the country."

Returning to Japan, the dojo, and Junko was nice. I had actually thought of Beppu as home while I was gone.

When I arrived at the dojo on Saturday, Chitose Sensei was there. Shirahama Sensei and Ito both asked me where I had been. "I was on a short tour of duty at Camp Hakata up north," I told them.

Chitose Sensei taught the class as Shirahama Sensei, Matsumoto Sensei, and Ito assisted. Our training covered stances with the major emphasis placed on seisan dachi. Wrist on the hip, shoulders twenty degrees off center when blocking, or lunge punching. Shoulders square when reverse punching or reverse blocking. Breathing had a one, two, three pattern. One was always an inhale through the nose about one second long. Two was always an exhale between the lips one second long. Three was an exhale of approximately four to five seconds long. Never exhale more than seventy percent of your breath; always maintain at least thirty percent in your lungs to eliminate a major weak spot. Chitose Sensei was covering a great amount of material, all of which made his style unique.

During class, the katas Zenshin Kotai, Shihohai, Niseishi Sho, Seisan, Rohai Sho and Dai, and Potsai were covered. A large amount of instruction was spent covering the finer points of Seisan and Potsai.

"Each kata has a personality," Chitose Sensei explained. "The secret of understanding a kata is to understand the personality of the person who made the kata. What is the kata's purpose? Is it to build strength, speed, evasive action, balance, or some other skill? Do you know the history of the kata? Who is the founder? What type of person was he? Knowledge of this type will enable you to understand and practice the kata to your fullest potential."

Upon completion of the class, some students left while others practiced kata. I, along with a few others, retreated to the makiwara along the outside of the building. Since I had torn my callus off of my right hand, my fist had almost healed. Once again I could slam my fist into the straw-covered post at full speed.

I was punching the makiwara when Ito-san walked up to me and informed me that I was to take my san-kyu test on Tuesday night.

"I am not ready to test," I objected.

"You not to decide, we decide!" he replied in a low guttural voice. "You pay fee, you test." He turned sharply and walked back into the dojo.

I realized at once that I had made a serious breach of etiquette. I went into the dojo to apologize. Mary saw me as I entered and realized that something was wrong. I told her what had happened and that I wanted to apologize.

"No, no! You must not do that," she told me. If you really want to apologize, you must pass your test. It was Ito-san himself who recommended that you be re-tested. If you fail, he will loose face."

Once again, with Mary's help, I completed my application to test and paid my test fee of one thousand yen.

I arrived at the dojo on Tuesday at 5:30 PM, changed into my gi and walked from the small dressing room into the training area. A table with several chairs had been set up at one end of the floor. Sitting at the table engrossed in the stack

San-kyu Test

Last Goodbye at Higashi's House.

of papers lying before her was Mary Shigamoto.

I stretched, did basics and practiced my test kata a few times. Others arrived; soon the floor had many people in white uniforms, kicking, punching, doing kata or stretching.

"Ki o tsuke!" (Attention!) someone yelled.

All motion stopped, and we stood at attention. Emerging from the small office area were Chitose Sensei, Shirahama Sensei and three very distinguished-looking men. Chitose Sensei was behind a little old man who was the first person in the line of four. They walked slowly to the table and took their seats. Mary rose from her chair, faced the group, and bowed to them. The first man who was obviously a great deal older than the rest had to be assisted. He was escorted to his chair at the middle of the table by Chitose Sensei. The others moved to the table and sat on both sides of Chitose Sensei and the older gentleman. The others bowed to the older man at the table and then they took their seats. The older man reached into the sleeve of his kimono for his glasses, adjusted the small round spectacles, and placed them on his face. He then spoke to us for a couple of minutes, referring quite often to a paper he was holding. He spoke very softly with a deep hidden strength, even for his age, and I understood only a few words. I was confident, however, that Ito would brief me later. When he finished speaking, he sat down. The formal testing was about to start.

As each student was to test, Mary Shigamoto called out his name. The student would jump to his feet and shout "Osu!" He then moved into the center of the test area and bowed to the test board. Shirahama Sensei would then announce the name of the kata he was required to perform.

The sixth student had completed demonstrating his kata and left the floor.

"Dometrichi!" I heard Mary say.

"Osu!" I replied. I sprang to my feet; my legs seemed to carry me mechanically to the center of the testing area. "Seisan!" Shirahama Sensei said.

"Seisan!" I replied, a little too loudly.

I remember nothing of demonstrating my kata. It was as if I had ceased to be. During my first test, which I had failed, I had to struggle with each movement, thinking of every technique as I performed the kata. At last I was done. I stood there shaking. Shirahama Sensei told me to sit down.

"Osu!" I replied, then left the floor.

Twenty-seven students were tested that day. Four were brought back to their feet. They were going to perform basics which would be randomly selected by the test board. Finally they were allowed to sit down. Another group of four rose to demonstrate their basics as requested by the test board. I was in the third group. Upon completing the basics, all of the students formed lines in the center of the testing area.

The names of those who were promoted were read aloud by Mary Shigamoto. "Harada, Nishimura, Takahashi, Ono, Dometrich, Nishikawa..." I had passed. The remaining names seemed lost in a blur. I had passed, I had vindicated Ito's selection of me to test.

Gichin Funakoshi and Tsuyoshi Chitose in 1954.

Once the last name was called, Chitose Sensei stood and spoke to us.

"What is he saying?" I whispered to Ito.

"He said that the true karate punch comes from the inside, the spirit and the heart. Karate, which is only physical, is like a corpse of a human. It lacks life force, and, in time, as a corpse will decay and stink; the karate without commitment will decay and start to stink."

We lined up, assumed the seiza position, meditated, then bowed to the test board and the kamiza. The test board arose from their seats, left the table and slowly filed from the room. I noticed that Chitose Sensei had taken the arm of the little old man to assist him as they left. Once again we bowed to them.

"Thank you, Ito-san," I said. "It is good to have a Sempai like you who is also a friend."

He looked at me for a moment. "We not friends," he said.

I felt for a moment as if I had said something terribly wrong. He looked at me and continued. "We not tomodachi (friends), we kyodai (brothers)." With that he did something totally out of character, he slapped me on the shoulder and smiled.

Two weeks later I was awarded my San-kyu certificate at the conclusion of Thursday night's class. Mary informed me that I should have it dry-mounted at the Post Exchange at Camp Chickamauga. "This will preserve the certificate and make it last," she said. Nine days later I picked it up at the P.X. and planned to secure it in the bottom of my footlocker for safekeeping.

Rocky, our houseboy, was moping the barrack's floors as I entered the building. I proudly showed my diploma to him. "Ahhhhhh!" he exclaimed rather loudly.

"What is the matter?" I asked.

"No matter! No matter!" he said softly. "You shoomeisho (certificate) sign by famous karate teacher."

"Who?" I inquired.

"Funakoshi Gichin," Rocky replied, as he half bowed to me and returned my certificate.

● ●

Chapter 12

Knowledge

The dewdrop slips into the sea, but it is not really gone. It is only a part of some larger thing, which shall go on, and on . . .

The Light of Asia, 1879 By Sir Edwin Arnold

Word was received a little over one week after I passed my san-kyu test that on May 9 Dien Bien Phu had fallen. The seemingly invincible Earthquake McGoon (James McGovern) had also been killed. His C-119 had been struck by anti-aircraft fire as his plane was making a pass over Dien Bien Phu dropping much needed supplies. He had attempted to make a crash landing on a sand bar near the Nam River but he did not make it. Many of the legionnaires whom we had met in Hanoi were now either killed in action or were prisoners of the Viet Minh.

The defeat at Dien Bien Phu caused me think a great deal about my own mortality. I realized for the first time that I was not invincible. Any of my friends in the 187th or I could be gone just as quickly as our newfound friends in the legion were. Life is fleeting and has only the meaning we give it.

My promotion to san-kyu had motivated me enormously. I had been getting complacent prior to the test but now felt as if I had a fire raging within me. Chitose Sensei traveled to Beppu on three different occasions during the weeks immediately after the test. His skill in the art of karate had always amazed me. During these visits, I became more aware of his technical knowledge. He was astonishing. His skill was so good; you did not have to understand Japanese to grasp the points he was attempting to get across to you.

His techniques were more precise than any of the other karate sensei who were less than half his age. The power he generated as he performed basic techniques could not be matched by any of the other sensei. I watched him demonstrate basics and kata and I would always wonder, "Where does the power come from?"

"One punch, sayonara," he was fond of saying, and then he would laugh and shove the palm of his hand toward the floor. He did this many times and it made an impression on me. On two other occasions, he took great pains to explain the power source. Even though Ito translated it, it was difficult to comprehend. Chitose Sensei said that we must strive for good basics and full body dynamics, that through constant practice and repetition we would develop the speed needed to allow us to have powerful kime.

Chitose Sensei became an enigma to me. My requests for information about him were seldom answered to my satisfaction. I was beginning to think that he might possibly be an enigma to everyone, including those who thought they knew him well.

I had spoken to Ito-san on several occasions concerning my desire to learn about Doctor Chitose's life. He informed me that he himself had rather limited knowledge about Chitose Sensei's background.

"He is from Okinawa and has studied medicine at Tokyo Medical College. On Okinawa, as a youth, he had been trained by the top karate instructors on the island. He had served as an officer in the Japanese Army Medical Corps for a little over a year but was discharged when he developed typhoid fever. He lives in a small town north of Kumamoto. He is a great karate teacher. This is about all I know about Chitose Sensei," Ito exclaimed.

Although it would not help my karate technique, I desperately wanted to know more about Chitose Sensei. Ito-san and the others who had been born in Japan would have an entire lifetime to study karate and to learn about O-Sensei, I would not. I would be returning to the United States when my military tour was completed. I went to Mary Shigamoto for additional information about Chitose Sensei.

"The person who knows him best is Shirahama Sensei," she informed me. "Let me speak to him and see if he will speak with you." Mary picked up a telephone and called him at his home.

"Shirahama Sensei is unable to do it tonight," Mary said, placing her hand over the phone.

"He has an appointment which he cannot break. Tomorrow night is the best time for him to talk to you. Can you come back tomorrow night?"

"Yes, tomorrow night will be fine," I answered.

Mary spoke into the phone, then hung up. "You are to be here at eight."

Knowledge

It started to rain ever so lightly as I left the barracks on Wednesday evening for the trip to the dojo. I was going to be early. The water falling from the heavens was more like a mist than rain. My rickshaw drove around the pedestrians and through light traffic as it headed toward the dojo.

Walking into the dojo, I observed a large group of judo-ka practicing. Shirahama Sensei and a younger sensei, Kazuhiko Tonai, a 3rd Dan, were assisting Masato (Kodama) Aso Sensei, a 6th Dan, with the class. I headed down the hall and looked in the office for Mary. She was nowhere to be found. On her desk was a note written in both English and Japanese. "Be back in fifteen minutes, Mary," the English part said.

Mary returned before the class was over and invited me to have some tea. Our relationship had blossomed into the type enjoyed by a big sister and her little brother. She had taken me under her wing, and although I could not prove it, I was sure that she acted as my guardian angel at the dojo. The judo class came to a close at 8:00 PM sharp. Shirahama Sensei came into the office. I started to stand and bow but he waved me back into my chair; he sat in the chair across from me. I was finally going to learn something about Chitose Sensei. Mary would act as my interpreter.

"May I take notes?" Mary asked. Shirahama agreed that it would be a good idea.

Shirahama Sensei settled himself into his seat, took a big breath, looked at Mary, then at me, and proceeded to tell me about the remarkable person known as Tsuyoshi Chitose, more commonly referred to by the higher-ranking black belts as O-Sensei.

"Okinawa, a small island a few hundred miles south of Kyushu, is the cradle of modern karate-do. My karate sensei, O-Sensei, Tsuyoshi Chitose, was born on this island on the October 18, 1898, in the Kumochi section of Naha City. Chitose Sensei learned from most, if not all, of the senior historically noted karate sensei. I have been told that his father, Chiyoyu (Masuo) Chinen, for reasons of poor health, did not practice the Okinawan art of "Te". His maternal grandfather was a great practitioner of the art of "Okinawa Te." His name was Sokon "Bushi" Matsumura.

"O-Sensei's first teacher was Arakaki Seisho Sensei. He spent seven years walking daily to Arakaki's where he trained on only one kata in his sensei's backyard. That kata was the kata Seisan. He was fourteen when Arakaki Sensei taught him his second kata. Arakaki Sensei died in May 1918. O-Sensei always considered Arakaki Sensei as his primary teacher. Under Arakaki's teaching, O-

Sensei learned many kata such as Seisan, Shihohai, Niseishi, Sanchin, along with a little of his early kobujutsu training.

"O-Sensei also studied with Sanda Chinen Ou, Chotoku Kyan, Chomo Hanagushuku, Kanryo Higaonna, Choyu Motobu, and many other of the great sensei of Okinawa.

"He moved to Tokyo in 1918 and 1919 so he could attend the Tokyo Medical College. During the early part of this century, many Japanese were prejudiced against the Okinawans. O-Sensei changed his name to a Japanese sounding name, Chitose Tsuyoshi. In the twenties and thirties, O-Sensei often assisted Funakoshi Gichin, who had also moved from Okinawa to Tokyo, and had made karate very popular. When Chitose Sensei was a young boy in Okinawa, his schoolteacher was Funakoshi Sensei.

"Chitose Sensei was a Major in the Japanese Army Medical Corps during the war. He contracted typhoid fever and was released after a little more than a year of service.

"O-Sensei held an Okinawan Kobudo Taikai (exhibition) in the Kabuki Theater in Kumamoto to raise money for the people of Okinawa who had been devastated and become destitute during the invasion of their island. It was during March 1946, that O-Sensei decided to develop his style of karate.

"As you are aware, Chitose Sensei lives in Kikuchi with his wife and several children. He also has another son your age living in Okinawa.

"Every day he puts on his gi and trains and improves. Sensei is now fifty-five, and is physically stronger than he was five years ago. His technique is constantly improving. He seems to be defying, or reversing, the aging process, through his practice of karate and other martial arts."

The telephone rang; it was for Shirahama. He excused himself, then proceeded with his telephone call. After a very short time he handed the telephone back to Mary and continued.

"What we call karate, 'empty hand', used to be called Tote, 'Chinese Hand', in Okinawa, or just hand, 'Te', during the last century. The karate of Okinawa had its roots in China. When, for political reasons, the name was changed from 'Chinese Hand' to 'Empty Hand', it greatly upset O-Sensei. He wanted to keep the old name because of the historical reference to China. Chitose decided to name his style of karate Chi-to-ryu. The "to" stands for China and our style's historical roots which are located there.

"I hope this information will satisfy your craving for details about Doctor

Chitose," Shirahama Sensei said as he looked first at me, then at Mary. He spoke to Mary as he nodded in my direction.

"Now that your appetite for knowledge about O-Sensei has been temporarily satisfied, Shirahama Sensei suggests that you concentrate all your energies on your training and not to bother him about such matters in the future," Mary said.

"Osu!" I said. Shirahama, Mary and I stood. I bowed and thanked them for their help. Shirahama turned and left the small office. I thanked Mary for her time and assistance.

"I will translate my notes into English and make you a copy," she told me.

I stayed an hour and a half after class on Thursday while Ito assisted Harada with the kata Sochin and me with the katas Potsai and Chinto. My Potsai was coming along very well; the kata Chinto was another matter. I had twisted my right knee during a parachute jump a couple of weeks before. The injury was not critical, but it hurt like hell. The 360 degree spin and jump kick at the beginning of Chinto was aggravating it. Ito told me not to jump or spin, but to concentrate on other movements in the kata until my knee was better.

Ito-san invited me to join him at a Zen temple for a special training called a Dai Sesshin. The Dai Sesshin was scheduled to start in three weeks and consisted of five days of Zen training under the direction of a senior Roshi.

"The training begins at 3:00 AM and finishes at 9:00 PM. It is an intense, eighteen-hour day. Would you like to attend with me and try it out?" Ito inquired.

Mary Shigamoto told me that if I were really interested in Zen, this would be my chance to experience it. "Dai Sesshin means, "to search the heart." It is an intensive week of meditation, usually held approximately four times a year in Zen monasteries. The week includes not only many hours of meditation, but lectures, dokusan (one-on-one meetings with the priest), services, and manual labor," she continued.

The following week, my unit was on another FTX at Mori Yama. As if nature had been at the planning session of the military training schedule, it started raining half an hour before our trucks left Camp Chickamauga. It rained all week, as scheduled, and stopped early Friday morning, just as we loaded back onto the trucks for our return trip to Camp Chickamauga.

"Ichi!" The class slid forward into right front shiko dachi as we did a leg block.

"Ni!" We pivoted on the heel of our left foot and reverse punched as our hips snapped around shifting our bodies into seisan dachi.

"San!" We repeated the first move as we slid forward into left front shiko dachi. Then on the count of "Shi!" we rotated on the heel of our right foot and reverse punched with the right hand. We continued this drill for several minutes. Saturday's class seemed easier than most. Chitose Sensei had taken the train from Kumamoto and was instructing the students in the finer points of kihon (basic techniques).

He emphasized several fine points during the training session. One fist distance between the front heel and the rear knee of the other leg when practicing seisan dachi, shiko dachi, and neko ashi dachi. We dropped down on one knee to check the distance and returned to our stance. Seisan dachi also calls for slight inward tension with the thighs while both feet push against the floor. In neko ashi dachi the feet should be far enough apart so the student can shift easily from neko ashi dachi into seisan dachi without stepping.

Front arm blocks and lunge punches with the hips at a twenty-degree angle. Reverse punches and reverse blocks with hips at a zero degree angle. Wrist on the hip. Hip motion places the feet; the feet do not place the hips. Maintain your center at all times.

"Even as you move back, your spirit and mind should be going forward. When you defend, you must defend as if the block is an attack. Blocks should be as dynamic as the punches and kicks."

During this single class, O-Sensei told us many things.

"Expansion and contraction of the body muscles make all techniques more powerful. Contraction of one set of muscles should result in the expansion of another set of muscles.

"Punches should not focus in front of the target or in back of the target. For optimum effect, the focus should be into the target.

"A weak technique on target is sometimes more devastating than a stronger technique which misses the target."

I had heard most of these comments before from Ito-san, Shirahama Sensei, Matsumoto Sensei, and others. Every time I heard them, I seemed to understand them better and get a new idea about how to make my technique stronger, smoother or technically correct.

I missed the Tuesday class the following week. The unit had an open locker and barracks inspection scheduled for Wednesday morning. Everyone was busy cleaning the barracks and their individual areas from top to bottom. We dusted, mopped the floors, spit shined our boots, blocked our backpacks with cardboard,

Knowledge

and did anything else we could think of. Rocky worked late to help us get ready for the inspection. After midnight we finally got everything shaped up.

"ATTENTION!" SFC Reese said as General Lindquist entered our barracks at 9:35 AM sharp Wednesday morning. The Regimental Command Sergeant Major, the Company Commander, Captain Carpenter, the Company First Sergeant and a Major accompanied the General. The inspection went well. Our platoon received a commendable rating, the only one in the entire company.

Howard and I had made plans to take the girls to dinner then to the Post Service Club on Thursday evening. After the meal we were going dancing at the Service Club. This date with Junko caused me to miss my class at the dojo, which I really did not mind. I had not missed many classes at the dojo and I had started training too hard again. I was not giving my body time to heal. Once again I was beginning to feel a little burned out. I thought that maybe I should follow Rocky's advice to relax and take time to smell the roses.

Our company was at the Oita drop zone at 8:30 AM on Friday. An old World War II C-47 transport was there painted with Thai markings. We were going to jump from 1,000 feet using the T-7 parachutes. We put our "Mae West" life preservers on under our parachute harnesses. Damn! I hated wearing a "Mae West". We needed them but if they deployed accidentally, because of the opening shock of the parachute, the jumper would be crushed to death. However, the "Mae Wests" were a necessary evil since we would be jumping over water.

Our unit's custom when jumping a C-47 was that everyone had a cigar. Everyone, that is, except Corporal Goodwin. He smoked a pipe. As we sat on the runway waiting for our turn to load onto the aircraft we lit the cigars and smoked them.

"Butt 'em out," one of the jumpmasters said. We were not allowed to smoke during take offs.

In single file, we loaded onto the C-47. Soon it was taxiing down the gravel airstrip and finally lumbering into the air.

"Light them up," the jumpmaster said as the plane passed the 500-foot altitude mark. The C-47 only had one door, on the left side, and one anchor cable. The door remained open throughout the flight. By the time the plane reached 1,000 feet, there was so much smoke rolling out of the door that it must have looked as if the plane was on fire if you were watching from the ground.

The plane made two passes over the drop zone. Each pass dropped eleven paratroopers onto the D.Z. My stick was the first to jump and had no problems; the winds were light and no one was injured. I rolled up my chute and was shov-

The author kneeling with a Thai C-47 in the background.

ing it into my D-Bag as the aircraft I had exited was beginning to make its second pass. Everyone stopped and looked up. Little black dots came tumbling out of the aircraft; small puffs of white appeared as the parachutes deployed. One chute did not fully deploy because of a partial malfunction.

"Pull your reserve! Pull your reserve!" several voices screamed from the ground and in the air. The soldier's reserve parachute tumbled out slowly, filling with air. Even with his reserve chute deployed, the soldier was still falling faster than the others in the air around him. He slammed into the ground – hard. Several men ran to where he landed to check on him. He slowly he got to his feet and crammed his deployed main chute and his deployed reserve into his D-bag. He then slowly walked off of the drop zone to the chute trucks and hoisted his D-bag onto the vehicle. The ill-fated paratrooper was Goodwin. His mouth was bloody and he had lost some teeth. Goodwin had exited the plane with his pipe in place and when the pilot chute on his reserve deployed, it hit the stem of his pipe and knocked out some of his teeth.

● ●

Chapter 13

The Stick of Infinity

Help! I am being held prisoner by my heredity and environment.

Dennis Allen

Corporal Donald P. Toney made his way through the various squad areas and barracks wishing everyone the very best. He was departing for the United States where he was to be discharged. He would be leaving for Tokyo within a couple of hours. A week earlier he had spoken to several of the platoon members concerning a dilemma he had. Corporal Toney had been in the Far East for two years. When he left the U. S. for his overseas tour he was engaged to a beautiful girl back home. However, since arriving in Japan, he had met another beautiful girl and fallen in love.

"I am really screwed up," he confessed. "I love them both and I don't know which one I love the most."

"What do you plan on doing about it man?" Corporal Medina asked.

"I guess I'll have to go home, see my girlfriend in the States and make up my mind," he said.

Corporal Toney ate his last meal with the platoon, told everyone goodbye, and boarded the bus which would take him to the train station. "Another little Japanese girl will have a broken heart," I thought. Many G.I.s promised to send for their Japanese girlfriends after they returned to the land of the "Big P.X." Some promised to return to Japan and marry their girls. The majority never intended to make good on their promise and the few that did plan to soon forgot about it once they returned to the U. S.

Chitose Sensei started training the members of the Beppu dojo on some techniques called the Hen Shu Ho. He told us that practice in these techniques would enhance our understanding of kata. The first technique seemed very difficult; no matter how I tried, it never seemed to work properly. I had more success with the other techniques although numbers twelve and thirteen also gave me trouble.

As the rest of the class advanced through the Hen Shu Ho, I continued to have trouble with number twelve.

I grabbed my opponent's elbow then kicked at his knee. I knew however, that I did not have sufficient control of my opponent. Chitose Sensei saw my problem and walked over to me.

Corporal Toney just prior to his leaving to return to the United States.

"Punchi," Chitose Sensei said. I slid forward and punched at him. Almost at once, I felt an electrical shock run through my elbow. As Sensei kicked me lightly in the side of my right knee, I felt another electrical shock that almost caused my leg to collapse. Under his guidance, I practiced the movement a couple of times but I still don't think I ever completely got it right.

While practicing Hen Shu Ho number thirteen, my opponent lunged forward and punched with his right hand. I placed my left foot behind my right and shifted into kosa dachi. I did a back fist strike to my opponent's nose with my right hand. As my opponent reverse punched with his left hand, I dropped my right forearm onto his left arm, bending it at the elbow. I continued bending my opponent's arm as I applied an arm bar technique. I had great difficulty making the arm bar effective.

"Punchi," Chitose Sensei said, as Shirahama Sensei and others looked on.

I lunge-punched, performing the attack for Hen Shu Ho thirteen. Chitose Sensei stepped to his right and performed a back fist strike to my nose; I reverse punched him with my left fist. Suddenly, I was bent over at a forty-five degree angle as Chitose Sensei applied the arm bar that had given me so much difficulty.

The entire Saturday class was devoted to learning and practicing all twenty-eight Hen Shu Ho. After class, with Ito's help, I tried to write down a description of the techniques. A few days later, as I tried to study my notes, I could understand very little of what I had written.

On Monday, Chief Warrant Officer Bell led the band in a rigorous workout. We marched to Chapman Field near the main gate. We practiced close order drill marching as we played "Stars and Stripes Forever," "Thunder March," "The

Dr. Tsuyoshi Chitose performing Chito-ryu kaisetsu (self defense) with a student.

Marine Hymn," and numerous other marches. Corporal Redwine, the Drum Major, directed us with his large baton as we marched around the field for four solid hours.

Finally we returned to the company area and our barracks. I headed toward the orderly room to prepare the paperwork for my seven-day furlough. Sergeant Munro was attempting to work his way through a mountain of paperwork, which lay stacked on his desk. Munro was a gruff but very fair person. Behind his back the troops affectionately referred to him as "Marilyn," after Marilyn Monroe, the famous movie star. We were positive that he was aware of his nickname although he never acknowledged it.

The good sergeant had been born in the Royal Maternity Hospital at Edinburgh, Scotland. His parents had immigrated to the United States when he was very young. He had served in the U. S. Army in Europe during World War II. In 1945 he was discharged and returned to civilian life. Before long, he realized that he had made a mistake and in 1948 he re-enlisted. (SFC Munro retired from active duty in the US Army as a Command Sergeant Major in 1979 and lives in Texas with his Japanese wife, Chiako.) Munro was as tough as he looked; he was one of the earlier soldiers to graduate from jump school back in 1943. I lived in awe of Sergeant Munro. His English always had a slight Scottish brogue to it. In my young eyes, he was certainly no one to trifle with.

After a short wait he looked up at me and in his deep voice said, "Yes? What do you want, Dometrich?"

I explained that I wanted to put in a request for a seven-day furlough. He opened his drawer, shuffled through some papers, and produced the form he was looking for.

"Fill this out and get it back to me soon as possible," he commanded.

I took the form, left the orderly room and returned to my platoon's quarters. I completed the form and dropped it off at the orderly room on my way to lunch.

The following week was a very busy one for me. I attended every class at the dojo, had a date with Junko, and attended services at the small Zen temple in Beppu with Ito-san.

"Our religion teaches that truth and virtue must be realized through spiritual evolution. These things cannot be acquired by merely assenting to creeds or believing in doctrines," the priest explained to me.

"Buddhism is a way of life – it is not a system of worship, nor does it concern itself with how the earth evolved, or its final destiny. Buddhism focuses upon life in this moment, the eternal now. Buddhism is awareness. To be aware means to be fully conscious of the importance of this moment, the eternal now. Seeking the way is, in itself, the way. Buddhism shows us oneness; as a person grows, he or she becomes aware of the self, then the family, then society, and finally the entire universe."

"How do I acquire this great understanding?" I inquired. "Just sit in seiza, count your breaths, lose your thoughts, and melt into your breathing," the priest said.

After a great deal of practice, I learned to sit comfortably in seiza for long periods of time. However, I was still absorbed in my thoughts and could not yet melt into my breathing. I eagerly anticipated my upcoming experience with Ito-san at the Dai Sesshin. Saturday evening I picked up my leave papers, packed my clothes, and went to bed early in anticipation of my trip on Sunday.

I met up with Ito-san at the Beppu train station early Sunday. We boarded the train and found some seats together; the train slowly pulled away from the station, and quickly picked up speed. We were scheduled to spend five days at the temple – I wondered how I would do.

As Ito and I hoisted our luggage off of the train, I received a pleasant surprise. At the station to meet us were two Buddhist monks. Ito-san introduced us.

"This is my friend, Gentai," he said as he introduced me to the taller one, who bowed.

"I am happy to meet you," Gentai said. Once again I had found a Japanese person who could speak very good English. I was constantly amazed by the intelligence of the Japanese, especially since I had heard so many negative things about them during the Second World War.

"This is my other friend, Mumon," Ito said as he motioned to a shorter and much rounder monk. The second monk could not speak English.

"Hajimemashite, dozo yoroshiku," the little monk said as we bowed.

Parked at the curb outside the station was a small, dilapidated car – this was to be our transportation to the temple. We loaded our luggage in the small trunk, opened the doors, and got in. It was a rather tight fit. Gentai drove up the mountain and told us how happy he was that we had decided to attend the Dai Sesshin. I learned that this Dai Sesshin was a first for Ito-san also.

"It was not an easy decision," I admitted.

Gentai honked the horn as we negotiated a very narrow curved spot in the

Yaguchi teaching Kata.

road to assure that there were no vehicles approaching from the opposite direction. As the car started up a steep incline he shifted to a lower gear and the vehicle lurched a little.

"We are only a kilometer from the temple," he told us.

We pulled into a small driveway on the left side of the road and then the vehicle slid to a stop on the loosely packed gravel. After we had retrieved our luggage from the vehicle, Mumon took us into the temple. Gentai parked the car and joined us a few minutes later. I learned that Gentai was only twenty-six years old but his manner led me to suspect that he was much older. As a Zen Buddhist monk he had no hair, making it difficult to judge his age. For a Japanese, he was very tall, almost five feet eleven inches. He had dark brown eyes, which matched his robe, and he moved without effort or noise. Wrapped around his waist was a black sash with a knot in the middle of his back.

Mumon, who was wearing an identical robe, bowed and excused himself then disappeared down one of the hallways of the temple.

Gentai-san took Ito-san and I on a guided tour of the area. We were shown the Zendo (where regular meditation services were conducted). It was not large and, at one time, had been rather picturesque. The temple had a rather neglected and somewhat run down look about it. I attributed this unkempt look to damage caused by the war and the poor state of the Japanese economy in the early nineteen fifties. We visited other buildings, including the kitchen, and a few of the smaller buildings that made up the temple grounds.

Ito and I received very detailed instructions after returning to our room concerning the procedures to be followed during the Dai Sesshin. Gentai told us about the procedures for sitting and walking meditation (Kinhin). Walking meditation is done between the brief periods of Zazen. Three times each day, we would go alone before the Roshi (Zen Master). The Roshi would assign us a koan. A koan is an exercise of the mind, beyond rational thought, which is prescribed by a Zen Master. Being able to solve a koan depends upon intuition rather than rational thought. The practice of appearing before the Zen Master, or Roshi, three times a day is referred to as Dokusan or Sanzen (spiritual counseling by a Zen Master).

Teisho (a lecture by the Roshi) is scheduled once a day and usually takes place in the Zendo around 2:30 or 3:00 PM. Ito-san and I were given a copy of the Sutra book (a book of chants, based upon sermons which were given by the Buddha). Unfortunately, my book was in Japanese and I could not make heads or tails out of it. The monks chant the sutras many times throughout the day.

"Once again, welcome to our temple. I wish you a good Sesshin," Gentai said. "Feel free to relax. The Sesshin begins tomorrow at 3:00 AM. Please be in bed by ten o'clock. You must not talk to anyone except the Jikijitsu (the monk who acts as the disciplinarian and go-between during the Sesshin) after midnight. The Jikijitsu is the only person in the temple that the participants may communicate with."

"Who will be the Jikijitsu?" I inquired. I was concerned about how I was going to communicate with someone who did not speak English.

"I am the Jikijitsu," Gentai said. "There is no need to worry."

Ito and I wandered around the temple grounds during our free time. They were beautiful. Moss-covered stepping-stones were placed in a perfect pattern. The stones were not set at a normal pace for a man wearing street clothes, but closer together for a monk wearing a robe. The stones and the plants were placed in such a manner that the garden looked natural – not man-made. It looked as if a Buddhist priest had wandered here centuries ago and discovered the temple just as it was. Everything was intended to produce the impression of innocence and graceful simplicity.

"Do you see the way the path is laid out?" Ito asked. "The way it curves and twists. That was not an accident, but the plan of an enlightened man, a person who has become one with the universe."

As I lay in the darkness on the hard, three foot by six foot tatami mat, I kept thinking to myself, "Why am I here? Did I do the right thing by coming here?" I wondered what the next few days would be like then dozed off to sleep.

DAY ONE

Klack... Klack... I awoke immediately. It sounded like someone was striking two pieces of wood together. A few seconds later, I heard a small bell in the distance. Ring... Ring... Ring... Ring... Several dim light bulbs in the ceiling came on. Ito-san, several other Japanese and I were sharing space in the Zendo, which was to function as our meditation area, our eating area, and our bedroom. Each person was assigned a tatami. To the rear of this area, our eating utensils were stored. Our clothes and personal gear were stored in one large drawer under the raised area. I glanced at my watch; it was three o'clock in the morning. What was I doing here?

I arose from the mat and dressed in a brown robe that had been given to me. Carrying my toothbrush and washrag, I made my way to the washroom. When I returned it was a little after three in the morning.

Monks were seated on both sides of the room on raised platforms. Many were sitting in seiza, a few sat in the lotus position. Others arrived and took their places. A bell rang three times – ring ... ring ... ring. I slowly shut my eyes to an almost closed position. I looked down at a forty-five degree angle toward the polished floor. Sitting there, quietly meditating, I could smell the incense.

After an undetermined amount of time, my legs and ankles started to hurt. Suddenly there was a loud KLAP; the first forty-five minutes of meditation was over. We stood and walked around the meditation hall. This exercise is called Kinhin (Sutra – Walking). It is a formal walking exercise to loosen stiff joints and to exercise the body between long periods of meditation. We left the hall and retrieved our sandals, although I actually had no sandals, only my shoes. We followed the lead monk single file over the various paths in the garden. Even as we walked, we were to maintain the spirit of Zen.

I assumed my seiza position after we returned to the Zendo. This was the easiest position for me to sit in. I then prepared to do the sutras (a scripture attributed to the Buddha) to the best of my ability. The clappers were struck – KLAP, the small bell rang – ring ... ring... ring. I stared at the paper I held in my hands (which Gentai had translated into English for me last night). A monk struck a large, hand carved, hollow wooden fish head with a mallet. KA-PONK... KA-

Kataka Sensei & Mr. Saito.

PONK ... KA-PONK ... KA-PONK ... came the sound. With each strike of the mallet, everyone recited a word of the sutra. Our first sutra was the Hannya haramita (The Heart of Perfect Wisdom).

KAN JI ZAI BO SA. GYO JIN HAN NYA HA RA MI TA JI. SHI KEN GO UN KAI KU. DO I SAI KU YAKU. SHA RI SHI. SHIKI FU I KU. KU FU I SHIKI ....

After a few lines, I found that my lips were not working properly. I would see SHIKI but my lips would say YAKU.

GYA TE. GYA TE. HA RA GYA TE. HA RA SO GYA TE. BO DHI SO WA KA. HANNNN NYAAAA SHINNNN GYOOOO.

We chanted very slowly as the sutra came to an end.

We stood again and performed Kinhin as we walked through another section of the gardens. Back in the meditation hall, we assumed our positions and resumed meditating, which lasted for only a few minutes.

I heard a bell in the distance that had a very strange sound – a double sound. Kla-lang, kla-lang, kla-lang. Monks jumped up and rushed from the meditation room – I followed. A line of monks sitting in seiza formed on a long porch. The bell would ring, kla-lang, and the line would move forward. Time passed. I ended up seated at the front of the line near the bell, which hung directly in front of me. A faint-sounding bell rang. It had a delicate sound – a tinkle, tinkle. I reached for the striker and struck the bell, Kla-lang ... Kla-lang ... I stood, walked down the porch, kneeled, slid open a shoji (Japanese door), entered the room, and bowed, my head touching the floor. I raised both hands, palms up. I advanced directly in front of the Roshi, Gentai Sasaki. I repeated the bow, both palms facing up as I raised them again.

I was surprised. The Roshi addressed me in fair English.

"You name Bill?" he asked.

"Hai," I replied.

"Where you home?"

"Clarksburg, West Virginia."

"Rong way," he said.

"Yes!" I said, "It is a long way."

He held a small stick, approximately twelve inches long in his hand, which I had heard referred to as his "stick of infinity". Suddenly he struck the floor beside him.

"You hear stick ... I hear stick... Buddha hears stick ... Jesus hears stick... God hears stick ... How does the sound of this stick unify you with me, Buddha, Jesus, and God? How does the sound of this stick unify us all?"

He struck the floor again.

"How does this sound prove your thingness; how does it prove your nothingness?"

I had attempted to think of what the Roshi was asking; my mind didn't seem to work properly. I hesitated as I started to speak. I had no answer. This was my initiation into "Sanzen", or "Dokusan". I looked at the Roshi dumbfounded. The Roshi reached for a small bell by his side. He grasped it and rang it gently. My first interview was over. I bowed, then left the room.

• •

Chapter 14

The Roshi's Roshi

*I take my refuge in Buddha, the teacher I take my refuge in Dharma, the teaching
I take my refuge in Sangha, the brotherhood.*

The serving of hot tea early in the morning prior to the second meditation session was a very interesting part of life at the temple. The tea warmed not only my hands, but also my spirit and made me feel more alert. The cup rested in the palm of my left hand. As my cup was filled, I raised my right hand sharply and the server would stop pouring.

Gentai informed us that Roshi Sasaki's Zen teacher was coming to visit the temple during the Dai Sesshin. He was in his mid-eighties and blind. To have him visit the temple was considered a very great honor. Roshi Sasaki wanted the temple looking immaculate when his teacher, the Roshi's Roshi, arrived.

Another aspect of temple life that I was unaware of was the daily work detail. The possibility that Buddhist monks worked had never occurred to me. No talking is permitted when working. Gentai, the Jikijitsu, communicated with everyone individually as the work was performed. Time was allotted each day to clean up the temple prior to the visit from Sasaki's teacher. I was assigned to the leaf-raking detail. After raking the leaves up, we stored them in bins, which were soon filled to the top. My work detail, which was made up of three others and myself, was then instructed to pull grass from around the steps leading to the kitchen. This was done by hand and was more difficult than I had anticipated. "If the old Roshi is blind," I thought to myself, "why bother with the fix-up? He can't see it anyway."

We pulled the grass out of the ground and carried it to the grass storage bins for disposal.

"Nothing is wasted in a Zen temple," Gentai told Ito and me during our first day when we arrived. "By wasting nothing, we achieve a balance with nature. This balance, once achieved, allows us to unify our body, mind, and spirit. The unification within assists us in our understanding of the oneness of all creation."

Gentai's statement caused me to reflect upon Chitose Sensei's words about karate kata:

"There must be no wasted movement in the karate kata. At first all motions in the kata seem difficult and unnatural. It is the same with a young child when he learns to walk. As he continues to walk, he perfects the skill of walking and, in a short time, becomes unconscious of walking – he just walks. The same is true of karate kata. Discussion and theory are secondary, the most important thing is to do the kata over and over until it becomes a part of us and we can do it without conscious effort. The importance of the perfection of basic techniques leads to the perfection of kata, and finally, to the perfection of self through motion without wasted motion."

DAY TWO

Daylight came as the sun slowly rose from behind the large mountain that surrounded the valley where the temple was situated. We had just completed another meditation and sat on our mats holding our eating utensils in a prescribed manner. Our eating utensils consisted of two bowls, teacup, chopsticks, spoon and a cloth used to cover the utensils when not in use. Breakfast began with everyone's hands together in gassho (similar to Christians' hands when they pray) and the chanting of the breakfast sutra.

SHU YU JU RI. NYO I AN JIN.

GOHO BUHEN. KYU KIN JO RA.

We ate in silence. Occasionally, slurping could be heard as the soup was drunk from bowls. Western cultures frown on slurping. In Asian cultures however, it is a way of showing the cook your appreciation. A loud crunch broke the silence as someone bit into a radish. After completing the meal, another sutra was chanted. The bowls were washed at the table and then we drank the water remaining in the bowls – nothing was wasted. We recited the Heart Sutra, wrapped our bowls, and then placed them to the rear of our tan (mat).

We left the building for a brief after-meal walk that was very similar to Kinhin. Our walk took us around the building and in the direction of the kitchen. A monk was standing by the kitchen steps where we had labored all morning pulling up every single blade of grass. He was scattering something on the ground. Gentai bowed and engaged him in conversation. Gentai bowed again and we departed. The monk continued with his work as we walked by. Gentai had inquired of the monk what he was doing. "Planting grass," the young monk answered.

After returning to the Zendo, we were given free time for personal affairs such as brushing our teeth, taking a bath, writing letters, or doing additional meditation. Our free time lasted for one hour. (We were given these one-hour breaks after each meal.) I came to realize that temple life was not much different from the military.

The noon meal was a solemn affair. Most Buddhist monks do not eat after twelve noon, but because of the large number of lay people attending the Dai Sesshin, we were to be served three meals a day. The food consisted of vegetables, soups, rice, tofu and other foods with which I was not familiar. It has been said that the food in a Buddhist temple makes the food in a Japanese prison look delicious. Never having been in a Japanese prison, I had no method of comparison. As at other meals, a Sutra was chanted before we ate lunch.

SHU JU SHI RI. NYO I AN JIN. GOHO BUHEN.

KYU KIN JO RA.

No one spoke during the meals. Instead, an elaborate system of hand signals had been worked out. As we received our food, we sat with our hands together in gassho. If we wanted only a little more food, we rubbed our hands back and forth very quickly, as if trying to warm them. If we wanted the server to stop, we thrust one hand upward very quickly.

During the second half of the day, we meditated and listened to a lecture by the Roshi. When dokusan time came, I went before the Roshi for the third time. I listened to the sound of the stick as it struck the floor. I could think of nothing. The Roshi's bell rang, I bowed, left, and returned to the Zendo to continue my meditation. That night I fell asleep as soon as my head touched the bed.

DAY THREE

I was alone in a field, the earth shook and thunder roared. The sky was coming closer – closing in on me. I tried to move, but could not. I was frozen in time and space. Suddenly, my eyes opened; it was dark, but the sound continued and surrounded me. A light came on. It was three in the morning and the beginning of my third day at the Dai Sesshin.

We weren't to speak, but I couldn't contain myself.

"Ito-san, what is that sound?"

"That is the Ogane, the large bell. It is only rung on special occasions. Now, get dressed."

During the daily Teisho, Roshi spoke to us about his understanding of the Buddha's teachings. Seated on both sides of the Roshi were Mumon and Gentai. As the Roshi spoke he would stop periodically and allow Gentai to translate his words into English – a kindness directed toward me for which I was very grateful.

"Many of you have come here to steal the secret of Zen enlightenment from me. For this I charge you some money." (Laughter.) "I must confess, I have no secret to give and have stolen your money." (More laughter.) "In my practice I have come to realize that Zen cannot be grasped by reading. I am sure that many of you have read books on Zen, but believe me; this is a waste of time. If you read about a great musician's music, that is fine, but it is not the great musician's music. When you read or talk about Judo, this will not allow you to obtain the skill of judo. Should you read a menu at a restaurant, reading the menu will not satisfy your hunger. To satisfy your hunger, you must eat the food. To satisfy your hunger for Zen, you must physically participate in Zen training. We do this not through reading or discussion but by sitting in zazen. Zen, which is the flower of Buddhism, is not restricted to Buddhism, but is available to all religions. Buddhism shows us that although we are individuals, we are not separate from each other in a broader sense. People spend years of study to master a profession, a sport, a musical instrument, or some other pursuit. These same people, however, will spend very little time on their spiritual perfection or enlightenment. A few visit a temple once or twice a month while many attend only once or twice a year when there is a special religious observance. The most important thing any person can do in his life is to know and understand himself. This task, which should be the most important in our lives, has the lowest priority. Civilization is beginning to fail and will continue to do so until all mankind rearranges their priorities," Roshi Sasaki said.

I thought a lot about Roshi's words during my next zazen even though I was supposed to be meditating on the sound of the stick. Roshi was a very wise man. I shook off these thoughts and forced myself to meditate on the stick koan.

After supper I was sitting on the mat in the Zendo when the bell announcing dokusan rang. I leaped up from the mat and followed the monks to the waiting area.

I entered the Roshi's room for the ninth time since I had received my koan.

Each time I had entered the room and sat before Roshi I had been far from answering the koan. I had not been interested in my koan until after the Roshi's Teisho. Now my interest in the koan was beginning to grow.

A light misty rain started to fall. I, along with several others, darted across the grounds of the temple to the Zendo. I took my seat and rocked a few times to settle my body and help myself get into a more stable position. A young person, approximately twelve years old, with head shaved, was seated directly across from me looking like a little Buddha. I thought that the young person was a boy but I later discovered that it was a fourteen-year-old girl, a young Buddhist nun. Her eyes were partially closed, sitting ramrod straight showing no emotion. She looked like a young statue of the Buddha. Occasionally, I would look at her although I tried not to. She never moved.

DAY FOUR

Late Wednesday night or early Thursday morning, while the majority of the members of the temple lay sleeping, Roshi's teacher arrived. The klack of the wood, the ding ... ding... ding... of the small bell then a few minutes later the large bell rang with a sound that felt as if it was coming into my body through my feet. I arose from my tan, dressed in my robe, and proceeded to the bath.

Mumon had gone to a village and located the largest pair of wooden geta he could find. They barely fit my size 13-C feet but I would make do. I wore the geta much to the delight of everyone. Rules against talking were enforced but laughter was commonplace.

I bowed low, head touching the floor, as I lifted my hands beside my head and entered the Roshi's room for my first dokusan of the day. When questioned about the sound of the stick, I proceeded to do some basic karate hand techniques and other motions like firing a rifle.

"Good!" said the Roshi, "You show thingness through you practice of karate and soldier boy work."

"Now! How you show nothingness?"

Suddenly I got a far away, out to lunch look in my eyes as my mind once again went blank. Roshi reached for his small bell and rang it; I bowed and left the room.

It was 10 AM when I entered the Roshi's room for my second dokusan of the day. My understanding in regards to the sound of the stick was no better than it had been the night before. "Ding," went the Roshi's bell. I bowed and returned to my tan in the Zendo to resume my meditation on the sound of the stick.

The Teisho that afternoon was by Sasaki Roshi's teacher. The eighty-some year old Roshi sat in the higher middle chair, which Sasaki Roshi usually occupied. Sasaki Roshi occupied the chair that Mumon usually sat in. Gentai was in his regular position next to the main chair as the old teacher started to speak.

"I would first of all like to express my thanks to my friend and student, Sasaki

The geta barely fit my size 13-C feet.

Roshi, for allowing me to return again during the Dai Sesshin and train with you." Gentai translated after the old Roshi had stopped speaking. "We must distinguish between two methods of training ... one is spiritual ... the other physical. Spiritual training is a very simple matter when realized to its full extent, but training in detailed techniques must not be neglected. Training should never be one-sided. Spiritual training and physical training are like the two wheels of a cart. If only one wheel moves you will go around in a circle. If one wheel moves slower than the other you will only go around in a larger circle – you will never get anywhere. Both wheels must advance together if we are to reach our goal."

The old Roshi stopped speaking, his sightless eyes looked across the Zendo. He hung his head. He was contemplating. Something miraculous, some great wisdom was about to come forth from this his lips – words of wisdom more precious than gold. A couple of minutes went by. I knew, as did the others, that the longer we waited, the more valued his words would be.

"Ho! Ho! Ho!" The old Roshi's body shook as be bellowed with laughter. "You know what? I fell asleep."

We all laughed with the Roshi. How different these monks and priests were from what I had imagined.

"I will now take questions," he said.

A monk bowed and asked, "How do I control this idea of technical and spiritual?"

"Any idea, however worthy or desirable it is in itself, becomes a disease when the mind is obsessed with it."

Another monk bowed and inquired, "How do I keep all of this in my mind?"

"Keep it not in your mind but in your deeds," came the reply.

A third monk bowed and asked, "What is the most important thing a man can do in his lifetime?"

"Know himself," the old Roshi answered.

A monk at the very end of the room bowed, "Roshi please explain the meaning of nirvana to me?"

"When you got out of bed this morning which foot touched the floor first?" the Roshi asked.

The monk thought for a moment and then answered, "Hidari" (left).

"There you have it," said the old, blind Roshi as he laughed.

Thursday's last dokusan of the day was totally different than the others. Upon entering the Roshi's room, I found the old blind Roshi seated alone in the middle of the room. I bowed, made my way in front of him and bowed again. He just sat there. Maybe he had not heard me enter. "Perhaps he does not know I am here," I thought. He looked like a small round boulder sitting there. I was not sure what I should do. He spoke in Japanese, I did not understand. As I sat there, I quietly started doing chest blocks, then I made motions, as if I was firing a rifle. I felt very foolish. "He can't see me," I thought. "Why in the hell am I doing this in front of a blind man?" The blind priest spoke again. I did not understand. My mind was blank. I sat there for a moment, dumbfounded, not knowing what to do next. He reached for the small bell, then rang it. I bowed and exited the room. I wondered how he knew what I had done.

DAY FIVE

My fourteenth dokusan before Sasaki Roshi was on Friday morning at approximately 9:30 AM. The line moved slowly. I sat in line with monks before and monks behind me. Slowly we moved forward as, one by one, we entered the Roshi's room and sat before him to answer our koan. At last I found myself at the front of the line. I waited for the sound of Roshi's small bell. After what seemed an eternity, I heard it. I stood and made my way to his room. I slid the small door open, entered the room, closed the door quietly, then bowed.

"How does sound of stick show your thingness?" he asked.

I had been half-right before so once again I did the karate techniques and the rifle drill.

"And your nothingness?"

Suddenly, I fell over at his feet lying prone on the floor before him, my eyes closed.

He leaned forward as I gazed up at him through eyes that were half-closed. "Are you sick, my son?" he asked.

"No, I am dead," I replied.

The stick flew down on me; he struck me with it several times.

"Shut up! Dead men do not talk," he replied.

I heard his small bell, bowed and left. Only one dokusan remained before the end of the Sesshin.

I was starting to sweat as I sat meditating, something I had never done before. I concentrated to the best of my ability, but it did not seem to help. Hanging in front of me in space was a freshly pealed boiled egg, then, as suddenly as it appeared, it was gone. The boards of the floor turned upward and looked like a wooden venetian blind. That too passed. A fly in the Zendo buzzed around my head. It landed on my face, walked around, then flew off again. I saw the fly and wanted to reach out and swat it. Suddenly, I saw myself sitting on the mat in the Zendo. How was this possible? I realized that I was seeing myself through the eyes of the fly. I was wringing wet. Then, as suddenly as it had come, the fly flew away.

The last dokusan was at 8:00 PM Friday night. My turn came. I heard Roshi's bell, reached for the small hammer, and rang the two-sound bell. I arose and walked to the Roshi's room for the last time. I entered his room, performed two full lifting bows, and sat before him.

Thwack, thwack, thwack. The stick hit the floor.

"How does this sound make you, me, Buddha, Jesus, and God one? How does it's sound show your thingness, and your nothingness?"

I stared at the Roshi; I became the egg, the wooden floor standing on end, and the fly from whose eyes I had seen myself. I became the Roshi, Jesus, Buddha, and God at that moment in time. I became all creation and all creation became me. The Roshi smiled, bowed, and said simply, "Bill San, please visit with us again."

I returned his bow. Slowly, he picked up the bell, rang it, and smiled. I did a full bow, left the room, and headed back toward the Zendo.

RETURNING TO BEPPU

Ito-san and I boarded the train at noon Saturday for our trip back to Beppu. Ito told me about what had happened to Mumon as the train picked up speed. Mumon had had to leave the temple because of a family emergency. Prior to departing, Mumon had an opportunity to tell Ito-san about what had taken place in the Roshi's room during his dokusan on Thursday with the old blind Roshi.

Mumon, who had trained under the old blind Roshi many times in the past, entered the Roshi's room for dokusan. He bowed, advanced before the blind Roshi, then bowed again. As he sat there before the old Roshi, a strange thing happened. The Roshi questioned him in a most unusual way.

"Mumon, is that you?"

"Yes, Roshi, it is I."

"I thought I remembered your sound. No one enters a room exactly like you."

"My son, you have a problem," the old Roshi stated. "What is it?"

After some prodding by the Roshi, Mumon admitted that he did indeed have a problem. Monday evening, the first day of the Dai Sesshin, he had received a letter from his father that he had not discussed with anyone. The letter informed him that his mother was seriously ill.

"You should have told us, my son," the old Roshi said in a sympathetic voice.

Group with Soke.

"I did not want to disrupt the Dai Sesshin," Mumon explained to the Roshi.

"Nonsense! You must go home to your father and mother immediately. If you do not have enough money, the temple will lend you a little and you may repay it upon your return."

Mumon was overjoyed. He bowed, thanked the Roshi, and made his way to the door. As he prepared to leave, he paused, looked at the old blind Roshi sitting there alone in the middle of the room. Mumon was curious and inquired, "Roshi, I never mentioned my letter to anyone, how did you know?"

"Was it not you who rang the Ogane (large bell) this morning?"

"Yes, Roshi, I rang the Ogane. But what does that have to do with it?"

The Roshi paused for a moment, then replied. "When you rang the bell this morning, it sounded troubled."

● ●

Chapter 15

The Unexpected

To leave home, a desire To return home, a dream.

Anonymous

It felt good to be back in Beppu and Camp Chickamauga after participating in the Dai Sesshin. The daily regimen at the Zen temple had seemed more difficult than my military training. In the military you can at least talk and move around. Sitting in seiza for approximately twelve hours a day without talking had been very difficult for me. Fortunately, the work details at the temple had given me the chance to occasionally get out of seiza. These daily details were what kept me from asking to leave the temple. I looked forward to returning to my military duties and resuming training at the dojo.

Ito-san and I continued to attend weekly services at the local Zen center. These weekly Zen services seemed much easier to tolerate and understand after my return from the Dai Sesshin. One day, almost as an after thought, I realized that I was no longer a Baptist. I had become a Buddhist. I had no idea when this change had taken place – the transformation had occurred so gradually that I had been completely unaware that it was happening.

On the 23rd of July, some units of the 2nd Battalion got into trouble with Regimental Headquarters, our higher headquarters (The Far Eastern Command) in Tokyo, and, most importantly, with the Japanese citizens who lived in Oita. The battalion had made a parachute jump onto the Oita drop zone. Upon landing, some soldiers of the 2nd started plundering the local watermelon fields adjacent to the drop zone. The incident, while not as bad as portrayed by the Japanese news media, did cause a lot of resentment towards us by the local farmers.

Dr. Chitose & Masako Tamia, translator.

I spent the next few weeks at the dojo practicing the katas Potsai and Chinto. My hip vibration was improved through better use of the hip muscles. Thrusting the hips upward then dropping them increased my ability to project power. My injured leg had healed; I no longer had problems with the spin or jump in Chinto. Under the critical eyes of Chitose, Shirahama, Ito, and other sensei, my ability to flow through the kata improved. I still was not satisfied with my skill level and knew that I had a lot more to learn and perfect.

The sirens of the Camp Chickamauga fire department woke me at about 5:00 AM on the 9th of August. The NCO (Non-Commissioned Officers') club was burning. Flames lit up the early morning sky. The Beppu City Fire Department sent two fire trucks to assist the post fire department but to no avail. The building was totally destroyed. However, members of Mike Company who were on duty as the regimental fire alert unit did manage to salvage some items.

Saturday, I made my way to the dojo through the rain-swept streets of Beppu, streets that I had come to know so well. As I entered the now-familiar dojo, I bowed greetings to those present then quickly walked to the dressing room.

I changed into my karate-gi, walked from the room, and entered Mary's office to pay my monthly dues. Mary informed me that a date had been chosen for the

The Unexpected

next test.

"You have been selected to appear before the board and test for sho-dan," she advised me.

"You must be mistaken," I replied. "I have not been a brown belt long enough, and besides, I am not ready."

"Your name has been placed on the list by Chitose Sensei, himself. I do not think you should refuse."

"I thought there was no test scheduled for the immediate future," I said to her questioningly.

"Shirahama Sensei had not scheduled a test, but Chitose Sensei asked him to schedule one for next month. Chitose Sensei told Shirahama Sensei that he wanted you and several others to test," she said.

I asked about the cost of the test, checked the yen in my wallet, took out the required amount, and paid Mary. I wondered why I had been selected to test; I had a lot of work to do before the test date.

Each week seemed to go by faster than the week before. The week before the test was no exception. I was scheduled for C.Q. duty (Charge of Quarters). A special detail assigned to Corporals and some Sergeants. The C.Q. was required to stay in the orderly room during the weekend to answer the telephone, distribute passes, relay messages, etc., and lucky me, I was scheduled for C.Q. during the weekend of the test. Corporal Jim Harvey agreed to work in my place – for a fee. Fifteen dollars later, we had a deal. Both of us went to see Sergeant Munro for his approval of the change.

During the final week, all of my spare time was spent on training in an attempt to sharpen a few of the fine points that Ito-san had told me to work on. I attended class on Tuesday and Thursday and practised at the post gymnasium on Monday, Wednesday, and Friday evenings. I had no real hope of passing the test but with the extra training perhaps I would not completely embarrass my teachers or myself.

I was confident that no problems would arise after I had solved the Charge of Quarters problem, but I was wrong. I learned on Thursday afternoon that my platoon was to be placed on alert status starting at midnight Friday. All leaves had been cancelled for seventy-two hours. I went to see Sergeant Munro about my dilemma. I told him about the test and that I had to be able to go to Beppu on the weekend.

"The damn Army comes first Corporal. What in hell do you think I'm running here, a boy's school?" he said loudly and rather abruptly. Then he told me in a softer voice that the seventy-two hour alert was a training alert and the company commander might be able to give me a little slack.

"Let me talk to the old man," he said, "and I'll see what I can do."

After supper Friday evening I was ordered to report to the orderly room at once. Sergeant Munro had kept his word; he had obtained a special pass for me, which had been approved by a lieutenant colonel at Regimental Headquarters. My pass stated that I had been assigned as special liaison to assist and coordinate the band's concert, which was scheduled to be held in downtown Beppu in a few weeks. The conditions of my pass stated that I would be allowed to come and go at will.

I arrived at the dojo early Saturday morning so I could have a little more training time prior to the test. When I arrived the floor was crowded with karate-ka. Some exercised, others performed kata while a few were practising basic sparring. At one end of the training area were the now familiar tables already in place and awaiting the test board.

"Ki o tsuke!" Matsumoto Sensei yelled. Everyone jumped to their feet and stood perfectly still. Walking slowly toward the tables were Chitose Sensei, Shirahama Sensei and two other older sensei.

As Chitose Sensei and the others took their seat, Mary Shigamoto arrived as usual and sat down off to one side of the main desk.

"Tsuzukeru," (Continue to practice) Shirahama Sensei said.

Students moved vigorously around the floor as they practiced kata and basics. Everyone present made the most of the time remaining before the test.

My required kata was a beautiful kata called Chinto. The kata had a 360-degree spin along with two jumps – it was a complex kata. Perhaps that was the reason it was so beautiful. Even though my knee injury had healed, the kata still caused me problems occasionally.

The kata Chinto seemed very difficult to me when I first started learning it. However, daily training and great instruction allowed me to learn and appreciate the difference between merely doing the kata to obtain technical skill and learning to appreciate the kata as a living thing that was to be mastered physically, mentally and spiritually. I accepted the fact that this perfection was something I might never accomplish. I prayed that I had learned the kata well enough so I would not be an embarrassment.

The Japanese students in the dojo seemed to have a little trouble with the kata but not nearly as much as I did. As a Westerner, I found that my legs did not work the same as those of my Japanese karate brothers. The last part of the kata was most difficult for me. I had never been able to perform it well. Many of the instructors, especially Chitose Sensei, would often walk over and stand on my back in an attempt to get me closer to the floor after the last jump kick in the kata.

We were called to attention and formed into lines. The students knelt in seiza and bowed to the test board. As the names were called, each student stepped forward, announced the name of the kata, and then proceeded to demonstrate it. As they moved, stepped, slid, and thrusted themselves across the dojo floor, their karate uniforms grew wet with perspiration. There were other requirements requested by the test board as well as the required kata. Kiai's resounded as every ounce of physical, mental, and spiritual energy was expended.

A few of the small children who were visiting the dojo unescorted started making noise and talking, as children the world over do when they become a little bored. It was obvious that their chatter was annoying the test board. Mary Shigamoto would quiet them down for a few minutes, then, within a short time they would become restless and start talking again.

O'Sensei and wife & I at his house in Kumamoto, Japan.

"Dometrichi!"

I jumped to my feet, stepped forward, and called off the name of my kata.

"Chinto!" I called out. My voice sounded strange and foreign to me. I bowed, shifted into my preparatory stance, then started the kata. The same sensation I had when taking my brown belt test returned. I had no conscious remembrance of doing the kata. I vaguely remember coming up off of the floor and doing a double punch as the kata came to a close. I stood there for several seconds, looking straight ahead at the test board but not focusing on them. I did not move. I just stood there in the center of the floor – waiting.

Shirahama Sensei's voice brought me back to my senses.

"Dometrichi," he said, as he motioned with his hand to back up and sit down. I bowed and backed away from the test area and sat in seiza on the floor.

After the last student had completed his kata, we were called back onto the floor in groups of three, where we demonstrated the basic technique requested by the test board. We were then informed that we were to demonstrate three-step and one-step sparring (sanbon kumite and ippon kumite) depending upon the rank being tested for. The test ended. We were given a few minutes to visit the benjo (restroom).

"Line up!" Matsumoto Sensei said.

We sat on the floor in seiza facing the test board and awaiting their decision. I knew that I had demonstrated the kata adequately but I didn't feel that it was my best performance.

The members of the test board whispered among themselves. Occasionally they would stop talking, look at us for a moment, and then resume their deliberations. During the deliberations, Mary shuffled paperwork, which she handed to them upon request. The test board members would mark on the papers and return them to Mary. Finally Mary handed several papers to Shirahama Sensei. He pushed his chair back stood up and looked at us. Calling off the names of those who passed, his voice reverberated throughout the dojo.

After what seemed an eternity, I heard my name. "Dometrichi! Shodan."

I bowed from seiza. "Osu!" I said. Then, like the others before me had done, I jumped to my feet and stepped forward. I bowed again as I held out both hands to accept my diploma from Chitose Sensei.

"Domo arigato gozaimasu," I said as my certificate was handed to me.

Shirahama handed a black belt to Chitose Sensei, which he, in turn, handed to me. I bowed again and said thank you in Japanese. I noticed that I was holding a new belt and not one of the dyed ones that was used so often.

I backed away from Chitose Sensei, returned to my original position and sat on the floor.

Other diplomas were issued. Within a short time the awards ceremony was completed. The class lined up and sat in seiza.

"Mokuso." We sat in silence.

"Mokuso yame." We opened our eyes.

"Rei." Everyone bowed to the little Japanese flag and then to the test board.

As a young black belt, I was to assist with the newer students although I knew very little about teaching.

Ito-san had been promoted to Yon-dan; Harada-san had been promoted to Ni-dan.

"Congratulations," Ito-san said. "Now your training will start in earnest."

"I don't feel that I deserve to be promoted," I said to Ito. He looked at me, his eyes becoming slits.

"You are not to question the test board," he said. "Besides, your karate training is now only starting."

I had traveled to Japan to learn the art of karate – obtaining rank of any kind had never occurred to me before. Now that I had my black belt, an advanced belt, I was being told that my karate training was just beginning.

I spoke to Rocky and told him that in my opinion there were others who had taken the test who looked better than I and they had failed while I had passed.

"Test board rook many ting," Rocky said slowly and with great difficulty. "Skirl one ting, check. Question test board, no good. Bill-san funny boy. You fail test, want quit. Pass test feel unworthy. You probrem tink too much."

Cleaning weapons took most of Monday. We cleaned the 3.5-inch rocket launchers, our M-1 Garands, and the B.A.R.'s (Browning Automatic Rifle). The 3.5's were easy to clean since there was not much to them. It was crucial that the electrical firing apparatus was functional; it was also crucial to see that the inside of the tube was smooth and round so the missile would not jam when it was fired.

Corporal Medina, Corporal Hall, and I cleaned the unit's B.A.R.'s. We completely field stripped the weapons, did a through inspection of all parts for abnormal wear, and cleaned them using oil and graphite to lubricate the moving parts, taking care to wipe off the excess oil which acts as a dust collector. After being reassembled the weapons were dry fired a couple of times to assure that the firing mechanisms functioned properly. The cleaning took most of the day. The company armorer was extremely thorough in his inspection and could find dust on a bug's butt at fifteen hundred yards. After two rejections all of the B.A.R.'s passed muster, were accepted by the armorer and returned to the armaments room.

Tuesday night I walked to the dojo as a black belt for the first time. Changing into my karate-gi, I felt strange when I wrapped the black belt around my waist. I left the dojo and walked out to the makiwaras. I had been neglecting my makiwara training during the past several weeks as I had devoted most of my training time to preparing for the test.

The Unexpected

It felt good to slam my fist into the straw-covered post once again. I attempted to use my left hand but it was awkward since I seldom used it when practicing on the makiwara. Matsumoto Sensei scolded me time and again about my poor makiwara habits.

"Better punchi both hand, one hand all time no good," he told me on many occasions.

I left the makiwara and returned to the dojo for class. I felt no different than the week before when I had been wearing a brown belt.

After class both Ito and Matsumoto walked over to where I was standing.

"Now you are brack bert," Matsumoto said.

"People in America now think you expert," Ito told me. "There are many degree black belt, now you just start black belt. Lifetime of hard practice ahead."

"Most important not to get big head. If do get big head, Matsumoto and I bust big head," Ito-san added with a smile.

"Osu!" I replied, trying to act very correct.

Shirahama Sensei gave a lecture about the importance of kata during Thursday's class.

"The main point of kata," Shirahama Sensei said, "is to develop and perfect strong physical actions of the body and simultaneously develop the spirit and the mind. If your kata are practised daily with this idea in mind, you will someday arrive at true understanding."

The students were ordered to line up by ranks for kata practice.

"Rohai Sho."

The class repeated the name of the kata then moved into uchi hachi dachi.

"Ichi." We moved into an iaigoshi dachi (kneeling stance) and performed juji gedan uke (lower cross wrist block).

"Ni." We sprang up into a shiko dachi, double side arm punch.

"Dame, dame." Sensei said. (No good, no good.)

He then proceeded to instruct us in the proper angle that the arms were to take during the double side punch.

"San." We stepped forward with the right foot and did a right elbow strike.

We practised Rohai for more than an hour. Each time we did the kata our timing and understanding of the various techniques also improved. In addition, we learned how to use the proper amount of power at the optimum time for applying each technique. Shirahama Sensei walked among the students moving an arm here, changing a stance there. He commented to the students about their techniques as he checked the tension of their stances. Occasionally he would kick the legs of the students to check their balance and muscle tension. One student collapsed onto the floor after having his leg kicked only to receive the wrath of Sensei for having a weak stance.

Our uniforms were, as usual, wet with perspiration as we completed Rohai Sho for the last time. The class was over; it was time to bow out. We sat in seiza and meditated as the sweat poured from our bodies. We felt exhausted both mentally and physically, comforted only by the fact that we had trained as hard as we could.

Dr. Chitose showing a technique to Famarez Alavi from Iran in Covington, KY.

● ●

Chapter 16

Oiya City

Does a dog have Buddha nature - yes or no? Be careful or you may lose your own Buddha nature.

On Saturday after class, I remained at the dojo to train with Harada-san under the watchful eye of Ito-san. For approximately an hour and a half we practised ippon kumite (one step sparring). During our training we only practiced five combinations. Gradually, our techniques became smoother and faster; we were both developing more power. Ito-san would stop us occasionally to make a correction or demonstrate a technique.

One hour and a half later we decided to call it a day. I bowed and retreated to the dressing room, changed clothes and said good-bye to Mary. It was an excellent day – breezy, warm, and pleasant. Stopping at a small store, I purchased several candy bars then ambled back into the busy streets of Beppu.

Junko had to work until 5:00 PM so I had not planned anything for the rest of the afternoon. I rented a bicycle and rode through the streets and alleys of Beppu. The bicycle was a one-speed model constructed from the parts of several other bicycles, which looked as if they had barely survived the war. The bike was in very poor shape; it was faster than walking, but not much.

I pedaled through southern Beppu. There at the inter-section lay highway #10, which led south to the city of Oita. I pointed the bicycle south and headed down the highway toward Oita. I checked my watch, it was 1:30 PM, still early enough to ride to Oita, sightsee, and return to Beppu in time to meet with Howard and go dancing with Junko and Kazuko.

I pedaled toward Oita with some anxiety. Members of the 187th had warned me about traveling to Oita City. The Mayor of Oita was reported to be a

Winners at our first tournament. Covington's Mayor awards trophys. Standing: Bob Yarnall, Shinichi Kumanomedo, G. Van Horne; Center: (two center) Terry Collis, Rich Hootesl; Seated left: Lawrence Hawkins.

Communist and very anti-American. He did not take kindly to American GIs being in his city. Some soldiers who had been there told me that if I behaved myself and got out of town before nightfall, I should have no trouble.

Upon arriving at the outskirts of Oita, I thought that I was back in Beppu, but as I approached the downtown area, I noticed that the buildings were much larger than those in Beppu; the majority of them were constructed of a dirty-looking grey stone. The buildings looked as if they had not been cleaned since before the war. I had an eerie feeling as I pedaled the bicycle through the streets. For such a large town, there were very few people out and about. Compared to the crowded streets of Beppu, Oita seemed almost deserted.

Ito-san had told me that during the final days of the war, Funakoshi Sensei and his wife had sought refuge in Oita. While I was in the city perhaps I could locate Funakoshi Sensei's home. Even though I had not planned to try to locate Sensei's home, I was confident that I would have no trouble finding it. I was positive that everyone in town would know such a famous Karate man.

Plan A was to stop people and ask directions. However, the citizens of Oita, unlike those of Beppu, spoke little or no English. I had trouble understanding those who did speak English. Despite our communication problems the locals were very kind to me and cooperated to the best of their ability. The big problem was my lack of knowledge of the Japanese language – a problem which could not be overcome.

No one that I came in contact with seemed to know Gichin Funakoshi. I thought that a great karate master would be well known by the masses – I was mistaken. Karate-do was still considered a foreign (Okinawan) art and was not as popular in Japan as judo and kendo.

I pedaled deeper into the city. Riding the bicycle through Oita was as different from riding in Beppu as a black and white movie was from a Technicolor one. Beppu was colorful – Oita was drab. The only color in Oita was the blue of the sky above me. The streets were wider than those in Beppu, but the entire city had an eerie feeling to it. I rounded a curve leading into an intersection and almost wrecked the bicycle as the front tire wedged temporarily in an old streetcar track. I momentarily lost control of the bicycle, but luck was with me and I did not crash. I stopped at a small store. The owner, a middle-aged man with round spectacles and a black and red coat with no sleeves, greeted me.

"Konnichi wa," he said, smiling.

"Konnichi wa," I replied.

I had learned a little Japanese with the help of Ito and Rocky. I hoped that the man could understand me. I asked him about Funakoshi Sensei.

"Funakoshi-san no uchi wa doko desu ka?" I asked.

He looked at me for a moment, scratched his head, and said something unintelligible to me. Again I repeated the phrase. This time I said it very slowly and placed great emphasis on "Funakoshi" and "no uchi". His face brightened. He took a piece of paper and, with a stubby pencil in hand, drew me a map. He motioned for me to follow him outside. There we stood in front of the small shop. A young American in sports clothes and a middle-aged Japanese attempting to communicate. We both looked a little crazy as we gestured with our hands and arms. He pointed down the street in the direction from which I had just come then he pointed to the homemade map. Using his finger, he pointed to the lines he had drawn on the paper. A symbol for a house was drawn on the map.

"Koko," (Here) he said. "Funakoshi no uchi," he said, with a smile of self-satisfaction. I bought a box of cookies out of gratitude and pointed the bicycle in the direction he had designated.

I used the map to retrace my route but still got lost twice. I came to a street with little houses of different shapes and sizes. This part of Oita was more like

Beppu. The shopkeeper had designated a house on a corner next to a bridge that crossed a small moat. I glanced at the map again; I was not sure that I was in the right place. There was a moat a few hundred feet from the corner – a small house was nearby. The door was open and I could hear activity inside. "Hello!" I called out in English. I repeated myself two times before I heard movement. Within seconds a woman with two small children was standing before me.

"Funakoshi Gichin no uchi?" I inquired. She looked at me quizzically. "Funakoshi Gichin no uchi?" I repeated.

"Chotto matte," (Just a minute.) she said as she went back into the house. She returned quickly with a small girl approximately thirteen or fourteen years of age. "I help you?" she asked in faltering English. I learned that she had studied English for two years in school.

"I am looking for the house of Funakoshi Gichin," I told her.

"You wrong house have," she said. "I never heard Funakoshi, my mother never heard Funakoshi."

"My father name sound a little like the name you mentioned but this is wrong house," she said. "We not know Funakoshi-san; I sorry."

I thanked her for her time and gave up on locating Funakoshi Sensei's home. It was now past 3:45 PM. I decided to find my way back to downtown Oita and then to Beppu. I was tired and a little saddle sore. I pedaled quickly through the center of Oita. Within a short time I arrived at the entrance of the Oita-Beppu highway, which curved northward around the bay. The traffic light at the entrance to the highway was red. A loaded flatbed truck pulled alongside me. I had what, at the time, seemed like a brilliant idea. Just as the light turned green, I grabbed onto the truck with my left hand and steered the bicycle with my right. The truck and I sped off to Beppu. It took only a few seconds for me to realize that I had made a big mistake by grabbing onto the truck. I wanted to let go but could not for fear of wrecking. After a short time, which to me seemed an eternity, the truck entered the southern limits of Beppu. The truck slowed down to make a left turn onto a side street. It was then that I said a little prayer and let go of the truck. I pulled off to the side of the road for several minutes in an attempt to stop shaking. Then, I continued toward the center of town, pedaled to the rental shop and returned the bicycle just as the rain started.

I started walking in the general direction of the Hanago Bar and Grill, dashing from shop to shop, trying to stay out of the rain as much as possible. I had a couple of drinks, then went outside and flagged down a rickshaw for the trip back to camp.

Inside the Yudan Dojo.

When I got there, I shaved, showered, and dressed in a polo shirt and slacks. Then I yelled into the other squad area for Howard.

"Howard, are you ready?"

"Sure am, buddy!" came the reply.

I told Mary about my trip to Oita when I arrived at the dojo on Tuesday night.

"I rented a bike and rode over to Oita on Saturday afternoon to locate Funakoshi's home but no one knew him," I told her.

I asked if she would check with Shirahama about the exact location of Funakoshi Sensei's house in Oita. Mary left the office and returned in a couple of minutes with Shirahama. After she and Shirahama were through talking, they both looked at me.

"Now, explain to me again why you went to Oita," Mary said.

"Originally, to sightsee," I said. "However, once I got there, I decided to look for Funakoshi Sensei's home. I was told that he had moved to Oita during the war," I avowed as I looked at Shirahama Sensei eye-to-eye.

Shirahama Sensei looked at me for a minute and smiled. It was the type of smile a person would display when taking pity on some dumb creature. Then he spoke to Mary.

"Shirahama Sensei said Funakoshi Sensei moved to Oita during the last days of the war, however he returned to Tokyo in the late 1940s. He now lives in Tokyo."

"He moved to Oita Ken, which is the prefecture in which Beppu, Oita and several other towns are located. He never did live in the city of Oita. Funakoshi Sensei lived on a cousin's farm where he and his wife took refuge during the final months of the war. He had been to the dojo on two previous occasions because he had come to visit his cousin who was seriously ill. His most recent visit had been to attend his cousin's funeral and console the family. Both trips were very hard on Funakoshi Sensei. He was very old and had not been feeling well. He felt compelled to make the trips because of his great respect and obligation to his cousin. When Chitose Sensei learned that Funakoshi Sensei was traveling to Oita Ken, he came from Kumamoto to visit," Mary explained.

Left to Right: Barbara Dometrich, the author, Dr. Tsuyoshi Chitose, Debbie Dometrich, small child Sherry Dometrich.

I thanked both Shirahama Sensei and Mary for their help. I felt a little stupid but not discouraged. I walked to the dressing room, changed into my street clothes, and headed back to camp.

● ●

Chapter 17

Chitose's Wonderful Power

If all the waves of the Zen stream were alike, innumerable ordinary people would get bogged down.

Zen saying

Several soldiers at Camp Chickamauga requested that I start a karate club on Camp Chickamauga. A post judo club had been organized several months before, which trained twice weekly at the post gymnasium. Although I wasn't interested in teaching and knew that I was not qualified to teach, I did feel that I should mention the idea to Shirahama Sensei. I spoke to him and Ito-san about the possibility of starting a small karate club at the Camp Chickamauga gym. I was positive that one of the karate sensei at the Beppu dojo would want to organize the post karate club. Shirahama Sensei told me that he would talk to Chitose Sensei about it. A small karate club had already been organized at Camp Wood in Kumamoto with the help of Masami Tsuruoka Sensei. Chitose Sensei thought the idea had merit but wanted to think it over. I would get my answer within one week. Six days later, Chitose Sensei had granted approval for the new club under two conditions.

"What are the conditions?" I inquired.

"You must organize the club and teach the classes. Occasionally an instructor from the Beppu dojo will visit and assist you but you must do most of the work."

"You mentioned two conditions," I said, "what is the second one?"

"You must charge 1,000 yen a month and the money is to be given to the 187th Rakkasan fund." (The Rakkasan Fund had been established to benefit the orphans at the Eidoin orphanage, which was managed by Sister Susuka Ogo.)

The post gymnasium was located near my barracks so having classes there would be very convenient. Posters were placed all over Camp Chickamauga advertising the formation of a karate club. Monday evening I arrived at the gymnasium expecting to find forty or fifty people waiting for their first karate class. I had grossly overestimated – only sixteen people were waiting. After a few weeks of hard classes, the membership dwindled to nine hard-core members.

Classes were scheduled for Monday, Wednesday, and Friday nights from 6:00 PM until 7:00 PM. I felt that the classes were not long enough but these were the only times that the gym was not being used by other groups.

All day Wednesday the band was lined up practicing for a parade at Chapman Field. Major General James B. Rigley, U.S.M.C., and some of his marines were scheduled to be the guests of our commander, Brigadier General Roy Lindquist.

A month before we had been issued light blue scarves and a blue rope to be hooked on our right shoulder and two little circular blue plastic disks that were to be placed behind the brass on our Class A uniforms. Some desk jockey at the Pentagon thought this extra junk would jazz up our uniforms. A few days before the big event, I headed downtown wearing my Class A uniform. Luck was not with me. One of my brass disks, along with a blue disc, popped off and rolled down the street. My brass stopped a few inches short of an open sewer which ran along the side of the street. My blue disk, however, took the plunge. I had no intention of attempting to retrieve a plastic disc from an open drainage ditch. The very next day during formation Sergeant Munro held an "in ranks" inspection and noticed that I was wearing only one blue disk. He questioned me about the missing disc and I made light of the fact that it was missing. He gave me one week's restriction to post for losing it. I attempted to reason with him jokingly but before I knew it I had joked my one-week restriction into a five-week restriction. I decided to shut up and lick my wounds while I could.

I continued to teach at the camp on Monday, Wednesday, and Friday nights, but could not leave the post to go to the dojo. Howard told Junko about my problem and she visited me on post. We would go dancing at the service club or take in a movie at the post theater.

Saturday, three weeks later, while I was lounging in my squad area, the C.Q. came into the room to tell me that there was a Japanese in the orderly room asking for me. I entered the orderly room and there stood Chitose Sensei. I introduced Chitose Sensei to the C.Q. and told him that this was my karate teacher.

"Can Papa-san break that desk?" Corporal Corral asked.

A small, folding Artillery desk was set up in a corner with nothing on it.

Chitose Sensei misunderstood and walked over to the desk and struck it, very hard and fast with his fist. Corral jumped up and ran over to check the desk. One leg was slightly bent and the top had been split. There was that sudden power again; I could only wonder.

Chitose Sensei had missed me at the dojo and came looking for me. I was flattered. I got my karate-gi and we both walked to the post gymnasium. Some of the boxers were there, as usual. We dressed and found an area in which we could practice and proceeded to do so.

"Hey Bill!" I heard a voice yell. I looked around and spotted Jake Morrison over in a corner punching a speed bag so fast that it sounded like a machine gun going off. Jake was one of the better boxers on the regimental team.

"Is that Papa-san your karate teacher?" he inquired.

"Yes," I answered him. He walked away from the speed bag and headed our way.

"Would Papa-san like to go a few rounds?" Jake asked in a joking manner.

I was going to explain to Chitose Sensei but he had already understood. He put his hands up in a shuto kamae (on guard position). Jake shot a left jab out, then he started dancing around Chitose Sensei and another left jab shot forward. The third jab struck Chitose in the temple. Chitose Sensei was not used to this type of treatment. His eyes became like slits as he moved slightly to Jake's left. Jake's left hand shot forward again. Chitose Sensei's left hand flashed out even faster than Jake's as he parried the jab. Chitose's left foot flashed forward and upward as his toes found their target – Jake's left armpit. Jake dropped to his knees with a scream as he grabbed his left armpit with his gloved right hand.

"What the hell is he trying to do – kill me?" Jake yelled.

"You should not have hit him, it is against the rules," I explained. "In karate we pull our punches. When you hit him you broke the rules."

Jake did not box for two weeks after his little encounter with Chitose Sensei.

Sergeant Munro lifted my restriction to post the next Friday – ten days early. I thought that I had earned time off for good behavior.

Karate class at the Beppu dojo was invigorating, especially after my restriction to post. After the Saturday class ended Chitose Sensei asked me if I wanted to go shopping with him again.

"Hai," (Yes.) I answered.

Ekimae Cho, one of the streets in the main shopping area, was crowded, but not nearly as crowded as it was in the Ginza Arcade. This Saturday was a special sale day. Chitose Sensei visited several stores and purchased many items. He would visit a small shop, buy a couple of items and inform me that these were for his children. He entered another shop to take a look at some merchandise. I waited outside; the shop was very small and there were always several people inside shopping. Chitose Sensei exited the shop; he had purchased a present for his wife.

"Wife," he said, smiling as he patted the package in his hand. "Dojo ni," he stated. We started walking back toward the dojo.

We turned a corner and suddenly a crowd was in front of us at the intersection, shoulder-to-shoulder and not moving. It was neither possible to pass through nor could we see what was causing the congestion. Chitose Sensei stood on his tiptoes, attempting to look over the heads of the people in front us. In desperation, he extended his hands in front of him, back to back, palms out, placed them between two people and opened his arms. The people leaned, then moved to the left or right. He continued to do this again and again. Soon we were at the front of the crowd where we could see the problem. A little girl was lying on the ground, her bicycle beside her. A drunk standing next to her had kicked her bicycle, causing her to wreck. The drunk staggered, yelling at the crowd and making threatening gestures. I did not know what he was saying but it upset Chitose Sensei.

"Damatte kudasai!" Chitose said to the drunk.

The drunk made a threatening gesture toward Chitose Sensei. Chitose flicked the drunk's hand away and with his right hand grabbed the drunk's arm at the elbow.

Someone had forgotten to insert the CO-2 cartridges in the life preserver.

The author, 2nd from left, with friends prior to a parachute jump on the Oita drop zone, Kyushu, Japan (1954).

The drunk fell to his knees in great pain. There was that wonderful power and speed again. In the distance, I could hear a bicycle bell ringing. A Beppu police officer on a bicycle arrived, jumped off, bowed to Chitose, and spoke to him for a second. He then confronted the drunk. The drunk had regained his feet and started shouting again, suddenly his feet were pointed straight up, the police officer threw him over his shoulder, handcuffed him to a telephone pole, got on his bicycle and left.

"Jidosha," Chitose Sensei said, making a driving motion with his hands as if he were driving a car. A police car would arrive soon and take the drunk to jail.

"Dojo ni," Chitose Sensei said. We started back in the direction of the dojo; I carried Sensei's packages.

We entered the dojo and went into Mary's office. He spoke to her, motioning to me as he did.

"Chitose Sensei is going to Tokyo in a couple of weeks to meet Funakoshi Sensei and some friends. He would like for you to go with him, if possible. Do you think you can go?"

I would have liked to go with Chitose Sensei. However, I was young and afraid that I might become separated from him, get lost in Japan, and never find my way home.

"I cannot make the trip," I lied. "It will be impossible for me to get a furlough at this time."

I did not make the trip and have regretted it ever since.

An airborne operation was scheduled for the regiment on Wednesday and was to be conducted at the Oita drop zone. On this jump we were not going to wear traditional Mae West life preservers. A new life preserver had been designed especially for airborne troops and our regiment was going to test it.

The troops who were participating in the operation marched to Chapman Field on Monday for an orientation about the new piece of equipment. The troops nicknamed the new life preserver the "double condom". I was informed that I had been selected to be part of the demonstration team.

Corporal Hall, one of my friends from Texas and a unit member, took my photo as I walked off the drop zone.

I stood in front of the troops the next day wearing my new life preserver, which fit neatly in two small packages under my armpits. Sergeant Reese, the narrator, stood behind a rostrum and informed those present of the advantages of this new life preserver over the old Mae West. Sergeant Reese motioned for me to pull the tabs and deploy the new life preserver. I pulled the tabs but instead of inflating, the bladders dropped straight down. Someone had forgotten to insert the CO-2 cartridges into the pockets of the life preserver. I looked up at the men in the audience and could almost read their thoughts – "This is BETTER?" Instead of building confidence in the new life preserver the demonstration had an entirely opposite effect.

I had a case of the butterflies; it had been several weeks since I had jumped. The plane, a World War II C-47, bounced its way down the gravel packed runway and then we were airborne. We circled the drop zone once; one paratrooper jumped to test the winds at our thousand-foot altitude. On the second pass, I jumped in the first stick of eleven men. I was second from last in the stick. I took off at a trot, then I was outside the plane falling earthward.

"One thousand, two thousand, three thousa . . . . I felt the opening shock of my parachute as it deployed. I hung there, looking over my shoulder at the aircraft as it headed out to sea, banked lazily, and turned for its next approach over the drop zone. My PLF (parachute landing fall) was a good one. I packed my chute into my D-bag and walked off the DZ to the pick-up point. Corporal Hall, one of the unit members from Dallas, Texas, was standing next to the truck.

"Hey Bill, hold it for a minute," he shouted. I turned to face him and he took my photograph as I stood there with my D-bag on my back.

The trucks bringing us back from the Oita DZ rolled through the main gate of Camp Chickamauga at 3:35 PM. I was beat and dirty; my shower felt good. I decided to lie down and rest for a while. Later that evening I dressed in civilian

When I first met Dr. Chitose, I looked upon him as a type of God. But after I came to know him better, I realized that he was just a human being, although a very special and talented human being.

Front Row: Hidimichi Kanazaki, Scino, Misho Chitose, unknown. Back Row: Denny Dickerson, Sam Morris, Kazanori Kawakita, the author, Dr. Tsuyoshi Chitose, Barbara Dometrich, Miako Chitose, Cherie Stepaniak.

clothes and headed to the mess hall for supper. The steaks, which we seldom had, were very good. The jump and my nap had invigorated me and I decided to walk downtown to Beppu. It had been a great day, warm but not hot, sunny, with enough cloud cover that it wasn't too bright. I strolled along the streets and alleys, stopping in small shops to browse around. I took my time and walked slowly, observing the people as they walked by on Yayoi Arcade Street. Most of the soldiers referred to these streets as the "covered streets." The little shops seemed endless and were great places to shop. I enjoyed the sounds, smells, and feelings of the people. They were very kind, intelligent, and hard working.

I walked down one narrow street and then I entered Nagare Kawa Street. I had walked just a little more than a block when an all-white rickshaw with lace curtains covering the windows pulled along beside me and stopped. The driver was dressed in a black chauffeur's uniform; he even wore a chauffeur's cap. The flap, which served as a door, opened. Stepping out of the rickshaw was the most beautiful Japanese girl I had ever laid eyes on. She stood before me wearing a white wedding dress as she flashed a dazzling smile. I knew who she was immediately. I had heard many stories about the beautiful Miss Beppu. She had won the first beauty contest ever held in Beppu City in 1951. Miss Beppu made her living as a prostitute. Her home was in the biggest hotel in town, approximately two blocks south of the Hanago Bar and Grill. Rumor had it that her bedroom was decorated in white.

"You rakkasan, ne?" she asked.

"Hai," (Yes) I answered.

"You know who I am?"

"You are Miss Beppu," I answered.

"Hai!" she said. "Rakkasan boy, you like take me to movie, buy me nice meal?"

"Watashi kane nai," (I don't have any money) I told her. She got a disappointed look on her face as she thought about it.

"I catchi payday," she said and smiled. "You come see me pay day, OK?" she said as she climbed back into the white rickshaw. She flashed that beautiful smile again then she closed the flap. I watched the white rickshaw as it drove down the street and then disappeared around the corner.

Everyone was sound asleep when Corporal Redwine, the band's drum major, staggered into the squad room where the platoon slept. He was a young, tall, thin, black soldier who was about as sharp as they come. He had memorized the U.C.M.J. (Uniform Code of Military Justice). His uniforms were always immaculate. He was one of the few GIs who had signed up at the post judo club and stayed. He was a little standoffish but very professional, and no one, absolutely no one – including officers – screwed with Corporal Redwine. The last time the unit was at Ashiya Airforce Base, an Air Force major who had been drinking a little gave him a very hard time for no reason at all. Corporal Redwine took his case to the Base Commander and won. The major was court marshaled and reduced in rank to Captain.

Redwine was very upset, his clothing was torn, and he had a black eye and a cut on his lip. He had been drinking in a local cafe, the "Cupid Beer Hall", when three GIs made some advances at his girlfriend who was a barmaid there. One of the soldiers punched Corporal Redwine and a fight erupted with the three other soldiers fighting Redwine.

The next day, we heard through the grapevine that three members of "F" (Fox) Company were in the hospital. They told the Military Police that they had been drinking sake and had been jumped by seven sailors. The joke around the platoon was, "Sake hell, what they had was too much wine – Redwine." The next morning, after a hot shower, Corporal Redwine was in pretty good shape, especially when compared to the three jerks he had put in the hospital. All that he had to show for his encounter was a little mouse under his left eye and a couple of bruised ribs.

I went to the dojo on Thursday night. I felt that I was getting worse in various areas of my training. I did not have as much time to devote to my training as I wanted. Now a great deal of my time was spent at the camp karate club.

"This is the way it is meant to be," Ito-san told me. "Chitose Sensei sacrifices his time to teach others; Shirahama Sensei sacrifices his time to teach others, and I sacrifice some of my time to help you and other students. This is life, and is one of the principle teachings of the Buddhist Bodhisattva Kanzeon Bosatsu." (Kanzeon is similar to a Christian saint. The statue of Kanzeon Bosatsu, represents people who sacrifice their time, effort and lives in the service of their fellow human beings.)

"Kanzeon is the Bodhisattva of great compassion. The ideal of Kanzeon is self sacrifice for the betterment of all society and is an example of how we must help other beings," Ito-san explained. "We all must sacrifice a little of ourselves for others."

In keeping with the ideals of "Kanzeon", the entire regiment, under the direction of Colonel (later General) William Westmoreland, had adopted the orphanage. The orphanage needed help and the paratroopers of the 187th had responded enthusiastically and without hesitation. A photograph of General Westmoreland hung in the orphanage entrance. The money from the karate club, although very little, would go to help the children of the orphanage.

On special holidays such as Easter, Fourth of July, Thanksgiving, and Christmas, the orphans and nuns were invited to participate in special camp functions and dinners. Thanksgiving was only two days away.

When Thanksgiving Day arrived, the camp was opened to the orphans and nuns of the Eidoin Orphanage. They were divided into groups and assigned to various companies where they would be welcomed to enjoy a turkey dinner with all of the trimmings.

One of my students at the post karate club was Staff Sergeant Gerald Z. Higgins. Gerald was a twenty-four year old saxophone player. A few minutes before we were to start eating, Sergeant Higgins arrived. He was driving a small, dilapidated motorbike, which he had purchased a few weeks before. He parked it next to the company commander's, Captain Carpenter, jeep. Sergeant Higgins had a big hangover, which was an understatement. Sitting behind him, legs sticking out at forty-five degrees and holding on for dear life, was Crazy Mary. Everyone claimed that she was in her thirties but she looked like she was in her

Inside the Mechanic's Garage in Covington, Kentucky. The author with Clyde Powell, Terry Collis, Herb Duncan and Fred Hill.

fifties. She had her dress hiked up around her hips, as she sat astride the back of the motorcycle smiling at everyone and showing us that she had less than half of her teeth. She too, was suffering from a hangover.

Captain Carpenter had encouraged the unit members to bring a guest to dinner, but to bring Crazy Mary to any type of function was asking for trouble. Mary was known to be more than a little crazy (she was nuts) and very unpredictable. During a regimental football game with the 9th Marine Regiment a couple of months earlier, a lone figure dashed from the sidelines and grabbed the football while the Marines were in a huddle. Hiking up her skirt with one hand she displayed the combat boots someone had given her. With the football tucked under her arm in true NFL (National Football League) fashion, Crazy Mary headed off the football field and ran toward a wooded area on the north side of the field. Thirty yards behind her were twenty-two football players. Both teams were attempting to retrieve the ball so the game could continue.

Upon entering the company mess hall, each soldier was seated with his guest. Howard was seated next to Kazuko, I was seated next to Junko, and Staff Sergeant Higgins was seated at the end of our table with Crazy Mary. The orphans and nuns were scattered among the tables with the soldiers. Several officers and ranking NCOs had brought their wives and children with them. The officers and senior NCOs lived with their families in the Camp Chickamauga housing area. Captain Carpenter welcomed the guests and told them that no one was to leave the mess hall hungry.

We had been eating for twenty-five minutes when suddenly, without warning, Crazy Mary climbed on her chair and started giving jump commands in broken but very understandable English.

"Gwet Ready."

"Stan ups."

"Hook ups."

"Checks equipments."

"Sounds off fors equipments cheeks."

She then proceeded to grab various private parts of her body and give equipment checks in English.

"This OK."

"This here is OK."

"This here is OK, too."

The Company Commander's face turned red with rage. It was obvious to everyone that he was struggling to maintain his composure. Staff Sergeant Higgins and Crazy Mary were escorted from the mess hall. Everything quieted down. The commander voiced an apology to the guests and we finished our excellent meal without further incident.

Staff Sergeant Higgins had been on probation prior to this incident. A week later, former Staff Sergeant, now Corporal, Higgins showed up again at my post karate class. Crazy Mary was barred from the post permanently for the FOURTH and LAST time.

● ●

Chapter 18

Sayonara

This is the place where we must sever —You go thousands of miles my friend. Once, forever, like the floating clouds, We drift apart. The sunset lingers like the feelings of my heart.

By Poet Li Pai

The day I landed at Sasabo and first set foot on Japan seemed so long ago. Yet, in another respect it was not long at all. I thought about my first sighting of Japan from the deck of the USS John J. Pope as the ship docked at Sasabo. Reminiscing about all that I had done, it seemed like I had been in Japan a long time. However, when I considered all that I had not accomplished, the time seemed much too short. My time in Japan was coming to a close; I was beginning to have mixed feelings. I looked forward to returning home to my family and friends but dreaded the thought of leaving. I was going to miss Japan, especially her cities of Beppu and Kumamoto. I would miss the many people with whom I had become acquainted – those who had befriended me during my stay. I was in a quandary; I wanted both to stay in Japan and return home – an impossibility. For some unknown reason I was apprehensive about returning home. Why did I feel this way? I had no idea. My final days in Japan were very confusing as my mind and heart were in conflict with each other.

The small karate club at Camp Chickamauga was doing okay. After a few lessons, several of the soldiers who had joined out of curiosity drifted away and never trained again. We did attract a few soldiers who joined and stayed. One of my students was promoted to san-kyu (brown belt) and was to take over teaching when I left. Ito-san, Harada-san and a few other sensei from the Beppu Dojo would occasionally come to the post to help with the classes.

It had been raining very hard most of the night and in the early part of the morning. Then, as suddenly as it had started, it stopped raining. As I took my last trip to the dojo by rickshaw the sky remained overcast. The little rickshaw bumped and rocked – its tires made a swishing sound on the wet pavement when it drove past Hock Shop Charlie's. I was more acutely aware of my surroundings than I had ever been before. The rickshaw neared the top of the hill where the road curved left then plunged down into Beppu. As we passed the Hanago Bar and Grill I took a long look at it and thought of the many good times I had had there. The rickshaw swerved as the driver turned sharply to avoid an old man who had walked in front of it without looking. I glanced down the wet side streets and alleys attempting to absorb the sights and sounds one last time. The faces, clothing, even the way the people walked, seemed to lock in my mind. The rickshaw turned north and in a couple of minutes pulled to a stop in front of the dojo. I paid the driver and entered the dojo just as the rain started to pour down.

This building had become a second home to me. I walked into the dressing room and changed into my karate-gi for my last class here. The training floor was getting crowded as many students warmed up before class.

I stepped into the office for a few minutes and spoke to Mary. Her help and caring had made my stay in Japan, and my training, more pleasurable. I told her I would see her after class. Leaving the office I walked to the main training area just in time – the students were lining up.

After meditation I bowed for the last time toward the wall with the little Japanese flag. The twenty-eight students and I stood and started doing warm up exercises and basics. We ran from the dojo a few minutes later and were surprised to find that it had started raining again. For the last time, I was following

Dr. Tsuyoshi Chitose in 1973 at Northern Kentucky University.

Shirahama Sensei and Ito-san to the base of Takazaki Yama (Monkey Mountain). As we ran northward, the cold rain striking my face invigorated me. I felt extremely alert; nothing seemed to escape my attention. I felt as if I had just been born. Many sights, which I had failed to see on previous runs, now caught my eye. How long had that old gate been hanging from one hinge? A dog behind a fence barked at us. I had heard the dog bark each time we ran by this old house but I had never noticed what it looked like – it was brown and white.

The rain started coming down harder as we approached the base of the mountain. Cold winds were blowing down from Manchuria. We turned and headed southward for our return to the dojo. As our bare feet fell onto the pavement with a slap... slap... slap ... rhythm, Shirahama Sensei led us home. Ito-san fell back to check on some stragglers. Water dripped from us as we entered the dojo. A combination of sweat and rain fell onto the dojo floor making it very slippery. Standing there in his karate-gi waiting for us as we entered the dojo was Chitose Sensei.

"Ki o tsuke!" (Attention) Shirahama Sensei yelled, as we stopped and brought our feet together.

"O-Sensei, rei." The class bowed to Chitose Sensei.

Chitose Sensei walked over to where Shirahama Sensei was standing, although, as always, he seemed to glide rather than walk. It was as if there was a thin cushion of air between his feet and the floor. After conferring for a few minutes, Shirahama Sensei said, "Kusanku!"

Several students and I sat down. I had seen Kusanku but had not learned it. The few students who remained on the floor were higher ranking black belts. They performed the kata several times. Chitose Sensei and Shirahama Sensei walked among them making corrections – a twist of an arm, a kick to a leg, a punch to the body.

"Sochin!" Shirahama Sensei said.

Many students, myself included, rose and took our places on the floor. We turned our heads to the left, then slid to our right into a shiko ashi dachi, and performed a double block, left hand in chudan (chest) and right hand in jodan (head) blocking posture. As we did the kata to Shirahama's cadence both he and Chitose Sensei walked among us, pointing out minor mistakes as we performed the kata. Once, we stood in the same position so long my leg started to cramp. When the pain became so intense that I didn't think I could stand it any longer, Shirahama Sensei called out "Ju-hachi!" (Eighteen!) and then we moved into

Training in Japan with students doing the kata Sochin. The author is in the middle, Dr. Chitose is to the right - hands on hips.

another technique and completed the kata. Next we did the kata again on only one count, adjusting our movements to the natural rhythm of the kata. Sochin flowed, stopped and snapped as the class moved, blocked, kicked, punched and fought its way through it. After that, we spent the next half-hour practicing Tenshin.

Chitose Sensei spoke to Shirahama Sensei. We were told to sit down along the walls. Chitose Sensei looked at us with a kind look, like a loving father looks at his children. He told us about opening a dojo during March of 1946 at the Nakamichi Kuma Fu Cho in the Kikuchi area of Kumamoto Perfecture. This was near Kikuchi City where he lived. After he had trained several students, he hosted a small karate demonstration at the kabuki theater in Kumamoto city to help raise money for the orphans of Okinawa. Chitose Sensei had no dojo as we picture a dojo today. What he did have was a back yard from which he taught those who would seek him out and whom he deemed worthy.

The dojo had no roof, no walls and no floor. It was a traditional dojo much like those found in many back yards of Okinawa during the past two hundred years. To those of us who practiced there, it became a sacred place of learning. "The most important thing is to practice, just practice, everyday," Chitose Sensei always told us. He would constantly remind us to, "Don't think, just do."

"The kata of karate is very similar to the koan of Buddhism. To master one koan is to understand them all. To master one kata is to understand them all. The kata and the koan are one – the only difference is how we perceive them," Chitose Sensei advised us.

We were told to line up once more. Shirahama Sensei informed us that we were going to do the kata Kusanku again and, again, several others and I sat down. After Kusanku kata was completed Chitose Sensei walked to the center of the dojo.

"Kusanku!" Chitose Sensei announced. He moved through the kata as if he were gliding. Each movement flowed into the next. The few times he projected power into his movements, I felt a small vibration through the dojo floor.

After completing Kusanku, Chitose Sensei yelled out, "Seisan!" He proceeded to demonstrate this, his first kata, even more skillfully than Kusanku.

Upon the completion of Seisan kata, Chitose Sensei motioned for everyone to line up. The students rose to their feet and lined up with those standing against the walls.

"Seisan!" Chitose Sensei said.

We practised Seisan five times as small corrections were made – foot position, breathing, sliding were all checked.

Finally the class ended. I bowed to the little flag on the wall for the last time, then to Chitose Sensei. I felt much older and very lonely. My last class at the dojo was over.

Junko had requested that we go out for supper later that evening. I picked her up at her home and hired a small cab to take us to our destination.

We arrived at the Beppu Daiichi Hotel at 7:30 PM and were escorted to a small room away from the main dining area. Waiting for us there were Chitose Sensei, Shirahama Sensei, Matsumoto Sensei, Ito-san, Harada-san and Mary Shigamoto.

"We wanted to have a formal goodbye party for you," Mary said. "Did we surprise you?"

"Yes," I answered. I shot a sideward glance toward Junko. She stood there looking at me with one eye; I could see a cute "I gotcha" smile on her face.

We ordered, ate, and made the kind of small talk which seems to go with any meal.

"Chitose Sensei wants to know what your plans are when you return to the U.S.," Mary inquired.

"I plan to enroll in college," I said.

"O-Sensei wants to know if you are going to keep up with your karate training," Mary asked.

"I will try," I answered, not wanting to make a firm commitment.

Everyone had a small going-away present for me. Money was scarce in post-war Japan and I knew that they didn't have much. This in itself made me appreciate their gifts all the more. They may have been poor in material possessions but these people were the richest I had ever known because of their outlook on life and their self-discipline. I no longer looked upon them as my Japanese friends; I looked upon them as my family.

"Mary, please tell them how very honored I am. I will never forget you or them."

I spent Sunday with Junko and her family. I paid my respects to her mother and father and prepared to leave the house. Her father bowed to me and then, almost as an afterthought, offered me his hand. I reached forward and took his hand in mine. I was very touched. As a retired Japanese soldier who had served a proud nation, I realized the effort that he had put into this parting gesture.

Junko and I took a short walk. I kissed her and held her tightly in my arms. I kissed her again, knowing that it was for the last time. I walked away, stopped, turned, and looked back. Junko was standing in front of her home, looking at me with one eye peering out from behind her bangs. I saw a lone tear streaking down her beautiful face. I waved, turned, and with a lump in my throat, walked out of her life forever.

I was up early on Monday. The day was cool, crisp, and overcast. Although there had been a threat of rain, there was none. My duffel bag and AWOL bag were packed. Several soldiers and I boarded a military bus and stowed our AWOL bags in the overhead racks. Our duffle bags had already been loaded onto some duce-and-a-half trucks which were to follow behind us. We were headed for the train station – the beginning of our journey home. We arrived at the station just as the train was pulling in and lined up in ranks on the station platform as a manifest was checked to make sure that no one was missing.

"Bill-san!" I heard someone calling my name. It was Mary Shigamoto along with Chitose Sensei, Shirahama Sensei and Ito-san. "We are so happy that we did not miss you!" Mary said. "O-Sensei was worried that we were going to be late."

Chitose Sensei stood before me in his western-style suit. He started to speak to me very slowly as he looked into my eyes. He bowed slightly as he presented me with a tube approximately twelve inches long and two inches in diameter.

"Chitose Sensei wants you to have this, your third certificate, before you leave Japan," Mary said.

"Why?" I questioned her.

Chitose Sensei spoke to Mary. I thought that I understood a few of the words, but could not be sure.

"Chitose Sensei has just told me that he believes you have good judgment. He has observed you in class. Your technique is improving. This certificate, however, is not for what you have done; it is for what Chitose Sensei hopes you will do. If you feel unworthy, then you must continue your practice until you feel worthy."

"O-Sensei's desire is that you will teach karate-do after you return to America. It will be very difficult and you must work very hard to establish karate there. Chitose Sensei wants you to accept this responsibility with his best wishes," Mary said.

I bowed to Chitose Sensei, "Domo arigato gozaimasu," (Thank you very much.) I muttered.

1973, U.S. Chito-kai National Tournament. Chitose awarding medals.

I paid my last respects to O-Sensei, Mary, Shirahama and Ito. After shaking hands and bowing several times, I was ordered to board the train. "I want to thank all of you for everything. Sayonara." I said, as I bowed for the last time, picked up my bags and stepped onto the train.

I could see their faces peering through the windows as the train started moving slowly away from the platform. Chitose Sensei, Mary and Ito waved; Shirahama Sensei stood there like a great stone pillar. I waved back – then they were gone. My time in Japan had passed so quickly, it seemed that only my memories remained.

Since I was returning home, I would have to perfect my technique to the best of my ability without the benefit of my karate teachers. There would no longer be an Ito-san, a Shirahama Sensei and, worst of all, no Chitose Sensei to correct me, guide me, or mold me. I was on my own.

I had experienced so much since I had joined the Army as a seventeen-year-old boy. I had learned about military life, karate, the people of Japan and their way of life. I did not know it then, but the events of the past three years would change my life forever.

As the train picked up speed and headed north, I thought about what Chitose Sensei had once told me.

"If you feel unworthy, you must not quit, but you must continue to train to go beyond mere technique. Karate training is not for a day, a week, or a year. It is for a lifetime. It is a quest for perfection which will never end."

Now I was saying goodbye to Japan – I was leaving Beppu and this beautiful, exotic land. It was Thursday, December 2nd, 1954 – a day I shall always remember. My training in Japan had only been a start, an initiation. A realization came over me that my journey was far from complete and that the remainder of my life would be devoted to . . .THE ENDLESS QUEST.

• •

Part 2

The Quest Continues

Chapter 19

The Voyage Home

In dwelling, be close to the land. In meditation, delve deep into the heart. In dealing with others, be gentle and kind. In speech, be true. In work, be competent. In action, be careful of your timing. Where there is no fight, there is no blame.

Grandmaster Chan Pui Wah Lum Kung Fu

The train from Beppu headed north toward Tokyo and sped past countless small tile-roofed houses. The houses were surrounded on all sides by rice paddies. The sky was clear and a sea of blue hung over the landscape. I relaxed to the best of my ability and unzipped my AWOL bag. I took out the long tube which I had been given at the Beppu train station to examine the certificate that O-Sensei had given me just a few hours earlier. I opened the tube, gently removed the contents, and studied the certificate as I held it in my hands. It was written in kanji (Chinese characters), the ideographs used in the Japanese writing system, and was exactly like my other two certificates. I wished that I could have read it but that was impossible. After a few minutes of looking at it, I rolled the certificate up, placed it back into its tube, and returned it to my duffel bag.

The sounds of the train's steel wheels drew my thoughts to them as they rolled over the tracks – clickety-clack, clickety-clack. The train seemed to be speaking to me, saying over and over: "Please come back. Please come back." I wondered if I would ever return. It seemed doubtful. Regardless of whether I returned or not, Japan would always hold a special place in my heart.

The train crossed a causeway then it sped over a bridge as we left the island of Kyushu. We proceeded onto the island of Honshu, the largest island in Japan. At Hiroshima the train stopped to pick up additional soldiers. The terrible destruction of World War II was still evident. I could see the steel skeleton of the domed structure at Ground Zero where the Atomic Bomb had been detonated on August 6, 1945. A few small buildings, mostly one-story ones, had been rebuilt. They did not, however, obstruct my view of the terrible devastation. The city was starting to recover from the massive destruction which had taken place on that terrible day in August nine years earlier. Many Japanese were wandering around the train station. Some were selling candy, others sold soft drinks, while a select few sold souvenirs to GIs. Countless others were scurrying around busily rebuilding their lives. It was obvious that years of hard work lay ahead of them before the city could return to normal.

Several military buses met us at the train station when we arrived in Tokyo. From there, we were to be transported to a U.S. military base located a few miles outside of the city. As we drove through downtown Tokyo, some bomb damage was evident, but unlike Hiroshima, Tokyo was making remarkable progress in its renewal efforts.

"Look to your right," our driver told us as our bus drove passed the main gate of the Imperial Palace. There was a rather ornate rock bridge of oriental design which spanned a large mote. On the opposite side was a large gate. Many trees grew on the island. Occasionally we would catch a glimpse of a building or the roof of a temple. The entire place looked so peaceful. I found it difficult to believe that this was where the war in the Pacific was formulated. The entire area was a little over three hundred acres and in truth looked like a large park.

Our stay at the transit Army post was supposed to be a short one. Our timetable called for us to board a troop ship for the trip home as soon as our paperwork was checked.

Everything on the base – rocks, fences – was painted black and yellow. This included a two hundred fifty foot smoke stack. The base had been home to the 1st Cavalry Division before their deployment to Korea. The division's colors were black and yellow. This explained the overzealous paint job, which was the object of many jokes told by the replacement troops and the locals, all of whom were sick of the black and yellow color scheme.

I repacked my duffel bag and AWOL bag as I prepared to board the ship in two days. I put my brown belt certificate, which I previously had mounted on cardboard at the Camp Chickamauga PX photo shop, at the bottom of my AWOL bag and covered it with a towel before placing other items on top of it. I still had extra space in my AWOL bag for my "pogey bait", (military slang for junk food) which I hoped would sustain me on the long voyage home. The two tubes that held my other certificates were packed in the center of my duffel bag with my uniforms packed carefully around them.

The Voyage Home

The ship home was very crowded. The Department of Defense has a tradition of shipping "short-timers" (soldiers with 90 days or less service remaining) home at Christmas. "Long-timers" (soldiers with more than 90 days left) are assigned to other units. I was a short-timer – I would be home for Christmas.

The waters of the Northern Pacific have very high waves and are notorious for their roughness during the winter months. The crowded conditions on the ship combined with the rough seas caused many tough soldiers to suffer from seasickness. My pogey bait saved the day and I was one of the lucky ones who didn't get sick.

Our ship took a northerly course across the wintry Pacific Ocean and stopped at the island of Adak, which is part of the Aleutian Island chain southwest of Alaska. We were scheduled to pick up a contingent of US Marines there. With them aboard, the sleeping bays were now stacked seven deep, making for a miserable trip to Seattle.

Once in Seattle we were transported to an overcrowded Fort Lewis. To state that Fort Lewis was overcrowded however, could in no way prepare you for the conditions there. Our buses stopped in front of the newly constructed post gymnasium where we were to be billeted. So many servicemen were scheduled to be released from active duty before Christmas that there were no barracks available. The only available space left in Fort Lewis to billet troops was the new gym. Five hundred folding cots, covering the entire floor, had been set up in the gymnasium. We were ordered to lean our duffel bags against the outer walls.

"Listen up!" a Master Sergeant yelled as we stood in ranks outside the gymnasium. "When you men get inside the gymnasium, pick out a cot. When you leave for any reason set your AWOL bag on the cot to mark it so it will be easier to locate when you return. No! I will repeat, NO duffel bags will be allowed by the cots. All duffel bags must be placed along the walls of the gymnasium. You are to see to it that your duffel bags are not blocking any of the fire exits. These regulations are necessary in the event of an emergency. We need to keep the area between the cots clear. The post fire marshal will be checking on us. Dismissed!"

For two days we stayed at the post gymnasium. During this time our paperwork was processed, mustering out pay was calculated, and airline tickets were purchased – all so we could be home by Christmas day.

On the morning of the second day, several of us had trouble locating our duffel bags.

"Out here!" a voice called, "There are some duffel bags out here on the ground."

I walked outside with several others to look for my bag. In the rear of the gym facing a wooded hillside were eight duffel bags. Although all of the bags had been securely locked, they had all been cut open and ransacked. My bag had been thrown over a hill along with another one. The contents were scattered all over the ground. The Christmas gifts, which I had purchased in Beppu city, were gone. Also missing were both of the tubes containing my certificates. "Perhaps this is God's way of telling me that I was unworthy to be a black belt," I thought. The Fort Lewis military police arrived, interviewed us and made a theft report. The contents of the eight bags were never found.

A giant aircraft, a Boeing Globemaster, carried a number of us to Chicago. After arriving in Chicago, we split into smaller groups with each group being escorted to flights that would take us to Army Bases scattered across the Eastern United States. Several soldiers and I boarded a Capitol Airlines DC-3 for the flight to Louisville, Kentucky. Upon our arrival there we were taken to Fort Knox, Kentucky, where our final out-processing would take place. Before that, however, we were given a re-enlistment talk by the post recruiter. Two soldiers decided to re-enlist but the majority of us were not interested. I just wanted to get home as soon as possible. On December 22, 1954, I was released from active duty.

With my DD-214 (release from active duty form) in a folder tucked into my AWOL bag, I walked to the Fort Knox Greyhound bus station. There I purchased a ticket to Cincinnati, Ohio. When I arrived in Cincinnati, I purchased a ticket on the Baltimore and Ohio Railroad for the final leg of my trip home. Little did I know that in the near future I would return to the Cincinnati area to live out the rest of my life.

• •

Chapter 20

1955-1959

If you wish to see the world, you must leave the shade of the family tree.

Ancient Indian saying

The train that I had boarded in Cincinnati several hours earlier pulled into the Clarksburg train station exactly on time. It was the 23rd of December and at last I was home. I was still wearing the same Class A uniform I had been wearing when I left Fort Knox, Kentucky. I went to the baggage master's office to pick up my duffel bag. Slinging the bag over my shoulder I walked across the bridge to the downtown area. At the Greyhound Bus Station I checked my heavy duffel bag in a locker. I would return later to retrieve it. A short walk later, I was on Pike Street.

Pike Street in Clarksburg was a pool player's delight. There were five pool halls grouped together with a total of approximately sixty tables. I stopped in the "Strand" pool hall and shot a few games of pool. I needed to kill a little time until four o'clock when my mother would quit work. I knew the pool halls on Pike Street well. My best friend, John Nelson, and I had both gone to Washington Irving High School and almost every day during our lunch hour John and I would walk from the school to one of the local pool halls and shoot pool.

As the clock on the wall neared 3:30 PM I left the pool hall and started walking to my mother's place of employment. I planned to surprise her; I had not told her I would be home for Christmas.

I was standing on the corner when I saw her walking up the street talking with several of her co-workers. I watched them for several seconds as they walked slowly toward me. I could almost reach out and touch Mom before she noticed me. When she saw me she broke into tears. She walked to me and took me in her arms. I felt badly because she was crying but she said it was because she was so happy. I felt that this was going to be the best Christmas ever. My dad was equally surprised to see me when my mother and I arrived at home.

The reservations and foreboding that I had felt about returning home had vanished almost immediately. I later discovered after speaking to many service men that most had had a strange fear about returning home after their first tour of duty overseas. A fear of what had changed, of the unknown. I too had had the same fear.

The author in his late 30s. Notice the old patch, it says Zen Nippon Karate-do Renmei - all Japan Karate-do Federation

After supper with my parents I walked to my girlfriend Wilma's house. I wanted to surprise her. I knocked on the door in anticipation of seeing her again. The door opened and she stood there looking at me – just as lovely as I remembered her.

"Well, I see you are finally back," she remarked coldly. It was obvious that our relationship was not going to be the same as it had prior to my leaving for Japan. Still, I was not going to allow this to ruin my first Christmas home in several years.

Clarksburg is one of those mountain towns where not much happens. It was often said that after the stores closed the cows were turned loose to graze downtown. New Year's celebrations were almost as exciting as watching the cows. John and I celebrated our return by drinking a few beers and shooting some pool.

On January 3rd, I visited with the local Veteran's Administration to check on my GI Bill benefits. I then enrolled at Fairmont State College; I started classes on January 10, 1955. Most college boys don't pick a major until their second year at the earliest. The first year is filled with the thrills of being free of their parents' restraints, learning the college halls, memorizing the locations of toilets, drinking beer, and chasing girls.

Since the army had been my home for the past few years, being away from my parents was not such a big thrill for me. I had drunk all of the beer I had wanted, and on a couple of occasions more beer than I needed. I was two to three years older than the average freshman. I had had both a Japanese girlfriend and an American one. Although, I thought, after the cool reception I had received from Wilma I wasn't so sure that I still had an American girl. Right now, I just wanted to get down to the business of going to college. I was ready to go and I would be damned if I was going to wear one of those freshman beanie hats!

At first I should have taken subjects I could have "aced" easily, such as history and geography. Instead I signed up for subjects in which I was deeply interested. I decided to pursue a physics major with a math minor and an additional minor in education. Three years in the army and away from a school environment had made my study habits very rusty. My choices of a very difficult major and double minor required me to spend every Sunday with a private tutor. In the end, my hard work paid off however, and at the end of my first semester in col-

Seated left to right: (seated) Roland Figgs, the author, Tsuyoshi Chitose, Yasuhiro Chitose, Shane Higashi.

The day Barbara and I got married - June 6, 1955. I was twenty years old; she was eighteen.

lege I had a 3.30 grade point average. This rose to a 3.6 during my second semester.

As busy as I was, I did find enough free time to start an unofficial karate club at the college. On Tuesday, February 5, I held my first class. The students there had never heard of karate and could probably have cared less about it. Still, my first class attracted thirty-seven curious college kids.

Unfortunately, my very limited teaching experience at Camp Chickamauga had prepared me to teach soldiers, not a group of college kids. Their mentality was completely different than the soldiers and Japanese I had been with. The warm up exercises were conducted as if the students were a platoon of paratroopers. I also taught the basics as I had been taught them – 1,000 punches, followed by 1,000 kicks and squat kicks plus countless repetitions of other techniques. Within three weeks I was practicing by myself. I came to realize very quickly that I was not qualified to teach karate and, more importantly, that I would need to modify the teaching techniques that I had learned and experienced in Japan to make the art more acceptable to Americans.

I broke up with Wilma on March 16, the day after my birthday. Two weeks earlier she had informed me that she wanted to start dating a college boy named Shady whom she had met but also wanted to continue to date me. I told her that I needed to think it over. I met her at the college cafeteria at Morrow Hall for lunch, after which I told her that I felt it might be best if we broke up so she would be free to date whomever she wanted. The break up with Wilma, although I initiated it, was very upsetting to me. But I didn't have time to play games.

I came to realize that in life, as one door closes, another one opens. During the next few weeks, I concentrated on my lessons and forgot about dating. In what little free time I had, I practiced my karate kata in my parents' back yard.

On Saturday, April 30th while walking on Main Street in downtown Clarksburg, I met a girl I had not seen for over three years. It was the same girl who was always asking Wilma about me and whom Wilma had written me about when I was in Japan. Her name was Barbara Ellen Webster, an eighteen-year-old senior at Roosevelt Wilson High School. I struck up a conversation with her and on Monday night we had our first date. I was smitten. I fell in love wholeheartedly, without any reservations, and within six weeks we were married. My marriage to Barbara was without a doubt the best and most important thing that ever happened to me in my life.

I continued going to college during the summer months while Barbara worked as a waitress at the McCrory's Five and Dime store. Other than her small salary and my $104.00 a month GI Bill, we had no money but we had each other and, as cliché as it sounds, that was what really mattered.

My marriage to Barbara and our love for each other were great but by August

Left to Right: Terry Collis, Al Johnson, Joe Copeland doing round kick, Lloyd Bridges attempting to bock.

I realized that it was going to be very difficult to remain in college and support a wife. I did not enroll for the fall semester at college. Rather, I started looking for work and during the next few months I drifted from job to job. October arrived and Barbara announced that she was pregnant.

I took a job with the Koblegard Company, a large warehouse located in the Glenn Elk section of Clarksburg in November 1955.

My karate training, which was becoming more difficult as I had less and less time, consisted of practicing my kata to the best of my ability. Each month I was able to train less and less and my ability to perform kata deteriorated at an alarming rate.

Barbara and I purchased our first car in March. It was a 1952 Nash Statesman four door. I thought it was a great car but it had a design flaw that required the water pump to be rebuilt every five thousand miles!

On May 9, 1956 Barbara gave birth to our son, William J. Dometrich, II. As she was wheeled from the delivery room she spoke to me.

"Well, there's three of us now," she said groggily.

Other than marrying Barbara this was the happiest event in my life up to that point. I had a son; I was elated.

I worked at the warehouse five days a week, eight hours a day. The pay was barely enough to get along on, but there was very limited employment potential in the Clarksburg area. Other than the coal mines, warehouses, or a couple of small plants, hardly any jobs existed. I did find out, though, that the Pepsi Cola distributor was looking for truck drivers and the position paid almost fifty percent more than I was making at the warehouse. I applied for the job and was hired as a truck driver. The hours were long and I was required to work on Saturday but the extra money came in handy.

I was still trying to devote an hour or two to my karate training in my limited spare time – mostly on Sundays. Slowly my time for training diminished until it finally stopped all together.

It became apparent that I was not going to be able to start back to college in the immediate future. My finances would not allow it. If my family and I were going to get ahead we would need to move to an area with a better job market.

My buddy John Nelson had moved to Cincinnati, Ohio, in January 1957. He had taken a job with the International Harvester Company. During the weekend of April 20, 1957, he returned to Clarksburg and Barbara and I went to lunch with him. He spoke to us about the job opportunities in Cincinnati and we both agreed that we should take a chance and move. When John returned to Cincinnati I went with him in the hope of locating employment in the area. After searching for a job for three weeks I was hired by the Liberty Mutual Insurance Company.

Barbara, my son Billy, and I moved to Cincinnati during May and I started my job as a sales trainee. My supervisor was a twenty-six year old man named James (Jim) Hinisch. He had become a manager at a very young age; this proved to me that the potential for advancement within the company was excellent. The only problem with this picture was that I soon found out that I could not sell a stove to a freezing Eskimo!

In June 1958, I said goodbye to the insurance industry and accepted a position as an assistant manager with the Associates Discount Corporation. The job entailed taking loan applications, investigating them, making loans and the collection of slow paying accounts. I worked at an office in Newport, a small town across the Ohio River from Cincinnati, for a year and really liked the job. However, one Wednesday morning we had a surprise visit from a company auditor. Two days later, on Friday afternoon, the district director arrived and informed the manager and all of the employees, including me, not to report for work on Monday – we would no longer be needed. I never found out what the office manager had done, but whatever he did, it resulted in the entire staff at that office losing their jobs.

The Endless Quest

One of the first things I did when I arrived in Cincinnati was to join the Army Reserve Unit on Seymour Avenue. The unit was a 105mm Howitzer Battery. After my job at Associates folded, I was offered a summer job by the unit commander of the artillery battery, Major Gary Lytle. I worked that summer for the Major and his father who owned and managed a farm implement company. My job consisted of forestry work for the owners of small farms. During this time I also took a police entrance examination for the Cincinnati Police Department.

Because the job at the Lytle's was only a summer job, I started looking around for other more permanent employment during August. I was offered a job by Ben Bishop, a manager of the Liberty Loan Company at 520 Elm Street in Cincinnati, and reported for work at the Liberty Loan offices on September 5, 1959.

I had worked at my newest job only three weeks when I received a telephone call on a Tuesday night from my Aunt Carrie who lived in Fairmont, West Virginia. She informed me that my father had died of a heart attack. The funeral was to be held in Clarksburg on Saturday. My father was only fifty-six years old. I was shocked. He had always looked very healthy.

Mr. Bishop told me to take off from work and was even nice enough to offer me a pay advance to travel home.

"Take as long as you need," he told me. "You will have a job waiting when you return."

Barbara, Billy, whom we called B.J., and I drove back to Cincinnati on Sunday, the day after the funeral. My mother had taken Dad's death very hard but she assured me that she would be fine and that I should return to work at my new job.

I had not been a good salesman with Liberty Mutual Insurance Company but I was an outstanding delinquent accounts collector. The delinquent customers would move, skip, and hide but I would always locate them and, in the majority of cases, get their payment. Within a very short time I was the troubleshooter for all of the serious delinquent accounts within the city. The accounts that other collectors had trouble locating ended up on my desk.

• •

Chapter 21

1960-1964

A flower is held up, and the secret has been revealed. Kasho breaks into a smile;
The whole assemblage is at a loss.

It had now been five years since I had returned from Japan. During this time my karate training gradually fell from two or three training sessions a week to one, and then, finally, it ceased altogether. I decided to resume my karate training on a limited scale after starting to work at Liberty Loan. My training started again on January 11, 1960.

I joined the Williams YMCA on East McMicken Street in Cincinnati. Two or three nights a week I would drive to the YMCA, don my karate-gi, and find a corner where I could practice by myself. Practicing alone like that brought back memories of my practice sessions at the Camp Chickamauga Gym. I spent most of my time getting into better physical condition and trying to remember my kata. One afternoon I was trying to remember the proper sequence of the kata Potsai when a young man walked over to where I was training and introduced himself. His name was Richard (Richie) Adams. Richie informed me that he was a brown belt in Judo and that his older brother Gene and a friend, Harvie Eubank, were also martial artists.

During the next few months I continued to train at home and the local YMCA. The years of neglect began to haunt me.

I gathered my daily accounts and placed them into my briefcase. I left the loan office on Elm Street and headed north on Vine Street. Stopping for a red light at 13th and Vine, I glanced to my left and saw a large hand-painted sign in the window at 1235 Vine Street. It was painted on a large roll of brown butcher-block paper and had the following notation: "Judo and Karate School to open

Sensei Raymond Hughes performing a judo throw on a student at the Yudan School of Self Defense in Cincinnati, Ohio.

here soon." The sign had two phone numbers to call for additional information. I got no answer at the first number but was more successful with the second. I was speaking to Harvie Eubank, the person Richie Adams had told me about.

Harvie was a black belt in Goju karate and had been a student of Yoshitaka Nishita. He was opening the club with the help of a partner, Raymond Hughes. Raymond was a sho-dan in Kodokan Judo. Ray had just recently been discharged from the U. S. Air Force where he had been a member of their famous Strategic Air Command judo team. At the United States National Judo Championships in 1960, Ray, who was a brown belt at the time, defeated several black belts, one of whom was a third degree black belt from Japan. Ray's performance so impressed the official representative from the Kodokan Judo Institute in Japan, Sensei Sadaki Nakabayashi, 8th dan, that he promoted Ray to sho-dan on the spot.

I met with Harvie and Ray on Tuesday night at their school's grand opening. I explained to them that I had trained in Japan. I told them

The advertisement place in the Cincinnati Enquirer newspaper by Ray Hughes in an attempt to attract some students to out small karate and judo club.

that I was out of shape, having brain lock with some of my kata and had very little money with which to pay dues. They both agreed to accept me as a third partner. Harvie was the president, Ray was the treasurer and I was the club secretary, a job taken over immediately by my wife, Barbara. During the first months of 1961 when we opened the small club on Vine Street, karate techniques were being demonstrated more and more on television in fight scenes. A few movies also had karate demonstrated in them. The United States and the world were on the verge of a karate and martial arts boom but we were unaware of it.

A large commercial martial arts school opened during April 1961 on Reading Road in Cincinnati. The name of the school was "The Cincinnati School of Self

An early karate demonstration (September 17, 1961) at River Downs Race Track. Master of Ceremonies is radio and TV personality, Bob Braun. Beside him is Ray Hughes.

Defense". It was owned and operated by businessmen who knew nothing about karate or judo. They were men who had a good feel for trends and felt that the time was ripe to open a self-defense school and start raking in the money. They hired Richie Adams and Nick Kurlas, a karate-ka who was said to have been from Columbus, Ohio, to teach judo and karate.

Harvie, Ray, and I named our little club on Vine Street the Yudan Dojo. We didn't know that the word Yudan should have been Yudansha. We did attract a few students but we were unable to compete with The Cincinnati School of Self Defense. They advertised heavily, something we could not afford to do. The owners soon opened three additional schools in Dayton and Columbus, Ohio, and in Indianapolis, Indiana. All of their schools were called "Self Defense" schools. Sensei Johnny Matsumoto, an early Pan American Judo Champion of the Chicago Judo club, was contacted by the owners of the Cincinnati School of Self Defense and hired as the chief judo instructor. The owners signed him to a long-term contract.

Approximately two months after the Dayton School of Self Defense opened, a young, good looking, well-built young man with military bearing visited the school. He was interested in continuing his karate practice; he said he had started training in Okinawa when he was in the Marine Corps. He was interviewed by one of the owners and during the interview he said he had married the head master's niece and claimed to hold a third degree black belt in karate.

The owner was very skeptical. He asked the young Marine to return on Tuesday night and to bring his rank certificates with him. On Tuesday night as agreed the young Marine returned. A karate class was in session and was being taught by Richie Adams and Nick Kurlas. The young Marine had the opportunity to kumite (spar) with both Richie and Nick and also to demonstrate his kata. After the class was over Richie and Nick motioned for the owner to come into the office with them so they could speak with him privately. They were very impressed with the young Marine.

That night, before he left the school, the young Marine was offered a job as the head karate instructor. One week later he accepted the position. His name was James (Jim) Wax and he had been a student of Matsubayashi Shorin-ryu. His teacher was Shoshin Nagamine, the founder of the style. Jim thus became the first person to teach Matsubayashi-ryu in the United States and while not well known today, he is the Father of American Matsubayashi-ryu.

A well-dressed man wearing a suit and carrying a small briefcase showed up at our little club on Vine St. during the second week of March 1961. He spoke to Harvie, Ray and me about the possibility of all three of us going to work for his firm which was located in Langly, Virginia. Ray had worked for Air Force Intelligence, Harvie was ex-navy and worked as an under water diver, I had infantry and parachutist experience.

"I would like to have the three of you come to work for my firm," he told us. "You will be gone approximately four to six months at a time and you will be paid well."

"How much does, 'paid well', mean?" I asked him.

"$1,600 dollars a month in gold will be deposited in your name in the Florida bank of your choice. The three of you will not need money because you will not be anywhere you can spend it. Your wives and families will also receive a check for $1,100 a month in addition to the gold we promised you."

This was an offer that seemed too good to be true. None of us were making anything like the amount promised to us by the stranger. At that time I was making approximately $120 a week, in a good week.

"What do we have to do?" Harvie inquired.

"Travel with me to Florida and train Cubans in military arts," came the answer.

"Do we just train them or will we be required to go into combat with them?" I inquired.

"If you train them, you would have to lead them. Don't you agree?" the man in the suit answered rather abruptly.

He informed the three of us that after we arrived in Florida we would be flown

Barbara, my wife, was exceptionally good at the art of karate. Years later, she held black belt rank in karate, iaido and kendo.

to the jungles of Columbia, in South America, where we would train the Cubans at a secret base.

"Have you ever parachuted from a C-47?" he asked, looking at me.

"Sure, several times."

"Good, because these are the planes we will be using."

"Just who do you work for?" Ray finally asked.

We discovered that the person with whom we had been talking was an employee of the Central Intelligence Agency.

Harvie, Ray, and I informed him that we would need to talk it over before making a decision. The three of us discussed the offer in great detail. Ray discussed it with his wife Sandy; I discussed it with my wife Barbara; Harvie was single and free to make his own decision. We did decide that whatever our decision, it must be a unanimous one if we accepted the job offer. I had my wife and my son B.J. (Billy) to think about and Ray's wife Sandy was expecting their first child. After much soul-searching and discussion the three of us felt very uneasy about the vagueness of the answers we had received.

The CIA man visited us on three different occasions during the next two weeks. On his last trip to the dojo he pressured us for an immediate decision.

"Gentlemen, I need a decision now. If you do agree to accept my offer, you must be prepared to leave by no later than tomorrow afternoon." We decided to turn his job offer down. On April 17, a few weeks later, the news media was ablaze with the story of the failed "Bay of Pigs" invasion. The invasion was a fiasco. If we had taken the CIA man up on his offer, we would have had less than four weeks to train the Cubans for this dangerous mission, far too short a time for any training to be effective. That night after we closed the dojo Harvie, Ray, and I went to the bar on the corner of 13th and Vine Streets and had a few drinks to celebrate our wisdom and good fortune in deciding not to join in on the adventure. We were thrilled that we were not dead or rotting in some Cuban prison.

The three of us struggled throughout the summer and into the fall attempting to establish a good judo and karate club in Cincinnati. The Cincinnati School of Self Defense was now advertising not only in the newspaper but also on radio and television as well. We could not compete with them. Another strike against us was our location. Our small club was established in "The Over the Rhine area", one of the toughest neighborhoods in Cincinnati.

On December 1, 1961, we decided to close our little club after only nine months. Our first attempt at founding a traditional martial arts club had failed.

Ray Hughes had become very busy with his job and told me that he did not have the time to dedicate to a martial arts school. Harvie had applied for employment with the Los Angeles Police Department and was off to L.A. for an interview. If he was accepted by the L.A.P.D., he would be moving to California in the very near future. Any further attempt to build a traditional karate club in the greater Cincinnati area would rest solely upon my wife Barbara and me. I didn't know it then, but my wife Barbara would prove to be instrumental in the development of traditional Japanese martial arts in the Greater Cincinnati area.

January 1962 arrived and I was on my own. No karate dojo, no karate students, and no help. I was invited by one of the better students from the Vine Street school, Carroll McGlasson, to temporarily relocate to the basement of his home in Hebron, Kentucky, a small town approximately fifteen miles from Cincinnati. We painted his basement and made a few cosmetic changes and soon we had a small dojo. Our membership never exceeded six or seven people. It was during this time that Barbara started her karate training. She had great ability and within a short time was making rapid progress.

I met John Osaka, a fifth degree black belt in judo, when he moved to Cincinnati to work for the Cincinnati School of Self Defense. Over the course of several months we became good friends. John realized that while I might not be the best martial artist he had ever met, I was sincere in my intentions. John was having major financial difficulties in March 1962, primarily because the Cincinnati School of Self Defense itself was starting to have financial problems. His last two paychecks had been returned from the bank marked, "Insufficient Funds." Even though they were low on money and their checks were constantly being rejected by the bank, the owners of the Cincinnati School of Self Defense refused to let John out of his contract which still had eighteen months to run. John mentioned his dilemma to me. He wanted to break his contract.

I told John to meet me at the First National Bank Building at 9th and Main Streets on Monday morning at nine o'clock. When I arrived at the scheduled time, John was already waiting for me. I introduced him to Mr. Arthur Schuh, an attorney who worked for the Liberty Loan Company. Mr. Schuh wrote a letter on John's behalf to the owners of the Cincinnati School of Self Defense. A week later John was released from his contract. Within a week he moved to Detroit, Michigan where he had been offered a job as the Chief Instructor of the Detroit Judo Club. The Cincinnati School of Self Defense closed its doors permanently in April 1962 and left several hundred local citizens stuck with loans for lessons they would never receive.

By May 1962 I knew that if I wanted my school to be successful I would need to move the dojo back into the city. After three weeks of walking the streets of Covington, I located a bingo hall called "Hollywood Hall" at 811 Madison Avenue. I could rent the hall for one hundred dollars a month. (At the time, Covington was a small river town of sixty-five thousand people. It is located directly across the Ohio River from downtown Cincinnati.) Bingo was held at the hall on Monday, Wednesday and Friday. I was allowed to use it on Tuesday, Thursday and Saturday. In June 1962, I started teaching karate classes on Tuesday and Thursday nights and Saturday morning. Three days a week, my students and I would arrive at the bingo hall and take a half-hour to stack the tables and sweep the floor before I could hold class. As it turned out, I inherited a few students from the Cincinnati School of Self Defense, one of whom was a very nice person named Fred Hill. Fred had been swindled out of almost $5,000 by the self-defense school.

On September 1st, my landlord at the Hollywood Hall, Mr. Herzog, approached me and offered to rent the building next door at 813 Madison Avenue to me for one hundred fifty dollars per month. This building would be used only by me and would be a karate school and nothing else. I agreed to rent the building. I knew that I could build a good karate school there.

The building had been a mechanic's garage and was filthy. Mr. Herzog agreed to let me have it free for two months. I was to use the rent money to fix it up during this time. After three weeks of cleaning, painting and fixing, we were ready to move into it. The first class was held on Saturday September 22, 1962. It had been ten years and seven days since I had taken my first karate lesson. Thinking back, I felt like I had come a long way in a short time. Ten years prior I never would have dreamed that I would be running my own dojo.

I placed third on the test for the Cincinnati Police Department. When I read in the newspaper that the Cincinnati Police had hired twenty-six new recruits, I wondered why I had not been called. I drove to the police academy and spoke to Lieutenant Colonel Kluge. I was advised that veterans who were Ohio residents got a ten percent bonus on their test. Living in Kentucky had disqualified me from the bonus. My name had dropped from third to twenty-eighth.

The Covington Police Department had scheduled an entrance examination for the last of September for the position of patrol officer. I gave up on becoming a member of the Cincinnati Police Department and took the examination for Covington. Once again, I did well on the test but no one contacted me. I was at a loss because I knew that I was the best candidate for the job – why couldn't they see that?

Now that I had a permanent location for the karate club and my competition

Photo taken in 1961. Front Row (L to R): Mr. Winfred Ho, Chitose Sensei, Mr. Thomas Morita. Back Row (L to R): Mr. James Miyaji, Mr. Bob Igadashi (judo and karate sensei).

was gone, the club started to increase its membership. Harvie Eubank had made two trips to Los Angeles for interviews and testing, but he, too, had heard nothing from the L.A.P.D. and was still in town. He assisted me with the teaching while Barbara took over the duties of office manager. The three of us worked full time jobs during the day, then we would go to the dojo three nights a week to teach karate classes. We usually made enough money to pay the rent. When we did not, Barbara and I would take our paychecks to make up the difference. This happened pretty often during the early years. To Barbara's credit, she never complained. She wanted to see the dojo succeed as much as I did. When Barbara was not in the office she could be found in the training area practicing.

Around this time, a black belt from the New York / New Jersey area moved into the Covington area. He visited the school and decided that he would like to join. His name was George VanHorne Jr. He was a sho-dan under Don Nagle, a very competent Isshin-ryu teacher from New Jersey.

1960-1964

One night before class started, Harvie showed me an advertisement he had received in the mail. The advertisement was about a karate tournament that was scheduled in November at Madison Square Garden in New York. Harvie and one of my students, Clyde Powell (who became my first black belt years later), and I drove to New York to attend. The tournament was sanctioned by Mas Oyama, the man I had read about years before in Readers' Digest who had slain a bull on the beach in Tokyo – with his bare hands. The chief referee was Sensei Peter Urban, a Goju-ryu black belt. Gary Alexander, a 6'3" tall Isshin-ryu practitioner from Union, New Jersey won the tournament. Five weeks earlier Gary had won the Canadian Karate Championships in Toronto, Ontario, Canada. This win made Gary Alexander the first United States, National and International champion. Jim Wax attended the tournament and was there with Ansei Ueshiro, an Okinawan karate teacher who was his Sempai.

Unknown to me at this time was that O-Sensei Chitose was in Hawaii for six months during 1962 at the request of Mr. Thomas Morita and some friends. Mr. Morita was appointed to represent Chitose Sensei in the United States. He was told to organize a United States Chito-ryu karate association by Doctor Chitose prior to Chitose Sensei's return to Japan.

Upon my return from New York I decided to write a letter to Chitose Sensei and inform him that I was still practicing karate and now had a small dojo. I also

Referees wearing their overcoats at the tournament in St. Louis on January 27, 1963. The temperature is in the upper 30s to lower 40s (Fahrenheit). Refereeing is Sensei Ansei Ueshiro.

wanted to see if he would allow me to affiliate with him. My major problem was that I did not have an address in Kumamoto to which I could mail his letter. To make matters even worse, I was not even sure about the proper English spelling of his name. I wrote him a letter anyway and told him about my dojo and the fact that my certificates had been stolen at Fort Lewis. I requested that he reissue the certificates which had been stolen. I sealed his letter enclosing it in a second envelope addressed to the Beppu Police Department. I asked for their help in getting my letter to Chitose Sensei.

Jim Wax told me that he and Ansei Ueshiro were going to hold a tournament in St. Louis, Missouri, during January of 1963. Carroll McGlasson, his wife Carol, Barbara and I drove to St. Louis for the event. As we headed west on Route 50, the sky in Northern Kentucky was clear. Before we got half way across Indiana it started snowing. By the time we arrived in St. Louis there was snow everywhere and it was getting deep. The temperature had dropped to a few degrees above zero. The weather kept many contestants away and the large field house in which the tournament was held did not have an adequate heating system. Inside the field house, the temperature hovered between 35 degrees and 40 degrees Fahrenheit. The judges wore shoes and coats over their karate-gi as they officiated the matches.

It was at this tournament that I met a young, tall, good looking, and impressive young man who studied Chito-ryu under Sensei Mamoru Yamamoto. The young man's name was Mike Foster.

> On the 3rd of February 1963, a letter arrived from Chitose Sensei. His letter was dated January 18. He was happy that I had continued my karate training and said that I should affiliate with him. He asked me to work hard and become a good instructor. In response to my stolen certificates, he informed me that he was promoting me to Yon-dan. My new certificate was in the mail and I should receive it soon. At the end of the letter was a:
>
> P.S. - I hope that you don't mind my writing the letter for Mr. Chitose. I hope you remember me.
>
> Mary Shigamoto

The promotion was greatly appreciated; however, it was the last thing I needed at that time. What I really needed was some help with my basics and kata. Chitose Sensei informed me to contact Sensei Tommy Morita of Honolulu, Hawaii. Morita Sensei was Chitose Sensei's official Chito-ryu representative in

On the left is James "Jim" Wax, the Father of Matsubayashi-ryu in the U.S. He is pictured with the author at the Covington dojo in August 1963.

the United States. I immediately sent a letter to Sensei Morita. I received no answer. I sent several more letters – none of them were answered. I advised Chitose Sensei of my plight and he then instructed me to contact Sensei Masami Tsuruoka, of Toronto, Canada for assistance. Sensei Tsuruoka was the founder of Chito-ryu in Canada and is known as the Father of Canadian Karate. Unlike Morita, Tsuruoka Sensei took time out of his busy schedule to write to me immediately. He invited me to visit with him in Canada.

During the last week of February, I received a package from Chitose Sensei. It was a round tube exactly like the two that had been stolen from me in Japan. I opened the tube and read the enclosed letter. In addition to my rank certificate, Chitose had sent me a teacher's certificate and a charter to teach Chito-ryu in the United States.

During May a young black man came to the dojo to observe a karate class. His name was Willie Stewart and he was a resident of Covington. After class ended he walked into the office, spoke to Barbara and applied for membership. Immediately, two students who had been with me since I had started the dojo on Madison Avenue told me they wanted to speak to me.

"You're not letting that nigger join the dojo are you?" the tall one inquired.

"We don't need any niggers," the second one stated.

I looked them straight in the eye and told them that Chitose Sensei had accepted me when I was not a Japanese citizen and I was most certainly going to accept the young black man who was an American citizen.

"If you accept the nigger as a student, we are going to quit," the tall one told me bluntly.

I sat there for a few minutes, thinking of their threats to leave. "I hate to see you leave," I said, as I looked both of them in the eye. "I am going to accept him as a student."

Willie Stewart joined my dojo the next week and started his karate training on Tuesday night. A total of five students quit the dojo. "You cannot keep everybody happy," I thought to myself. I knew that I, as an American, had made the proper decision.

First trip to Canada in the summer of 1963. Left to right: Kay Tsuruoka, Masami Tsuruoka, Albert Johnson, Randy Goodhew and the author. Tsuruoka Sensei was a complex person. Very nice off the training area and a complete non-forgiving martial artist on it.

1963 Canadian Karate Championships. The author is kneeling at the far left.

The Covington dojo needed a name so I named it the "Kushin-Kan", using the Japanese kanji which meant "self truth school". It was growing slowly and was doing well. I now had enough students to meet the monthly rent with a little left over to improve the facilities.

During June 1963, I received time off from Liberty Loan so I could visit and train with Tsuruoka Sensei. Barbara was pregnant with our second child and was unable to travel. Two of my brown belt students, Albert Johnson and Randy Goodhew and I drove to Canada.

I arrived in Toronto on a bright, sunny Saturday in July. I was finally going to meet Tsuruoka Sensei, the legendary fighter of Kyushu Island during the early 1950s whom I had heard about when I was in Japan. Tsuruoka was envied by some and feared by many. The thought of meeting him face to face worried me. I wondered if he would want to kumite and beat me up during our first meeting!

Upon meeting Sensei Tsuruoka, I found it very difficult to believe that the little mild-mannered person standing before me was the famous Masami Tsuruoka – the terror of Southern Japan. Tsuruoka Sensei and his lovely wife Kay drove us to a nice Chinese restaurant. We ate, then drove to his dojo where we changed into our karate uniforms. My students and I dressed while Tsuruoka Sensei took care of a telephone call. Finally, he retreated to the dressing room and changed into his karate-gi. As he walked onto the training floor I noticed that a complete change had come over him. I no longer had any doubt. The

My first day of work as a Police Officer. Left to Right: Wayne Pelfery, Captain Joe Megerle, the author, Charlile Mitchell.

mild-mannered Masami Tsuruoka whom I had met a few hours earlier was gone. Standing before my students and I was Tsuruoka Sensei, Go-dan. He had undergone a complete metamorphosis into the ultimate karate warrior. I bowed as he walked onto the training area. Sensei Tsuruoka was a no-nonsense, straight to the point type of person. I was a little afraid of him. He was a very hard-nosed, unforgiving taskmaster, but he was never brutal. He helped me greatly and never failed to answer any question I asked him.

During October, several of my students and I attended the Canadian Karate Championships which were sponsored by Tsuruoka Sensei. The tournament was held at the YMHA (Young Men's Hebrew Association) in Toronto. Harvie Eubank had planned on attending but he had been accepted by the L.A.P.D. and he had to leave for California. Barbara was still expecting, so she stayed behind. The tournament was a good one. One of Tsuruoka Sensei's new black belts, Shane Higashi, won the black belt division.

Barbara gave birth to a beautiful baby girl November 21, 1963 at Saint Elizabeth Hospital in Covington, Kentucky. We named her Cheri Lynn but the doctor wrote her name down as Sherry Lynn. We liked the name Sherry Lynn better and kept it.

I had just returned home after working all day at Liberty Loan. It was a Monday evening in January 1964 when the telephone rang. The caller identified himself as Lieutenant Lyle Schwartz of the Covington Police Department. He wanted to know if I was still interested in becoming a Covington police officer. It had been so long since I had taken the written test that I had forgotten about it. I was sworn in as a Covington Police Officer on February 24, 1964. Captain Joe Megerle was our training officer; after thirty days of training I would be assigned to his shift. During the first week of training I came down with flu-like symptoms. My doctor gave me some antibiotics, which kept me going and a few weeks later I was feeling much better. Also during my first week of police training I wrote to Chitose Sensei and informed him that I had become a police officer. I then made the mistake of telling him I was not feeling well. By the time my letter arrived in Japan I was well. A letter arrived from Japan expressing concern over my health and informed me that Mary Shigamoto planned to write to me.

The first United States National Karate Championships was scheduled to be held in Washington, D.C. during the month of April. I was unable to attend because of my new job with the police department. Seven of my students wanted to attend so I loaned them my automobile for the trip. The problem with my car was that it was a small 2-door Plymouth Valiant. Gene Adams got out of the vehicle in Columbus, Ohio and caught a bus back to Cincinnati. The car was

Two early U.S. Chito-ryu students spar under the eye of the referee, Albert Johnson, 2nd Dan (1964).

Seated center: Tsuyoshi Chitose; author to his left; Hidemichi Kugazaki to his right.

just too crowded for Gene. Tom Schonecker, a young student who was a 4th kyu (and who would one day become an Assistant Chief on the Covington police department, a second degree black belt, and my brother-in-law), won his division.

I decided to make an attempt at holding a karate tournament myself. I rented the gymnasium at the First District School on Scott Street and scheduled it for Saturday, May 30, 1964. I made some flyers and mailed them out to the few karate Sensei I knew of. I believe that this was the first karate tournament ever held in Kentucky and one of the first held in the mid-west United States. Tsuruoka Sensei, Ansei Ueshiro, Jim Wax and many others supported it. A young Japanese exchange student named Shinichi Kumanameido of Gensei-ryu attended. Bob Yarnell, a student of Jim Wax's, won the event.

Sensei Tsuruoka held his annual tournament during October 1964. Several students, along with Barbara and I, drove to Canada. This was Barbara's first trip to Canada, or anywhere outside the United States for that matter, but it would not be her last. The tournament was very exciting. A young Okinawan named Zenpo Shimabukuro from the Seibukan Dojo won the event.

A month after returning to Kentucky from the Canadian tournament I received a letter from Chitose Sensei, which was dated November 16, 1964. Mary Shigamoto was worried that I might still be ill and enclosed a small note with Sensei's letter. She said that she was praying for me.

• •

Chapter 22

1965-1969

Focus on making things better, not bigger.

Life's Little Instruction Book

I survived my probation as a rookie officer on the Covington Police Department. I had finally found a job which I enjoyed and was good at. I was assigned to the patrol bureau where my job was to ride in a two-man police cruiser. Harold Musser, a six foot four inch tall, thirty-seven year old, sixteen-year veteran of the police department was my training officer. It was our job to patrol sector number three, handle trouble calls, and maintain law and order.

My landlord at the karate school, Mr. Elmer Herzog, came to see me during the spring of 1965 and asked me if I wanted to rent the second floor as well as the first floor of the building I had rented for my karate school. He agreed to let me have the second floor for an additional fifty dollars a month. I needed the additional space so I accepted his offer. The second floor was renovated and a second training area was added which included a weight lifting area and a small apartment with a toilet; this became the women's dressing room. Up until this time the women had been required to change in the dojo office. The addition of the second floor to our training facilities was very timely because our student enrollment was increasing.

On March 22, 1965 I received a letter from Chitose Sensei. He had purchased a better house at 175 Matsuzaki Shimizu Machi, also located in Kumamoto. I was to send all future letters to him at the new address. His letters inspired me to train to the best of my ability. Often when I was very tired after a hard day's work at the police department, I would re-read his letters to find the motivation for my training.

The summer of 1965 found me training a great deal with Sensei Shinichi Kumanameido. Shinichi, a student at Miami University in Oxford, Ohio, spent the summer with me. A young Gensei-ryu stylist, he assisted me with precision of technique and taught me the kokutsu dachi stance, a stance not used in Chito-ryu karate. I also learned four of his Gensei-ryu kata: Chino, Sansai-dai, and Koshoku Sho and Dai. The kata were fast, snappy and designed for a smaller person.

During the last week of July, Mike Foster arrived in Covington and spent a few days training with Shinichi and me.

The author doing a demonstration with the Tonfa.

Mike, a giant of a man, was very intimidating. One day, Mike admitted his one weakness in karate to me. "I get lazy and need someone to stay on me who will make me train hard," he said, "This is one of the reasons I am going back to Japan in a couple of months," he continued, "so I will be forced to train consistently."

The next afternoon while Mike and I were at my dojo we engaged in a friendly sparring match on the 2nd floor training area. Our sparring had none of the intensity that it would have had if Mike had been serious. I assumed a defensive position and allowed my right arm to drop inviting Mike to attack. Mike, not being one to waste a target area, launched a punch at my side. I blocked his punch with my elbow, then counter-punched him with a jab to the face which was so effective it surprised me as well as him. We were both enjoying ourselves. A few days later Mike left Covington to return home and prepare for his trip to Japan.

After the Saturday class ended I looked through my mail. There was a letter from Chitose Sensei dated June 18, stating that I was being considered for Go-

1965-1969

dan. I wrote to him immediately to inform him that it was a great honor but for me to accept a promotion to Go-dan at this time would cause me problems. I felt that I wasn't qualified to be a Go-dan.

On August 3rd of 1965 I was working the night watch (3rd shift) at the police department. We received a radio dispatch to respond to an auto accident on 19th and Freeman Streets. Upon arrival we discovered that an older gentleman had a slight fender bender with a second auto inhabited by several youths. The vehicle with the youths had the right-of-way, the accident was minor, and no one wanted to press charges.

After the accident report was completed, one of the kids, a short, rather cute one, dressed in boys clothing walked up to me and asked, "Hey! Aren't you the guy who runs the karate school?"

"I sure am," I answered.

"Can I come down and watch a class sometime?"

"Anytime you want to," I said.

As we drove away in the police car, I turned to my partner Harold and asked him, "Was the little kid who was bugging me about the karate school a little boy or a little girl?"

"I do not know," he said and then added, "But whatever it was it was cute."

Little did I know then that this small four foot eleven inch tall kid would someday play a major part in my life, my wife's life and in karate in general.

One Tuesday evening a couple of weeks later (after I had transferred to the second shift – we rotated shift from first, second and third on a regular basis), the young fourteen year old, four foot and eleven inch kid arrived at my dojo to observe a karate class. Because I was working I was unable to be at the dojo on that night. The kid met my wife and was very enthusiastic when talking about karate. After observing a basic class of karate the kid returned to the dojo office where my wife was working. Finally, in desperation, because she was unsure of the sex of the young person, my wife inquired, "Are you a boy or a girl?" Standing up as straight as she could at four feet eleven inches, the kid looked my wife in the eyes and announced a little indigently, "I'm a girl."

On Thursday evening the young girl showed up at my dojo again, this time wearing a dress, but still looking every bit the tomboy that she was. Her name was Devorah Wear. She was referred to as either just plain Debbie, Deb by those young boys and girls who wanted to get a punch in the nose, or the "Termite" (her chosen nickname) by those who wanted to stay on her good side. She joined the karate school that very night and would in her lifetime become a living legend within the traditional martial arts community in both Okinawa and the United States of America.

Barbara and I soon learned that little Debbie had no permanent residence. She would stay with one of her girlfriends for a few nights, then moved in with another girlfriend, and a few days later move again. We had a small apartment on the second floor of the dojo. It was offered, and she moved in. Within a couple of weeks after she started her training, my wife and I both discovered that she had a God gifted natural ability for karate training.

The Dojo was attracting many students and I decided to start holding an annual tournament. During the past four years I had been sponsoring a semi-annual dojo tournament, which helped me gain valuable experience. For this tournament I rented the gymnasium at the Covington Catholic High School. The tournament was a success and resulted in the development of a referee and judges training course. In the sixties no manuals existed on how to run a tournament; it was a "learn as you go" experience. Many other instructors and I shared information on what had worked and what had not – tournament operation was a truly cooperative learning experience.

Chito-ryu karate students training on Kyushu Island, Japan. Left front is Hitomi Hayashi. Behind her, at 5 o'clock, is Kazunori Kawakita. Hitomi's father was one of Dr. Chitose's top students and her sister married Sensei Mamoru Yamamoto of the Yoshukan dojos.

The black belt champion of our first large tournament was a good technician but his attitude was a disgrace. I presented him with his 1st place trophy and whispered to him so that no one else could hear:

"Here is your trophy. You have the worst attitude of any person I have ever seen. Take it. You are a disgrace to karate. Take it and never again come to any of my tournaments."

He reached out and accepted the trophy with a look of disbelief on his face. He said nothing. He never returned.

I received a letter from Chitose Sensei dated October 19, 1965. He told me that he was happy that I was working hard for the development of Chito-ryu karate-do in America. His next remark stated, "I can understand what you mean about the problems of your fifth dan black belt." I had hoped that Chitose Sensei would appreciate my feelings and would not promote me. I knew that I was not qualified to be a Go-dan at that time.

Mike Foster visited me a few months after his return from Japan. He said his months of training in Japan were very beneficial but too short and he was planning on returning to Japan as soon as possible. While in Japan he had practically lived in the dojo. Training at Mamoru Yamamoto's dojo was rough and tumble and involved a lot of kumite, especially in the 1960s. Many karate students would seek out an easier dojo in which to train, but not Mike. He relished the rough kumite, strict discipline, and strong spirit that such dojos can provide.

After some small talk we donned our karate-gi for a little friendly kumite. I assumed the same position as I had several months earlier when I counterpunched him so successfully. I wanted to see if his visit to Japan had sharpened his reflexes. My answer came a fraction of a second later. Mike reverse-punched me exactly as he had several months earlier. This time his punch exploded as his fist shot forward and tapped me lightly. He had developed an exceptionally fast punch with perfect control. His hand was back on his hip before I realized I had been struck. A few months later Mike entered the United States Karate Championships and won, overpowering opponents with his size, speed and power. He was unbeatable at that time in his life. Mike won the United States Karate Championship for four years in a row. I personally felt that if Mike Foster set his mind to it and trained faithfully, he could have easily defeated the top five karate fighters in the U. S. in one day without even raising a sweat.

The 1966 National Karate Championships in Washington D.C. was sponsored by Joon Rhee, a Tae Kwon Do instructor; it was the biggest tournament on the East Coast. My students were excited about the tournament. Barbara inquired

Devorah Wear being awarded First Place trophies for both kata and kumite at the National Championships of 1966 in Washington D.C. Movie star Robert Culp of "I Spy" fame, made the presentation.

about renting a bus at the Greyhound Bus Station. It would cost $37.00 a person if we could fill all forty-two seats. A week later a bus loaded with forty students, Barbara and myself was on its way to the nation's capitol.

Karate was still young in the United States and no competitors had yet gained the nation's attention. Several people worthy of that attention were at the tournament. Bruce Lee did a demonstration and explained his ideas. The winner of the men's black belt kumite was a handsome, young ex-Marine named Joe Lewis. Joe was well built, strong, fast, and did not seem to care if he got hurt, as long as he could hurt the other guy too! When Joe assumed his soon-to-be-famous side stance and stared at his opponent, his blue eyes seemed to turn green. The other contestants sparred, Joe fought – a big difference. The second place kumite winner was a fantastic fighter from New York, Tommy LaPuppet. I saw Tommy pin his opponent by stepping on his foot then kicking him in the head with the other foot. Third place went to Victor Moore of Cincinnati who had taken his first karate lesson from me at the old Yudan Dojo on Vine Street. He was now a member of Robert A. Trias' U.S.K.A. organization. Debbie, who had continued to train rigorously, traveled with us to Washington, D.C. Still a white belt, she easily won both the women's kumite and kata divisions beating out several female brown and black belts. This tournament was the third United States

National Championships (1964 being the first) and the first National Tournament to allow women's competition. With just a little under nine months of training, Debbie became the first Women's National Champion of the United States. Robert Culp, an actor in the television series "I Spy", awarded the trophies.

Barbara and I started a small news bulletin to let people know about the Midwest Chito-ryu Karate Organization. We had articles about tournaments, special training, and general interest items about some members that were in the service in Vietnam. Several copies were mailed out to our students and key

Seated center is Doctor Tsuyoshi Chitose. Kneeling to his left is Hidemichi Kugizaki. Many students came daily to Dr. Chitose's home to train in his back yard and learn Chito-ryu karate-do.

karate personnel in the United States. Barbara mailed several copies to Chitose Sensei for distribution in Japan.

Barbara and I received a letter from Chitose dated April 26, 1966. He had received the news bulletin and enjoyed it very much; he wanted us to keep up the good work, as always. He was attempting to gather the names and addresses of Americans who had taken Chito-ryu. Sensei mentioned that Shane Higashi was staying at his home in Kumamoto for a couple of months' training and sent his best regards to me. As I continued to read the letter, I thought, "Why me?" Chitose Sensei said that I had been promoted to Go-dan. Two weeks later a round cardboard tube arrived at my home. It was my Go-dan certificate. Only my wife knew of the promotion. I told her not to mention it to anyone. I rolled the certificate up, put it back into the tube, and then hid the tube in my sock drawer. I still had not been able to accept the fact that I was a Yon-dan, let alone a Go-dan! What I really wanted was to go back to Japan and train to gain more knowledge and skill along with the ability to teach better. My students were never told of my promotion and that was the way I wanted it.

October arrived and many U.S. Chito-kai students prepared to head for Canada. It had become a ritual that I, along with many of my students, would drive to Toronto, Canada, to participate in Masami Tsuruoka's Canadian Championship.

The author receiving congratulations from the ranking black belts at the Canadian tournament upon being elevated to Go-dan during the fall of 1966.

Many high-ranking sensei attended the tournament. Ansei Ueshiro, Jim Wax's sempai, was there. Yamagami Sensei, the 1966 Japanese kumite champion, and Tsutomu Ohshima, a legend among karate practitioners throughout North America and the world, were also in attendance.

During a short break in the finals my name was announced over the loud speakers. I was requested to approach Tsuruoka Sensei who was standing at the head table where the honored guests were seated. I approached the table, stopped, bowed, and stood at attention. Tsuruoka Sensei picked up a roll of paper, slowly unrolled it, and then started reading from it.

"William J. Dometrich, United States Chito-ryu, is hereby promoted to Go-dan, 5th degree black belt, by orders of O-Sensei, Tsuyoshi Chitose," he said into the microphone. He reached across the table and handed the certificate to me. I bowed as I put both hands out to accept it.

Where and how had Tsuruoka Sensei obtained a second Go-dan certificate!? I found out when I returned to my seat that my wife Barbara had taken the certificate from my sock drawer and smuggled it to Toronto on the orders of Tsuruoka Sensei and Chitose Sensei. I was now officially a Go-dan whether I wanted to be one or not.

Several karate magazines were flooding the shelves of the local newsstands. In one of the magazines there was an interview with Hidetaka Nishiyama, one of the top sensei of the Japan Karate Association (JKA). Parts of the article were rather derogatory toward western (American) karate teachers. Nishiyama was quoted (or misquoted) in the article as saying that most western karate teachers were unqualified. The general tone of the article gave the impression that he had substituted the word "unqualified" for "fake". It was true that most of us westerners were (at that time in history) unqualified when compared with our Japanese counterparts, but we were not fakes. We were as dedicated as many of the Japanese. If it wasn't for the American servicemen who had returned to the United States and started teaching karate there would be very few karate dojos throughout the country. The problem was not that the Americans were unqualified or fakes but that the Japanese instructors were better trained and educated in karate, mostly because it was a part of their culture. I wrote an extremely critical letter to Nishiyama Sensei which I planned on mailing the next morning on my way to the dojo. That night I had a dream in which Nishiyama Sensei came to Covington looking for me. He then proceeded to kick me all over a dark intersection. The next morning I rewrote my letter. It was still to the point but more courteous. I was glad that I rewrote it. In the very near future I would meet Nishiyama Sensei. My rewritten letter made our initial meeting more amicable. Nishiyama Sensei turned out to be both a kind and knowledgeable person. Over the years, whenever I had an opportunity to train at one of his clinics, he was always helpful and kind enough to answer many of my questions concerning karate techniques, kata, kumite and history.

I drove to Philadelphia to visit Teruyuki Okazaki's dojo in January 1967 with two of my students, Terry Collis and Al Johnson. We left on Thursday night traveling in a 1963 Volkswagen bus, which had a top speed of about fifty miles per hour on level ground. We arrived in Philadelphia at noon on Friday. Stopping by the karate school before we located a motel, we were surprised to find that Okazaki Sensei was there. He told us that a class was scheduled for 1:00 PM and we were invited to attend.

We put on our karate-gi and got ready for class. There to assist Okazaki Sensei were Keinosuke Enoeda, the 1963 All Japan kumite champion, and Kisaka Sensei, the 1965 Japanese kumite champion. Kisaka Sensei did the warm up

An example of Chito-Ryu Tournament in the 1970s.

exercises.

Slowly, he did a full split and then leaned forward and started turning his head from side to side touching his ears to the floor. I knew immediately that I was in trouble. The class consisted mostly of basics with a few kata thrown in for good measure. Everyone on the floor was soaking wet by the end of the class. Once the class ended we received a polite, "Thank you for coming," from Okazaki Sensei. Then he said, "We have a black belt class scheduled at 7:00 PM tonight, would you like to attend?"

"Yes, Sensei, we would," I replied.

We located a motel a few miles from the dojo and finally got to bed at about 3:20 PM. We told the main desk to wake us at 5:30 PM sharp. It seemed like we had just lain down when the phone rang; it was time to get up. We were all sore and stiff. Kisaka Sensei had really put it to us during the first class. Arriving at Okazaki Sensei's dojo at 6:40 PM, we had to stand on a bench and help each other put on our karate-gi pants. Our legs refused to bend. It was our good fortune that Kisaka Sensei was not present at the night class. He was teaching at a branch dojo. Okazaki Sensei and Enoeda Sensei were tonight's teachers

Approximately seventeen black belts attended the class. The training was very demanding and informative. The entire class stood in zenkutsu dachi performing gyaku tsuki (reverse punch) for over an hour. Enoeda Sensei walked among the students punching their "lat" muscles and checking their tension. A few of the students were knocked off balance and fell to the floor. After the class was over both Okazaki Sensei and Enoeda Sensei took the time to help us with our technique and give us some pointers. We greatly appreciated their assistance.

Back in the motel I phoned an old friend, an excellent karate-ka I had known for some time, Sensei Walter Dailey. A student of Zenro Shimabuku of the Seibukan dojo in Okinawa, Walter was a Shorin-ryu stylist. His Kusanku kata was the best I had ever seen. He invited the three of us to train with him on Saturday morning at the Valley Dojo, which was located on the outskirts of Philadelphia.

At 10:00 AM the next morning we bowed in with the class at the Valley Dojo. Yamagami Sensei, the 1966 Japanese kumite champion whom I had met at Tsuruoka Sensei's tournament, was the instructor. Terry, Al and I were still sore but not as sore as we had been the night before. We did stretching exercises and a half hour of basics before we started one-step sparring. When we started doing san-bon kumite, Yamagami Sensei stood to my right. Directly across from him was my student, Al Johnson, who was a very good technician and extremely quick. The line Yamagami and I were in was to attack. We both stepped forward into zenkutsu dachi as we punched to the face of our opponents. I saw a flash to my right. Yamagami's face punch was so fast that it was at Al's face before he could react. Yamagami Sensei threw two more punches using his right hand; the punches followed each other in rapid succession.

At the police department it seemed that everyone smoked either big black cigars or cigarettes. The favorite cigar was a local Cincinnati brand named "Ibold". Riding in a police cruiser during the winter months with officers who chain-smoked cigars or cigarettes with the windows rolled up to keep the cold out began to cause me to have serious lung problems. My ability to breathe properly deteriorated rapidly. Within a short time I started getting winded very easily while training at the dojo. After a few minutes of very hard training I would be forced to rest because I was short of breath. To escape the enclosed confines of the smoke-filled police cruisers I decided to volunteer for duty with Traffic Bureau which had only one officer assigned to a car.

"I wish I had known last week that you wanted to transfer into the Traffic Bureau," the traffic chief, Lieutenant Colonel Ralph Bosse, told me. "Unfortunately, I just filled the last vacancy for a traffic cruiser last week."

I thanked him, turned, and started to leave his office. "Can you ride a motorcycle? I need a motorcycle rider," he said before I reached the door of his office.

"Yes," I lied in desperation as I turned and walked back to his desk. I had never been on a motorcycle in my life but I would do anything to escape the smoke of the cruisers.

Officer Bill Mason, an experienced motorcycle officer, was assigned to break me in. We arrived at the garage where the motorcycle was parked. It was Unit 917, the jinxed motorcycle. On Unit

Doctor Chitose with Mamoru Yamamoto at the Greater Cincinnati Airport.

917, officer Don Ronnebaum was killed on the I-75 expressway. He had been off the motorcycle at the time investigating an accident when he was struck by a truck. His replacement officer, Mike Hebbler, was on an emergency run when he was struck by a car at 6th and Main Streets. Mike went to the hospital and died a year later from complications. The motorcycle was repaired, and now I was going to get my chance to try out Unit 917.

"How do you start it?" I inquired.

A few months later I was an accomplished motorcycle officer.

Chitose Sensei and one of his top students, Sensei Mamoru Yamamoto (three time Japan kumite champion and Mike Foster's Sensei), flew to Canada in September 1967 for a visit with Tsuruoka Sensei and his wife, Kay. Uncertain if Chitose Sensei's schedule would allow him the free time to visit Kentucky and meet my students, Barbara chartered a Greyhound bus so forty-two of my students could travel to Canada to meet Chitose Sensei. Barbara, my daughter Sherry, who was now three years old, and I drove to Toronto a few days earlier in our 1963 VW Camper. We found a campground near the center of Toronto. The next morning after an early breakfast, the three of us drove to Tsuruoka Sensei's home on Indian Road. I looked forward with great anticipation to meeting Chitose Sensei again. I knocked on the door and prepared myself for my first meeting with Chitose Sensei since I had waved goodbye to him at the train station in Beppu thirteen years before. After climbing the stairs to the second floor,

Dr. Chitose during his visit to Kentucky in 1967.

I entered the dining room. Sensei was sitting at the table looking at me. He looked exactly as I remembered him. He had not changed a bit. I felt a lump form in my throat; my emotions were so high that nothing I said could possibly explain my feelings.

Tsuruoka Sensei had enlarged his annual tournament in honor of Chitose Sensei's visit to Canada. The tournament was going to be held at the Canadian National Exposition Center near Lake Ontario. It was a three-day affair with several excellent demonstrations. Higashi Sensei demonstrated the Sakugawa No Kon Sho bo kata. Mike Foster and Mamoru Yamamoto demonstrated a bo and sai defense. Finally Chitose Sensei moved into the center of the arena. He demonstrated self-defense against two opponents who were attempting to grab or pin him. With vice-like hands Chitose Sensei threw his attackers in different directions simultaneously. The crowd applauded wildly with approval. Chitose Sensei bowed then started performing a segment of the Chitose family kata. His movements were precise, beautiful and extremely fast and lethal. No sooner had he completed the last movement of the kata when the crowd of about 5,000 people jumped to their feet and gave him a standing ovation. The National Karate Association of Canada made a film of the tournament.

Fortunately for the Kentucky Chito-ryu students, there was enough time in Chitose Sensei and Yamamoto Sensei's itinerary to allow them to travel to the United States. After the tournament in Toronto ended, they flew to Kentucky.

It was during this visit that Chitose Sensei requested that I change the name of my dojo from "Kushinkan" to "Yoseikan". Yoseikan was the name of his school in Japan and he wanted me to use the same name. During his stay in Covington, we trained daily in basics and kata. Training with O-Sensei in my own dojo brought back fond memories of my training years earlier in Japan.

Yamamoto Sensei stayed with us a few days before flying to Tampa Florida to visit Mike Foster and his students.

At the time of Chitose Sensei's visit, our small dojo operated as the Midwest United States headquarters for Chito-ryu. I hired a young Japanese lady, Masako Tamia, to assist me in translating English to Japanese and vice versa, so Chitose Sensei and I could communicate more effectively. Masao Morita, a young Japanese man who had been a karate black belt student of Osamu Ozawa who had joined my dojo to train in Chito-ryu karate-do, also assisted with the translations.

Photograph taken during 1967 of the author, Dr. Tsuyoshi Chitose and Mamoru Yamamoto, one of Chitose Sensei's top students.

During Sensei's visit, I learned that Sensei Tommy Morita of Hawaii was no longer a member of the Chito-kai. As we sat around the kitchen table one evening Chitose Sensei informed me that he was appointing me to organize a United States Chito-ryu karate organization. I was to function as the Chairman and Chief Instructor of the new organization. I protested but to no avail. I explained to Chitose Sensei that both my wife and I worked full time jobs and that we had two children to raise. It would be next to impossible for me to build a large organization under these conditions. Chitose Sensei placed his hand upon mine as we sat there at the table. He looked into my eyes and spoke softly to Masako Tamia.

Chitose Sensei says, "Build a good honbu, produce good students, and build a good organization," she told me. "He is not asking you to build a large organization, only a good one."

The next day as I was training with Chitose Sensei, he told me to punch him.

"Punchi," he said.

I stepped forward and punched. O-Sensei knew that I was taking it a little easy on him. He was nearing seventy and I did not want to hurt him. He slapped my fist out of the air.

"No!" he admonished me.

"Moichido." (Again.) "Speedo."

I moved toward him once more, as my body and fist snapped forward. His hand flashed; I only caught a very quick glimpse of it before I landed on the floor with Chitose Sensei standing over me, looking down and grinning. It was at that moment that I understood that Chitose Sensei was a MEIJIN, a most gifted karate saint.

While we sat at our small kitchen table, Chitose Sensei told me stories about his life and early training. He said that his first teacher was a famous karate teacher by the name of Arakaki Oh. In the old days when he had started his karate training, very few basics were taught. Most of his training was in kata. O-Sensei told us that he had trained for seven years on one kata, the kata Seisan. Sensei stated that today this type of training would be impossible, since people are not patient enough to take their time learning. He also said that almost all of the students would quit.

Yamamoto Sensei arrived back in Covington after spending a week in Florida. From there Yamamoto and Chitose Sensei would return to Canada, then on to Japan. As they flew to Canada, I finally realized that the dojo in Covington had, for better or worse, been designated as the United States Chito-ryu Headquarters with me serving as the Chief Instructor. I was very nervous about O-Sensei's decision but would do my best. I knew that the organization would be successful because I had a secret weapon – my wife Barbara.

My students and I were now operating with a renewed level of confidence. I looked forward to 1968 with great expectations.

As the newly designated Chief Instructor of Chito-ryu for the United States I wrote to Chitose Sensei after he returned to Japan and once again requested the names and addresses of the Americans who had studied with him in Japan. After I received the names I planned to contact each of them to see if they would join me in building a strong United States Chito-kai. I did manage to obtain the names of a few of Tommy Morita's Chito-ryu students in California and Hawaii through the use of Black Belt Magazine, which had a "Who's Who" section at the back of the early editions. My attempts at locating other people were less successful. However, I did manage to locate Sensei Bernard Moore and Harry

Kualaanni. I knew that there should also be a few ex-military students located around the U. S. In Cincinnati, I located Dave Stewart, a member of the 187th Regimental Combat Team, who had been stationed at Camp Wood in Kumamoto. Dave had been promoted to Sho-dan in Chito-ryu by Chitose Sensei. It was challenging to build an organization from nothing. I had to locate students any way I could since Japan never did supply the names I had requested.

Chitose Sensei had always stressed the importance of having a good, strong, devastating punch and front kick. I felt that I needed to make a few changes in both my teaching and grading plan to aid me in the teaching of Chito-ryu.

Based on the experience I had gained in Chito-ryu and, more importantly, my exposure to other styles, I had trouble accepting the first kata, Zenshin Kotai. The hand and foot techniques were very simple with straight forward and backward movements. A simple turn to the right and left performed with a chest block, then two punches using hip snap to deliver them, none of which seemed to create a powerful punch. The next part of the kata had two side kicks which were very difficult for beginners to perform. I felt that Zenshin Kotai was not an appropriate kata for beginners. My opinion on this has never changed.

A karate teacher's first and foremost obligation is to teach new students one or two strong techniques – techniques that could be used effectively if the student were attacked. I had learned to appreciate the focus or "kime" of Japanese karate techniques and had come to believe that one fast, powerful, devastating technique is more beautiful than a hundred lesser techniques. To assist me in teaching this principle, I adopted the kata Taikyoku Shodan, renaming it Taikyoku Ichi. Taikyoku Ichi thus became the first kata learned by United States Chito-ryu students.

In addition to changing the kata structure, I also initiated a nine kyu ranking system. The non-Japanese Chito-ryu kata would be taught at the levels below sixth kyu, which was the entrance level in Japan. After my students reached the rank of sixth kyu they would be taught Chito-ryu karate. I felt that this would protect the style from unscrupulous individuals and demonstrate to the students that they needed to qualify to study Chito-ryu.

A local film distribution company contacted my karate school about doing a series of demonstrations on Friday and Saturday nights at the RKO Albey Theater on Fountain Square in Cincinnati. For two weeks, several students and I gave one demonstration on Friday and two demonstrations on Saturday. On Sunday night after the last weekend of demonstrations, I flew to New York to visit Sensei Peter Urban and S. Henry Cho's dojo, along with other schools in the city.

1965-1969

Sensei Urban's dojo had moved from the 14th Street area to Canal Street in Chinatown. His classes were always very spirited and he was doing well. I congratulated him on his book, "The Karate Dojo," which was excellent. Sensei S. Henry Cho was in the process of completing his manuscript, "Korean Karate Free Fighting Techniques." He was kind enough to allow me to review his book's rough draft while I was visiting with him.

I wandered the streets of New York on Wednesday and came upon a small dojo in an old rundown building. I walked up the narrow stairs leading to the second floor. There I had the distinct pleasure of meeting forty-six year old Sensei Duk Sung Son, a ninth degree black belt in Tae Kwon Do. Sensei Son was definitely a practitioner from the old school. He demonstrated a few techniques for me. When he did shutos (sword hand techniques), his hand position was exactly the same as Chitose Sensei's. He took great pride in his makiwara and enjoyed showing me how hard he could punch it. I felt a great kinship for this Korean sensei and spent the better part of the afternoon with him. I phoned Barbara Wednesday night to check in with her on how things were going at the dojo.

"You have to come home at once," Barbara told me. "The manager of the Albey Theater is going to show the movie, 'Our Man Flint' for two more weekends and needs you to do the demonstration at the theater." Cutting my trip to New York short, I flew back to Cincinnati on Friday's early-bird flight. That evening my students and I were back on the stage of the Albey. While we were doing the demonstrations for 'Our Man Flint', my dojo's membership tripled.

One of the owners of the old Cincinnati School of Self Defense returned and started another chain of schools, which he named The National School of Self Defense. One school was located in the Newport, Kentucky, shopping center. His other school was located in Cincinnati on Vine Street. Phil (his first name) hired Takayoshi Nagamine, the son of Shoshin Nagamine, founder of Matsubayashi Shorin-ryu, as his karate instructor.

The National School of Self Defense quickly went out of business. History was repeating itself. Many students had outstanding loans that they had to pay off to the local loan company. Nagamine Sensei felt an obligation to the abandoned students. He moved across the street and rented a small building which he turned into a dojo so the students would have a place to practice. He slept in a small room in the rear. It was during this time that a student from the Newport school, Dr. Robert Taylor, joined my dojo. Within a few weeks, he introduced me to Takayoshi Nagamine. We soon became good friends and then later, almost like brothers.

I received an invitation to a tournament in St. Louis, Missouri. The tournament was sanctioned by the Japan Karate Association, the All-American Karate Association, and the Amateur American Karate Federation. Several students, Barbara and I traveled to St. Louis for the tournament. Going to the tournament almost caused one of my students, Albert O'Mera, to get divorced. We left the dojo late Friday evening and when we got to Terra Haute, Indiana, Al announced that he needed to make a telephone call. He called his wife, who had expected him home hours earlier – they had a date to go out and celebrate her birthday. He then informed her that he was on his way to St. Louis to attend a karate tournament and wished her a happy birthday.

As I changed into my karate-gi at the gymnasium in St. Louis, Sensei Shojiro Sugiyama called my name, "Dometrich-san!"

"I'll be there in a minute, Sensei," I answered.

I worked my way through the crowded dressing room to where Sugiyama Sensei was standing.

"Dometrich-san, please allow me to introduce you to Sensei Hidetaka Nishiyama." Nishiyama Sensei was standing there with a slight smile on his face.

"Osu!" I replied in awe, as I bowed.

Nishiyama Sensei returned my bow, then shook my hand as he said, "I think you wrote me a letter once."

"Yes, Sensei, I did." At that moment, I was very happy that I had rewritten the letter before I had mailed it.

The kata competition at the tournament was above average. The majority of those attending had received excellent training. One young black belt demonstrated the Tekki kata. I have never seen it done better before, or in all of the years since. The young man's name was Ray Dalke. He really did an excellent Tekki kata.

During the sparring, Fred Wren, a rough and tough fighter, was warming up and preparing for his match. Fred's nickname was the "Texas Whirlwind." After sparring with Fred you usually felt as if you had been hit by a tornado. Some local, non-traditional schools had been invited to participate. The instructors of these schools operated by a different set of rules than the Japan Karate Association or the Japan Karate Federation schools. The person that Fred drew to fight was from one of these independent schools. Just before Fred entered the ring, he was advised by one of his students that the black belt he was scheduled to fight was really a brown belt whose teacher had instructed him to wear a black belt. Fred had a reputation to uphold. When it came time for Fred's match with the "almost black belt," Fred walked into the ring, looked at his opponent standing across from him, and waited.

"Hajime," the referee said.

Fred moved like a streak of lighting and the fight was over. Fred had knocked the guy out. After a meeting of the referees, Fred was disqualified for excessive contact.

"It was worth losing my entry fee," Fred said as he walked out of the ring. "He'll think twice before wrapping a black belt on again," he said with a grin.

In 1968 I made nine trips to Canada in my little 1963 Valiant to train with Tsuruoka Sensei. Each time I was amazed by his knowledge. One afternoon Sensei and I were the only people in his dojo. We started sparring. I was very confident that my one hundred seventy-five pounds could out-muscle his one hundred thirty pounds. I later found out that I had made a big mistake. I was muscling my technique and attempting to bully him around the dojo. Suddenly, Sensei's leg flashed out in a side thrust kick to my stomach. I slapped it down with both hands, and his foot struck me, full speed, in the groin. Tsuruoka Sensei stopped the fight at once.

"Did I get you?" he asked, with a worried look on his face.

Standing there, I felt absolutely no pain. "No, Sensei," I said, "I don't think you got me."

A few seconds later, the pain hit me and I literally spun around and screwed myself into the ground. Two days later I had a bruise from my kneecaps to my chest. In spite of the few injuries Tsuruoka Sensei had inflicted upon me, he was an excellent karate teacher. His theory was, "one ouch is worth one-thousand be carefuls." I always returned to Kentucky with more knowledge and a great many more bruises than I had left with. His teaching was very difficult and no one was ever cut any slack. Because of this hard-nosed attitude, Tsuruoka Sensei lost many students who had only joined to "play" at karate. At Tsuruoka's dojo, you worked from the time you entered the dojo until the time you left. If you played, you paid. I learned this lesson the hard way.

The lung problems I had developed from second-hand smoke were still with me. Riding a motorcycle with the traffic bureau had kept me from getting additional exposure to smoke, but the damage had been done. As a result of the lung problems, I had spent all of my time teaching and no time training or working my reflexes in preparation for competition. While at Tsuruoka Sensei's tournament in Canada in 1968, I got the crazy idea that I should enter black belt

Kazunori Kawakita, 4th Dan. A student of Mamoru Yamamoto, he was good kata technician and an excellent kumite champion.

kumite. I had not trained for the tournament and entering was not one of my better ideas. My opponent was a 19-year-old boy named Wally Slocki, the current Canadian kumite champion. Before the match was over, Wally broke my nose; it took five minutes for the bleeding to stop. He received a warning. I dropped him with a groin kick, which took him two minutes to recover from and get to his feet. I also received a warning. Then Wally finished me off with a picture perfect punch and won the match. It had been a fun match even though my nose took a long time to heal.

Just before Christmas on December 20, 1968 a Japanese karate instructor arrived at the Cincinnati airport. He was to spend a year with us. A few of my students, Barbara and I arrived at the airport early to greet him. Walking through the arrival gate was Kazunori Kawakita – five-time all Southern Japan kumite champion. "Kita-san", as we affectionately learned to call him, was a top student of Mamoru Yamamoto. In one hand he carried a small handgrip with his clothes. His karate-gi was rolled up and tucked under the other arm. We walked to the baggage claim area to pick up his large suitcase. To our surprise this large suitcase was crammed with Japanese food. Kita-san was pleasantly surprised a few days later when I took him to Cincinnati and introduced him to Ben Yamaguchi, a good friend and owner of The Soya Food Company which processed and distributed Japanese food for the tri-state area.

Saturday, the day after he arrived, Kita-san went to the karate school with my wife Barbara. I was on motorcycle duty with the police department and was unable to attend class. Kita arrived at the dojo wearing a kimono and wooden geta. Under his left arm he carried a rolled up karate-gi. Al Johnson was teaching class. Kita sat in the spectator area for approximately twenty minutes as Al taught. Then he walked to the dressing room, put on his gi, bowed onto the training area, and proceeded to warm up in a corner of the dojo while the class continued. Walking to the center of the floor, he motioned for everyone to sit down except Al.

"We fight," he said.

For about two minutes Kita allowed Al to attack him. Then it was Kita's turn. Five seconds later Al flew backwards into the dojo wall as the result of a hard and accurate back kick. With Kazunori Kawakita as the resident instructor, 1969 looked like it was going to be a very interesting year.

Kita participated in three tournaments that year in kumite, all with disastrous results. He usually got disqualified. The last tournament Kita-san was in took place in St. Louis. We had been invited to participate by Bob Yarnall, who was hosting the tournament. At this tournament, Kita-san's first and only opponent was a young Tae Kwon Do stylist.

"Hajime!" the referee commanded.

The Tae Kwon Do opponent threw a near perfect back kick, which found its way between Kita's arms and struck him in the chest. Kita brushed the dirty footprint off of his uniform; the Korean stylist was awarded a point. Kita assumed his "on guard" position.

"Hajime!" the referee commanded again.

The Tae Kwon Do stylist fired a strong front thrust kick, followed by a lunge punch. Kita side-stepped the kick as he slid to his left and blocked the punch with his open left hand. Then he struck his opponent with a hard right hook punch into his solar plexus. The opponent's body crumpled, bringing his chin down and into contact with Kita's fist; he was unconscious and still on his feet, but starting to fall. Kita continued moving as his right foot round kicked the opponent's relaxed left hand, breaking it. Without hesitation, he placed his right foot on the floor and spun as he threw a devastating back kick with his left leg. Kita's opponent flew out of the ring, hit the floor on his back, and slid ten feet. Kita was immediately disqualified.

"Dometrich Sensei," Kita said, as he walked over to me, "I am sorry to disgrace you. If you want to send me back to Japan, I understand."

Takayoshi Nagamine walked over to where Kita and I were standing and spoke to Kita in Japanese.

"What did you say?" I asked.

"I told him not to feel so bad. He lost the contest but he won the fight" Takayoshi said with a devilish grin on his face.

With Kita's help our school's ability to kumite increased greatly. Kata, however, was a different matter. Kita was good at kata, but great at kumite. We continued to train, and train hard. Many students started to fade away under the severe training.

The U. S. Chito-kai National Tournament was held during October 1969. As was my habit, I had invited schools of other styles to attend, participate, and demonstrate. During the demonstrations, one group had trouble breaking three boards with a jump kick. They dropped down to two boards and still were not successful. At last, they were down to one board that finally broke on the fifth try.

Kita looked at me. "Get seven boards," he said.

We picked our two biggest students with big hands to hold the seven boards, and then supported their arms and shoulders with those of at least five others. Kita walked to the center of the gym, measured his distance, and snapped his hip and body for a perfect spinning back kick. The boards shattered with a loud "crack!" Kita looked at the instructors from the other style, then bowed. They stood and left the tournament.

The final match was between Mike Foster and Bill "Super Foot" Wallace. Bill won, but it was not an easy match for him. After the match, Mike informed me that he did not even see a couple of Bill's kicks.

"You know," Mike confided to me, "when you see the techniques and still can't block them, you know you need to increase your speed. When you don't even see the techniques it may be time to retire."

A few months later, I saw Bill Wallace at a Midwest tournament.

"After your tournament and competing in the finals, I was so beat up I have not been able to do anything for a month," Bill said. "I felt as if someone had beaten me with a crow bar."

In the middle of October 1969, Mike Foster arrived at the dojo with Yuki Koda, who was a good friend of Kita-san, and a younger, nice looking Japanese man named Fujitaka. Mike and Yuki had trained together with Kita-san in Japan at Yamamoto Sensei's dojo. We had a good time while they were at my dojo. We trained hard, fought hard, and partied hard. Mike and Yuki headed back to Florida and left Fujitaka with me at my dojo. Within two weeks I knew this was a huge mistake. Fujitaka propositioned almost every girl in the dojo – including the married ones. I had some big problems with him.

On Thursday night as class was getting ready to start, Fujitaka arrived at the dojo with a young female student with whom he had spent the day.

"Get your gi on!" I told him.

"I am not going to train tonight," he responded.

Kita-san was standing there. I looked at him. "Kita, tell him to get his damn gi on. I am not asking him to get dressed – I am telling him to get dressed."

Before the class ended I held a kumite session. I sparred with three different students before Fujitaka stood opposite me. I could tell by his face that he knew something was up. We had only been sparring for a few seconds when he caught me with a great back kick that hurt me, but not enough to drop me. I immediately round kicked him very hard in the stomach, reverse punched him in the face and then foot swept him.

"Get your gi off!" I ordered. "You are going back to Florida tonight."

"I don't have a ticket," he said.

"You have a ticket, I reserved you a seat this afternoon."

"My clothes are at your house, I must pack first," he pleaded with me.

"Your clothes are already packed and in the trunk of my car. Get dressed, we're going to the airport," I informed him in a 'get your butt in gear, or else' tone of voice.

Prior to getting dressed, he walked into the office to say goodbye to my wife Barbara.

"Okusan, do you think Dometrich Sensei is mad at me?" he asked.

Barbara looked at his bloody face. "I think he is a little upset," she said.

Fujitaka had caused me more headaches in the two weeks he had been at my dojo than all of my other students had in seven years. A few of the husbands and fathers wanted to kill him.

A few days before Christmas we drove Kita-san to the Greater Cincinnati Airport and bid him farewell. He boarded the plane for his return flight to Japan. The year had gone by so quickly. It seemed as if he were only in the Covington area for a few months.

● ●

Chapter 23

1970-1974

Our words flew off like arrows, as though we knew what was right and wrong. We clung to our own point of view, as though everything depended on it. And yet our opinions have no permanence; like autumn and winter, they gradually pass away.

Chuang Tsu - Inter Chapters Gia-Fu Feng and Jane English

Our little house on Hazen Street felt empty after Kita-san returned to Japan. The dojo also seemed emptier. The attendance at the dojo, which had been great when Kawakita Sensei arrived in December 1968, had dwindled to such a low point that I seriously thought about closing it. The "tough guys" who thought they couldn't learn karate without a Japanese instructor had been the first ones to leave the dojo because of the hard training Kita-san provided. During the year that he taught at the Yoseikan Dojo, Kita had broken no less than ten sets of ribs while sparring as well as creating numerous other injuries.

Ron Taylor, one of my black belts and a former United States Marine, was chosen to assist with three step sparring during our quarterly testing on March 14, 1970. Ron's job was to be the opponent for the white belts during the test. Ron would do the attacking as the white belts demonstrated their ability or lack of ability to defend themselves. One white belt kept hitting Ron during the counter-punch of the sequence – a few times were fairly hard.

I yelled, "Pull your punches!" several times, but to no avail.

Ron, being the country gentleman that he was, pulled his punches continually. I allowed them to continue the san-bon kumite for several sets. The white belt always hit Ron, even though he had been told to pull his punches.

It was obvious that Ron was beginning to get a little upset with the white belt. At the end of the seventh set, Ron completed his blocks then he counter-punched and knocked the white belt out. The test board had to stand up, and look over the desk to see the white belt lying on the floor. I thought of Tsuruoka Sensei's saying, "One 'Ouch!' is worth a thousand 'Be carefuls.'" That white belt had learned a valuable lesson.

Making several trips a year to Canada to train with Mas Tsuruoka Sensei in Toronto had become as natural as breathing. When I first started driving to Toronto, the trips seemed very long. I soon started seeing them as a pleasant way to spend a weekend. Occasionally I could wrangle three or four days off from work to drive to Tsuruoka's dojo. Tsuruoka Sensei would critique my kata by pointing out little areas where he thought I needed improvement. After two to three hours of kata and basics came kumite time. I always returned home with bruises I hadn't had prior to the trip.

Tsuruoka Sensei had adopted the European system of belt colors for the kyus. He still had six kyus, and his belt colors were white, yellow, orange, green, blue and brown. I adopted a modified color system for my nine kyu ranking system. I used white, yellow, and orange belts to designate ninth, eighth and seventh kyus, a green belt with stripes to designate sixth, fifth and fourth kyus, and a similar striping system to designate the third, second and first kyus, who wore brown belts.

At tournaments I divided participants into four divisions by belt rank. The white belt division was made up of white, yellow and orange belts. The green, brown, and black belt divisions were made up of first, second and third degree green, brown and black belts. The system worked well.

Several of the students expressed a desire to learn more about Buddhism – particularly Zen Buddhism – so Zen meditation services were started on Sundays. I founded the "Greater Cincinnati Zen Buddhist Society" and within a short time the attendance at meditation services grew to over a dozen people. Our services' format followed that with which I had become familiar in Japan:

Meditation – 45 minutes
Kinhin (walking meditation) – 5 minutes
Meditation – 45 minutes
Kinhin – 5 minutes
Sutra Chanting – 10 minutes
Teisho (lecture) – 5 minutes
Dhammapadda (Buddha's teaching) – 5 minutes
End

The two hours went by very quickly. Over a period of years, attendance

Vic Moore (left) squares off against Joe Lewis (right) in round-robin final match. The author - hands on knees - referees.

totaled over fifty people on several occasions.

Most of the classes at the dojo were spent on kata and basics. After a year of hard kumite my goal was to rebuild the dojo membership and put it on a sound financial footing. I received an invitation from Sensei Robert Trias of the United States Karate Association to be the chief referee of the USKA Grand National Championships, to be held in Anderson, Indiana. The tournament was sponsored by Glen Kenney, a friend of mine and an excellent karate-ka. Sensei Trias informed me about some trouble that had occurred at one of his tournaments earlier in the year. A contest between Joe Lewis and Victor Moore had turned into a "no-holds barred" brawl. Both men disliked each other immensely and Sensei Trias felt that I was one of the few referees who could keep both men in line. I had known Victor Moore since the beginning of his karate career – I was his teacher at the Yudan Dojo on Vine Street in Cincinnati. I did not know Joe Lewis but remembered him from the 1966 Nationals in Washington D. C. He was a hard, fast, no-nonsense type of fighter with devastating punches and kicks.

In the first match, Joe totally overpowered Vic Moore. He then prepared to fight Bill Wallace for the championship. Both men were in excellent condition and top form. Both had a great respect for each other's abilities and moved around the ring cautiously. They each threw several ineffectual techniques before, finally, Joe Lewis threw a reverse punch at Wallace's midsection. Bill simultaneously leaned forward throwing a lightning-quick backfist at Joe's temple. Bill's technique was a fraction of a second faster and won him the championship.

"Ippon!" I yelled as my hand shot up into the air toward Bill.

Joe Lewis had lost the championship by a fraction of a second. As far as I am concerned, he was then, and still is, my idea of the ultimate karate fighter. Bill Wallace is also one of the greatest karate fighters of his era. Joe Lewis, Bill Wallace and Victor Moore had all conducted themselves as perfect gentlemen during the contest. I gained a deeper respect for all of them.

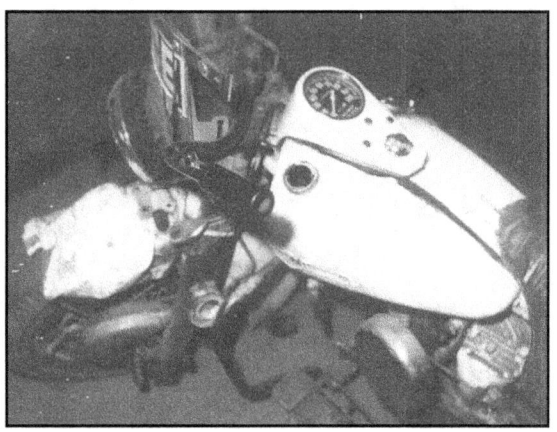

My motorcycle had the frame bent back of the seat. It was a total wreck. I was very lucky to have not been more seriously injured or even killed.

While I was visiting Sensei George VanHorne in Frankfort, Kentucky in July 1970, we discussed the need for a second basic kata which stressed reverse punches, hip rotation, the five basic blocks and front kicks. This brainstorming session resulted in our developing a kata that we named Taikyoku-nidan, now known as Taikyoku-ni. Taikyoku-ni became the second kata taught by the U. S. Chito-kai and was now the requirement for the 7th Kyu, orange belt test.

Wednesday, September 15, 1970 was a very eventful day in my life. At eleven o'clock that morning, while on duty with the police department, I stopped by the karate school to see my wife Barbara and to check on how the morning karate class was going. My motorcycle patrol area was in the vicinity of the dojo and I

1970-1974

would often stop by when things were slow. I parked the Harley Davidson motorcycle by the front door of the dojo keeping the radio on so I could hear it. I was only in the dojo for about two minutes when a radio call for backup was transmitted from a police cruiser only ten blocks away. They were in pursuit of a wanted suspect and needed assistance.

"I'll be back," I told Barbara as I ran out the door and jumped on the Harley. I had traveled seven blocks constantly changing my direction as I monitored my radio. I pulled in front of one police cruiser and was speeding through an intersection when a Ford Thunderbird failed to give me the right-of-way. I hit the car head on. I went over the handlebars shredding my left knee in the process. As I hit the windshield, my helmet was torn off and ended up at the next intersection. According to the other officers, I was thrown approximately twenty feet straight up then came crashing down on the rear of the T-Bird and bounced onto the street. I was stunned but conscious. I shook my head, and looked at my wristwatch – it was 11:20 AM. I couldn't believe my watch was still running.

The jinxed death cycle, Unit 917, had not killed me, I had killed it. It was destroyed. My left kneecap however, was shredded and would have to be reconstructed. Three weeks after the operation my knee would not bend properly. The doctor informed me that if my knee did not start bending soon I would need another operation. I went to the dojo and laid a heavy bag on the floor, in front of a makiwara. I put my left leg on the heavy bag, grabbed the makiwara and forced my leg to bend. I did this two to three times a day. Each time my knee would swell up and I would be forced to stop temporarily. To my doctor's amazement within two weeks my knee was bending properly. I would not need another operation.

While I was recovering I began thinking of ways to improve the karate school. I wanted to locate a building which I could buy, then rebuild it into a traditional dojo. I started checking the newspapers and real estate bulletins for property I could afford.

While I was out of commission I also planned to create a third Taikyoku kata. I felt that a third Taikyoku was needed to augment the first two. I wanted to combine lunge and reverse punches and speed up the timing of the punches to make them more realistic.

I returned to work on crutches five weeks after my operation. I was assigned duties in the office working in the traffic records section with Mary White, the traffic clerk. Later when I was able to walk without crutches I was fitted with a leg brace. By the last week of November, I was back in uniform on the street.

The building I purchased during March 1971 and for which I was unable to obtain a Building Permit.

I developed a third Taikyoku kata, Taikyoku San, after I was well enough to return to the dojo. Wearing a leg brace, I experimented with various techniques and selected those I felt would be the most beneficial to newer students. The third kata combined elements of the first two – hip thrust, hip rotation, punching, blocking and kicking – along with other more challenging movements.

During the last week of February an older student of mine, Arthur Rott, came to me and asked me if I wanted to purchase a building he had for sale on Martin Street. Art, a local businessman, was retiring and moving to Florida. He became aware of the fact that I was looking for a building one day when he heard me discussing the prospects with one of my ranking students.

Sensei Mamoru Yamamoto arrived at my dojo to spend a week and train with me before I had an opportunity to check out Art's building. Yamamoto, Barbara, and I trained together daily during the seven days that he was in Covington. On the last day of his visit, a Saturday, he presented me with two certificates from Chitose Sensei. The first was a Rokudan diploma; the other certificate was for the honorific title of "Renshi".

"Doomo arigatoo gozaimasu," I said, as I bowed and accepted the certificates. My students stood and clapped in appreciation.

Sunday afternoon, Barbara, Masao Morita and I drove Yamamoto Sensei to the

1970-1974

Greater Cincinnati Airport in Boone County, Kentucky. I thanked him for taking time to visit with us.

"Please tell Chitose Sensei that my promotion was totally unexpected but greatly appreciated and thank him for me," Morita-san translated for me.

Monday morning I rose, ate a small breakfast, then drove to 22 Martin Street. It was time for me to take a good look at Art's building. The building was just a shell, and not a complete shell at that. The west wall had not even been completed. There was no electricity, gas, water, plumbing or sewers. Upon entering the building it was possible to take a good look at the future west side of the building, which did not exist. It used the wall of the building next door as protection from the elements. It was going to take a tremendous amount of work before the building would be suitable for karate classes. However, the price was right and I couldn't afford anything else so I bought it. Art and I closed the deal on my birthday, March 15, 1971.

The police department was not going to replace the motorcycle that I had

The modern front of the Yoseikan U.S. Hombu as it is today.

totaled. I was reassigned to a Traffic Department car and worked the radar detail. My hours were excellent. I was assigned to work permanent first shift, leaving my evenings free for karate.

I had taken the Sergeant's test a year before but had heard nothing so I decided to enroll back into college on my nights off from the karate school. I enrolled at the University of Kentucky's Northern Extension College. The first course I took was police administration.

During May, a week before I was to complete my police administration course, I was promoted to Sergeant and transferred back to the patrol bureau. My shift commander was the person who had taught me how to ride a motorcycle, Bill Mason. Mason had been promoted to Lieutenant when I was promoted to Sergeant.

After purchasing the building at 22 Martin Street, I spent all of my limited spare time working on it to get it ready for classes. I was still paying rent to Mr. Herzog on the building at 813 Madison Avenue where the karate classes were currently being conducted. For a time, I was making monthly payments on the new building and paying rent to Mr. Herzog. I needed to come up with additional money so I could complete the repairs on the new building and transfer the karate club there. To cover the repair costs I sold a small motor home that Barbara and I had purchased a couple of years before. At the same time, I established a four-month timetable for having the new building ready for the transfer of classes.

My first major obstacle was the city of Covington. The city's Housing Department refused to give me a building permit. To them, the building was an eyesore and should be torn down. I argued with the bureaucrats but to no avail. In desperation I started building without the permit. To accomplish my four-month goal, I had to spend every waking moment at either the police department or the building on Martin St. I did not have the time to continue with college. There were many nights when Barbara and I spent the entire night installing large wooden beams that were to support large sheets of dry wall for the ceiling. Every night I would catch a couple of hours of sleep, a shower, then go back to the police department. After completing my shift at the department, it was back to Martin St., change clothes and dig the trench for the sewer lines in the front yard. Throughout this time Barbara was my most important helper. Some students would donate their time; however, they would only be there once or twice and I would not see them again.

Little Debbie was by now unofficially adopted by Barbara and I and she now went by the name of Debbie Dometrich. She worked side by side with Barbara and I as we struggled to get the building fit for habitation. Some of my students, such as Don Rigsby, Dennis Dickerson and others, also helped build the new dojo. Others, such as Maurice Prather, furnished much needed material and other items. Nothing would have been accomplished, however, without the help of my student Joe Schertler. During the five months that I was working on the new dojo and getting it ready for classes, Joe took charge and did seventy percent of the teaching at the Madison Avenue dojo.

Luck was with us during one stage of the construction. A young man stopped in one day as we were working and wondered what we were building.

"A karate school," I told him.

"I have always wanted to study karate," he said. Then he saw the two story unfinished concrete block wall. "Who's doing your block work?" he inquired.

"I guess I am," I responded.

"I am a professional block layer," he informed me.

Within five minutes, Christopher Alsip was a student working for his karate instruction by putting up the wall. One of the first things I did after I purchased the building was to clean up the front yard, which was an eyesore. I built a six-foot high wooden fence with a Japanese gate in the center. A small Japanese garden was scheduled for construction in front of the dojo after the interior work was finished.

The city building inspector paid me a visit in May and informed me that I was to stop building at once, or face a day in court since I had no building permit. I again attempted to obtain a building permit without success. I spoke to an attorney and then went to City Hall to visit with the city manager.

"I am going to file a 2.5 million dollar law suit against the city," I told him. "Who do I list on the lawsuit, you, the mayor, board of commissioners and the building inspector?"

"Hold on a minute," he told me. "What is this all about?"

"I am building a karate school and a Buddhist temple at 22 Martin Street. The building department won't issue me a permit. I either want a building permit today or a letter stating that that the city refuses to allow me, the founder of The Greater Cincinnati Zen Buddhist Society, to build a Buddhist temple at that location. If I get the permit, I will continue to build; if I don't get the permit, I'll see you in federal court. I intend to sue the city for religious discrimination."

He looked at me for a minute and said nothing.

"Can you wait until tomorrow for the permit?" he asked.

"No problem, and don't worry. When I'm finished, 22 Martin Street will be one of the best looking places in the city." I received the building permit the next day.

During July, Don Rigsby worked on the heating system and Denny Dickerson, an electrician, did the electrical work. A few others would come in to help get the building ready to occupy. I needed to make one last great effort so we could move into the new dojo by August 1st. During the last week I worked on the new dojo an average of twenty-two hours a day. Six days later, the dojo, while not finished, was at least ready to move into. During that last week I didn't have time to think about sleep; I was down to my last ounce of energy. The week also marked the end of these last and most difficult days of construction. During that week I had worked a total of one hundred and fifty some hours.

Front door of the Yoseikan Hombu Dojo in Covington, Kentucky. This is the same double door as is seen in the photo earlier in this chapter.

After working all night at the department I arrived home on Wednesday morning, July 28, 1971 at 7:00 AM. I had the next two days off and planned to rest and do absolutely nothing. We planned to move into the new dojo over the weekend. I sat on the couch to rest before going to bed. When I awoke it was 1:30 PM . . . on Thursday! I had slept thirty hours in a chair.

On August 1st we moved into our new dojo. It wasn't perfect, but it was ours. We would continue to build, add, and improve, far into the future.

Four of my students, Denny Dickerson, Sam and Minnie Morris and Cherie Stepaniak, along with Barbara and I, boarded a plane for Kumamoto, Japan in October 1971. Barbara and I refinanced our home to have enough money to make the trip and to have additional money for more repairs on the new dojo.

We checked in at the Keio Plaza Hotel after we landed in Tokyo. I looked up

1970-1974

Hanshi Gogen Yamaguchi, Head of Japanese Goju-ryu, received us with a warm welcome and took us on a tour of his dojo in Tokyo.

a Buddhist priest named Akagawa, a friend of Sensei Takayoshi Nagamine. We walked to a local restaurant to eat sushi and drink some beer. He ate a lot of sushi and drank a little beer. I on the other hand ate a little sushi and drank a lot of beer.

The next day we caught a cab and made our way to the home and dojo of "The Cat", Gogen Yamaguchi. Walking up the path from the large main gate, we were met by Mrs. Yamaguchi, Sensei's wife. "Chotto matte," she said to us. A couple of minutes later Yamaguchi Sensei, along with his little dog, came out to greet us and invited us to come inside. I told him that I was a student of Tsuyoshi Chitose. This brought a smile to his face; he informed us that he and Chitose Sensei had been friends for many years. We were given a complete tour of the dojo – all three floors of it. Upon completion of our tour several students were starting to arrive for class. Yamaguchi Sensei invited us to stay and observe a class. As we were getting ready to leave, he presented me with an autographed copy of his book "Karate - Goju-ryu by the Cat." His eighteen-year-old daughter, Wakako, went with us by bus to the local taxi stand. She was to ensure that we got back to the Keio Plaza without getting lost.

We caught the train to Kumamoto the next morning. The train would allow my wife and students to see what Japan really looked like. From 30,000 feet all countries look pretty much the same.

Chitose Sensei and several of his students, including Masaru Inomoto, Hidemichi Kugizaki, Hironi Minoda, and many others met us at the Kumamoto train station. I asked how Shirahama Sensei was doing. Chitose Sensei hung his head for a moment before answering.

"Shirahama Sensei died of cancer in 1967." he said sadly.

The thought of the loss of Shirahama Sensei caught me by surprise. "Is Mary Shigamoto OK?" I inquired.

"I spoke to her last week and told her you were coming to visit me." Chitose Sensei answered. "Now that you have arrived I will phone her and invite her to visit."

Photo taken by the author of Yamaguchi Gogen at his home in Tokyo in 1971

"How is Ito-san?" I inquired.

"I don't know." Chitose answered. "It has been several years since I have seen him."

We were transported in several automobiles to Chitose Sensei's home at 175 Matsuzaki Shimizu Machi. Chitose Sensei and his family graciously made room for us in their home during the short time we were there. After getting settled we rested for the remainder of the day fighting off the last effects of jet lag.

The next morning after eating a great breakfast, Sensei said we should go and train. We dressed in our karate-gis and met Sensei in the back yard for practice. Being back in Japan and training with Chitose Sensei again brought back fond memories of my training there as a teenager. We practiced kata all morning. Sensei pointed out the areas where we needed improvement and we followed along. Helping Sensei with the training were Nakahara Sensei and two of Sensei's younger students, Seino-san and Watanabe-san, who were both in their twenties. After completing our last kata, Potsai, we stopped for a lunch break.

Chitose Sensei said he wanted to take us on a tour of Kumamoto Castle. After

Arriving at the Kumamoto train station. Left to right: Unknown, Kugizaki, Inomoto, Minota, Dr. Chitose, the author, Barbara Dometrich, Denny Dickerson, Cheri Stepaniak, Minnie Morris, Sam Morris, Unknown.

lunch Chitose Sensei, Barbara, Miako-san (Sensei's twenty-four-year-old daughter and our driver) and I got into Sensei's Toyota sedan for the trip.

The other students climbed into the two remaining vehicles for the trip to the castle. We spent the entire afternoon sightseeing, touring, taking photographs, buying souvenirs and soaking up Japanese history.

After supper, we dressed in our karate-gis again as we prepared for more training. Nakahara Sensei, Seino and Watanabe had returned. Hidemichi Kugizaki, one of Chitose Sensei's better and more dedicated students and instructors, also arrived to train with us.

Starting with the kata Chinto, we progressed to Sochin kata. Chitose Sensei also taught us "bunkai" (basic defense applications) from the katas. We trained until it got dark, at which point Nakahara Sensei and Kugizaki Sensei bid us good night and went home.

Chitose Sensei's bathroom was very small and the girls were invited to use his small hot tub. Denny Dickerson, Sam Morris and I traveled to the local hot bath with Seino and Watanabe. On our way to the baths, Seino stopped to get four large bottles of Asahi beer. Up to our necks in hot water, four of us drank beer from paper cups. Sam, being a non-drinker, got a soda from the local vending machine.

Chitose Sensei thought that Barbara and I should get remarried in a Japanese ceremony while we were in Japan. The next day he located a kimono for her, and the proper attire for me so we could fulfill his wishes.

We spent the majority of our time the day after that training in the back yard. Cherie and Kugizaki gravitated to a corner of the yard and practiced a double bo kata. Denny, Sam, Barbara and I trained with Chitose Sensei on kata. Sam's wife Minnie was in the kitchen with Mrs. Chitose showing her how to cook southern fried chicken.

A quaint sight of contrast in downtown Kumamoto. Monks crossing the street give a sign of greeting with a large Coca Cola sign in the background.

Early the next morning Chitose Sensei and I took time to discuss the U. S. Chito-kai. I briefed him about the new nine-kyu system I had adopted and the reason for it. Next I explained my reasons for adopting the Taikyoku katas, their use and development. Then I demonstrated the katas to him. When my students reached the rank of 6th Kyu, they were taught the historical Chito-ryu kata. He agreed to allow me to use the Taikyoku kata, then reminded me that seisan dachi was a more practical stance than the lower and longer stance of zenkutsu dachi. I assured Sensei that I realized seisan was more practical; the goal of the Taikyoku katas was to develop leg strength, hip rotation and hip vibration. When he had visited with me in Kentucky during 1967, I had told him I would build a good U. S. Chito-kai Honbu. I now told him about the new dojo on Martin Street and showed him some photographs of the new Yoseikan. He was very pleased with the new location and acknowledged that the U.S. Chito-kai had come a long way in only four years.

Chitose Sensei made a request which I felt was too great an honor and I refused. He wanted for me to go downtown to Kumamoto with him and to legally change my name to "Tsuyoshi Chitose."

Japanese wedding photo taken in Kumamoto, Japan, during October 1971.

"Sensei, this is indeed a great honor but I can't do that," I told him as I turned down his request. At that time I did had not have the slightest idea as to why he would want to do such a thing. Only years later would I understand his motive.

I had four ranking black belts in the United States in October 1971. All were Ni-dan. I had been tight with promotions, even though mine had come rather easily, since I did not want Chito-ryu to become a laughing stock in the United States. At the same time, I worried about who would be prepared to run the organization if something should happen to me. My motorcycle wreck was still fresh in my mind even after a year and I realized that I needed a person who would keep an eye on things in the event that I got sick or something happened to me at the department. So I nominated Charlie Williams, an older student who had started with me in 1963, to be elevated to the rank of yon-dan. After explaining my reasoning, Chitose Sensei agreed. I paid for Charlie's promotion myself and upon returning to the states, I awarded Charlie his promotion; I never asked him to reimburse me for the cost of his promotion.

We stayed at Chitose Sensei's house and trained for a few more days. Mary Shigamoto arrived on Thursday to visit me. We spent a pleasant day together reminiscing about my early training in Japan. I felt very honored that she had traveled so far to visit me. She looked tired and informed me that she had cancer. As the three of us reminisced, some of the memories caused paroxysms of laughter. With Mary there to visit with us and watch us train in the back yard, the day seemed to fly by.

We finished training just as it got dark on Thursday. Upon entering Sensei's home for a snack, Chitose Sensei handed me a telephone. I looked at Mary. She

Training in the kata Potsai (Bassai) in O-Sensei's back yard. Left to right: Cherie Stepaniak, Dr. Chitose, the author, Dennis Dickerson.

explained the problem that Chitose Sensei was having with Yamamoto.

Chitose Sensei was having some difficulty with Yamamoto Sensei. Yamamoto Sensei headed a group of Chito-ryu dojos called the Yoshukan. Yamamoto had, without consulting Chitose Sensei, changed the name "Yoshukan" to "Yoshukai". This change was a direct slap in the face to Chitose Sensei. One "kai" cannot be a part of another "kai." By changing the last Japanese character from "Kan" to "Kai", Yamamoto had elevated himself in authority and importance to the same level as Chitose Sensei. Chitose Sensei had no Japanese students who would confront Yamamoto about his breach of etiquette, even on the telephone.

"You! Dometrichi, Yamamoto, call, talk, Yamamoto. Yamamoto, good boy OK, no good boy, out Chito-kai."

"Tell Sensei I can't do that." I said to Mary. "Tell him that I will not talk to Yamamoto on the telephone."

It was obvious that Chitose Sensei understood – he looked at the floor disheartened.

"I must travel to Yamamoto Sensei's dojo to see him in person. I need to talk to him face-to-face," I said.

Mary informed Sensei about what I had told to her.

"Good boy." Chitose said smiling as he patted me on arm.

"It is getting late and I have a long way to travel," Mary said as she rose to leave. I thanked her for coming to visit with me at Sensei's home and to meet my wife and students.

"Is there anything I can do for you?" I asked her.

"Bill-san, you know what type of food I miss most from America? Candy corn and the big German pretzels I used to get when I was a child at the baseball park in Cincinnati. If you could send me some pretzels and some candy corn I would really appreciate it."

"When I return to Kentucky, I'll send you some candy corn and large pretzels," I assured her.

Dr. Chitose trains with one of his top students, Hidemichi Kugizaki.

I bid Mary good-bye, kissed her cheek, and gave her a hug as she prepared to leave. Sadly, I knew I would never see her again.

The next day Chitose Sensei, his students, along with my students and myself, drove to a local park for a karate demonstration. Denny Dickerson took his Sho-dan test. He was required to do three kata, demonstrate basics, and after sparring with both Seino and Watanabe, he passed. Chitose Sensei presented him with a black belt certificate. I presented Chitose Sensei with an oil painting of himself, which was done by one of my students. Then I was called forward. I stood before Chitose Sensei and Nakahara Sensei. Two large certificates were handed to Chitose Sensei. A short speech was made and I was promoted to Shichi-dan (7th Dan). I was also awarded the title of Kyoshi.

All of this happened less than seven months after I had been promoted to Roku-dan. I had been a karate student for nineteen years. Sooner or later my

Standing before Chitose Sensei in 1971 and receiving my 7th Dan diploma along with the title of Kyoshi. Nakahara Sensei is looking on and my wife Barbara is in the background.

promotions would level out. Little did I know that twenty-eight years later, I would still be a seventh dan. Barbara tested before the Japanese Chito-kai Test Board and was promoted to Ni-dan.

Two days later Barbara, my students and I boarded a train for the trip to Kita Kyushu and Yamamoto's dojo. I telephoned Kazunori Kawakita to inform him that I was coming to speak to Yamamoto and that I would need a good translator when I arrived to talk with him.

Upon our arrival at Kita Kyushu, Yamamoto Sensei, Kita-san and several of Yamamoto's students met our train at the station. Our luggage was loaded in the rear of some small trucks. A short time later we pulled up in front of Yamamoto's dojo.

"Hold it!" I yelled. "None of my students are to go in – only me. After Yamamoto Sensei and I talk and reach some type of agreement, you may go in. If we do not reach an agreement we will return to the train station for the train to Tokyo tonight."

We walked through the dojo to his home, which was in the rear of the building. We sat on the floor in the little kitchen. Yamamoto sat across from me, Kita sat beside him and the little Japanese who was to translate was seated on my right.

After some small talk, I looked at the translator and told him, "Tell Yamamoto

Japanese students of Chito-ryu bow to the author at the left, November 1971.

I am going to speak to him in truth. If he speaks to me in truth, I may not agree, but I will respect him and stay in his dojo. If he lies, my students and I will refuse to stay in his dojo."

Suddenly the little translator was on all fours crawling away from me toward

Dennis "Denny" Dickerson testing for Sho-dan and fighting Seino Sensei (1971).

the side door of the kitchen. I grabbed him by his belt and asked him where he was going. "If I tell him that he may hit me," came the reply.

"I am closer than he is, and if you do not tell him, I will hit you," I told him.

Right center is Chitose Sensei, over his left shoulder is his daughter Meiko, to his right is Barbara. The author is on the left taking a bite of lunch.

"Remind Yamamoto that these are my words and not yours."

Yamamoto looked at me, he held up his index finger. "Me one tongue, not two tongue," he stated.

An hour later Yamamoto and I had discussed the pros and cons of his dojo's name change from Kan to Kai.

Yamamoto felt that it was time for him to move on. He wanted to do his own thing.

"Do you know everything about karate?" I asked bluntly.

"No," he admitted.

"When I have a question, I go to my karate father, Chitose Sensei," I said. "Who are you going to go to now?"

"I don't know," he said sadly.

I decided that at least we had been candid with each other and my students could come in. We stayed at the Yamamoto home for two days; then with Yamamoto and some of his students we headed to the city of Miyazaki in three cars. We were to assist with a demonstration. From Kita Kyushu we headed southeast – our trip would take us through Beppu city.

We arrived in Beppu at night. Barbara and I rode in the lead with Yamamoto Sensei and the driver. Our driver, not being familiar with Beppu, got lost. At one point I said, "Migi!" and the driver made a right turn.

Beppu city had changed a little since I had been stationed there seventeen years earlier, but I could still recognize most of the streets in the city.

"Massugu," (Straight.) I told him. After we traveled a little further, I said: "Migi," and we turned onto the main highway, which led south to Oita. It was nice to see Beppu again but I wish we had had time to visit Beppu in the daylight.

At Miyazaki, the demonstration went very well except for one major problem. Kita-san broke his foot attempting to back kick through a block of ice not much

Dinner at Mamoru Yamamoto's house in Kita Kyushu, Japan, 1971.

smaller than a telephone booth. We spent the night at Yamamoto's father's home. The next morning I rose early and took a walk around the small town. A little grocery store was open early so I purchased some cookies and a Coca Cola.

"You karate boy?" the little storeowner asked, in very understandable English.

"Hai," I replied.

"You Yamamoto house stay?" he asked.

"Hai," I answered again.

"Me brother karate boy," he told me.

"Everybody's brother is a karate expert," I thought to myself. I ate my cookies and drank my Coke. As our conversation progressed, I learned that his big brother was none other than "The Cat", Gogen Yamaguchi himself!

"May I get a photo with you?" I asked.

He asked one of the women heading out to work in the rice fields if she would take our picture. She consented so I handed her my camera and the rest is history.

We left the town after breakfast and headed for Mount Kirishima, a resort where we spent the day enjoying the hot baths. We stopped at the home of Akira Tsuruda Sensei, a 7th dan student of Chitose Sensei. Many karate people arrived and we had a beer party late into the night. Seated on the floor, I could hear someone talking about Chitose Sensei and it was not flattering. My Japanese language skills were very poor, but not so poor that I couldn't pick up the drift of the conversation. I slammed my hand down onto the table – hard.

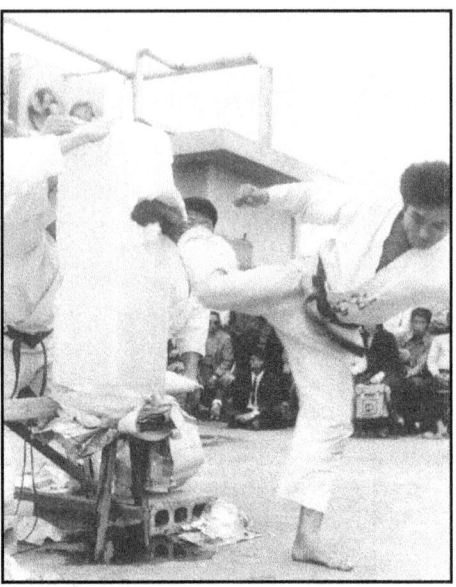

Kazunori Kawakita broke his foot at the demonstration during his third attempt at kicking a large block of ice.

"Yakimushi!" (Shut up!) I yelled loudly. "Chitose Sensei, watashi no Sensei. Yakimushi!" (Chitose Sensei is my teacher, shut up!) The talking ceased immediately. When it did resume, it was much more subdued and I do not think Chitose Sensei continued to be the object of the conversation.

Three days later we arrived in Tokyo with Yamamoto. We were to attend the annual Kyokushinkai tournament at the Taikan. I met Mas O-Yama again and reminded him that I had first met him in Madison Square Garden in New York approximately ten years before.

Denny Dickerson had been entered in the tournament by Yamamoto Sensei and was scheduled to fight in the full contact tournament in Tokyo just one week after being promoted to Sho-dan. Denny fought three matches before he was defeated. Between each match the remaining contestants were required to demonstrate "Tameshiwari" (breaking of boards). After Denny was defeated we caught a taxi to the Budokan where the FAJKO (Federation of All Japan Karate-do Organizations) was sponsoring a tournament. There were many more prominent Sensei there – including Gogen Yamaguchi, Masatoshi Nakayama, Hidenori Otsuka, and many others.

The next day I returned to Gogen Yamaguchi's home and showed him a photo I had taken while in Miyazaki. He looked, squinted his eyes and finally took his reading glasses from the sleeve of his kimono and looked at the photo again. He laughed and thought it was very funny that I had met his little brother in Miyazaki.

After returning to the United States I made plans to expand the Chito-ryu within the Greater Cincinnati area. In January, Yukinori Kugimiya, a student of Chitose Sensei, arrived in Covington, Kentucky. He reminded me of what Chitose Sensei must have been like when he was a young man. Kugimiya was a nice, polite, man with excellent karate technique. His arrival proved a blessing. No sooner had he arrived than I suffered a severe lung infection, which kept me from working at the department or the dojo for over two weeks. Kugimiya cheerfully taught the classes at the dojo and we were made aware of all of the kata modifications, which seemed to be a never-ending process. After I was released from the hospital, Kugimiya and I did get several opportunities to train together before he left to visit his brother in California.

Photo of myself with Sensei Gogen Yamaguchi's little brother at the family store in Miyazaki, Japan.

During the latter part of 1972 Debbie joined the Air Force and shipped out to Lackland Air Force Base in Texas for her basic training. Upon her completion of basic training, she was assigned to Rickenbacker A.F.B. at Colombus, Ohio. She did there exactly what she had done with karate; she excelled in every aspect of her training. A couple of months after she was assigned to Rickenbacker A.F.B., she started a bi-weekly karate class at the base gymnasium, which soon attracted

Photo taken at a farewell dinner for Sensei Kugimiya. Left to right: Yukinori Kugimiya, Devorah "Yoshiko" (Dometrich) Wear, Takayoshi Nagamine (son of Shoshin Nagamine - Chairman of the Okinawan Karate Federation), the author, Barbara Dometrich.

several dedicated students.

In the fall of 1972, I started a college karate course at Thomas More College. I was given the opportunity to teach the course for credit. The first class at Thomas More drew forty-four students to the new karate club. It was then that I started making plans for another class at Northern Kentucky University. I met with Dr. James Claypool who gave me the final approval to start a karate course for credit at NKU starting in January 1973.

The class at Northern Kentucky University attracted one hundred and thirty-three students to the first class. A month later I started the Cincinnati Athletic Club branch. The Cincinnati Athletic Club had a membership composed mostly of businessmen, doctors and lawyers who had offices in downtown Cincinnati.

I held a three-hour training clinic at Northern Kentucky University's Regents Hall in March 1973. There were three hundred and fifty-seven participants. After the clinic I decided that I could draw enough people to hold a tournament that would make enough money to send for Chitose Sensei. I chose a date in May for the tournament and wrote to Chitose Sensei. He agreed to attend the tournament.

I joined the AAU Karate movement on April 13, 1973, and brought five clubs into the organization with me. By April 23rd, all five clubs were certified as members by Ed Clott, the Ohio AAU Treasurer. At that time, Boone, Kenton and Campbell counties of Kentucky were in the Ohio AAU and not under the Kentucky AAU.

An election was held for Chairman of the Ohio AAU karate committee, which I won with a little over ninety two percent of the vote. At the same time a Kentucky AAU Chairman was elected. His name was George VanHorne Jr., a student of mine who had a dojo in the state capitol of Frankfort, Kentucky.

We were notified that a national AAU karate meeting was scheduled on May 11, 12 and 13 and was to be held in Albuquerque, New Mexico. We prepared to fly to New Mexico for the meeting. In New Mexico we were informed that we were to be assigned to groups of seven to eight people and each group was assigned a specific task. At this meeting I was informed that the existing alliance between the All American Karate Federation (AAKF) of Sensei Hidetaka Nishiyama was cancelled and that the AAKF could no longer claim it represented the AAU.

I felt extremely honored when I was chosen to be the chairman of the AAU karate organizational committee. Our task was defined as "To establish a national structure for an efficient and effective AAU karate organization which would provide for a tournament structure at the state, regional and national level." Provisions were made for a Junior Olympics, certification of officials, a Women's division, etc. This task took most of the day.

An early seminar at Northern Kentucky University where the students trained and got ready for Dr. Chitose's visit to the United States in April of 1973.

O-Sensei doing a kata at Northern Kentucky University in 1973.

The next day I was appointed as the chairman of the Officials and Contestants' Certification Committees. I was fortunate to have many very qualified sensei on both the Organizational and Official and Contestants' Certification Committees. Among them were; Robert A. Trias, Teruyuki Okazaki, Greer Golden, Ernest Lieb, Joe Corley, Ralph Castro, Caylor Adkins, Sam Allred, Don Buck, Wally Barber, Jack Coleman, Lynn Nichols and Gary Fredericks.

Finally, on the last day, we were informed that we did not have enough members present to make a quorum and because of this, a vote could not be taken for an AAU National Chairman. We would need to wait until the national AAU convention in West Yellowstone, Montana. This was to be held in October. Until then a temporary Chairman would be appointed. Ernie Lieb of Michigan was appointed to the position. Other assignments were: Tournament scheduling - Ralph Castro, Public relations - Chuck Portnick, Legal Section - Jon Evans, Finance Committee - Sam Allred, Women's Committee - Ann Small, Appeals Committee - Phillip Skornia, Juniors Committee and Administrative Committee - Don Buck, International Affairs – Dr. Don Small, Ranking and Time In Grade - Caylor Adkins. As mentioned before, I headed the Organizational and Official Certifications Committee. During the short tenure he had in office as Chairman, Ernie Lieb did a good job but he was not in the position long enough to leave his mark.

Chitose Sensei arrived in Kentucky with Hidemichi Kugizaki as his traveling companion during May after I returned from Albuquerque. Tsuruoka Sensei and

1970-1974

his wife Kay came to Kentucky, as did Shane Higashi from Canada. From California, Yukinori Kugimiya, a student of Dr. Chitose arrived a few days earlier. Shojiro Sugiyama of the Japan Karate Association of Chicago traveled to Northern Kentucky to visit and pay his respects to Dr. Chitose. Sensei Takayoshi Nagamine and Kiyoshi Nishime of the Okinawan Matsubayashi dojo in Cincinnati, Ohio, were also present. The tournament was a huge success with a crowd of over three thousand in attendance.

One night as Chitose Sensei and I sat in my kitchen I questioned him about religion.

"Chito-ryu," he answered bluntly.

"What do you think about God?" I asked.

Without hesitation he placed his index finger on the rim of an empty water glass sitting on the table. He tipped it on its side. "God is dead," he said with authority.

A second later, he placed the glass back into an upright position with his finger. "God lives," he exclaimed. He stood up, smiled down at me, and left the table.

A few days after the tournament, Chitose Sensei and Kugizaki Sensei flew to Toronto, Canada, and visited with Tsuruoka Sensei.

It was about this time that Charlie Williams, one of my students, approached Barbara and I and asked if we could hire him as a full time instructor. At this time he was working as a service manager for a Chevrolet new car dealership in Norwood, Ohio.

"I have never really thought about it," I told him. "Let me think about it for a couple of days."

After a few discussions Barbara, we both agreed to hire Charlie and pay him the exact same salary he was making at the car dealership.

"I can't furnish you a car like the dealer," I told him.

He assured me that he had no problem with the arrangements and I gave him a job at the dojo. Charlie got a pretty good deal because at the Chevrolet dealer he had to work forty or more hours a week. At the dojo his teaching schedule was one and a half hours on Monday and Wednesday, three hours on Tuesday and Thursday. I promised him every Friday, Saturday and Sunday off. Nine hours a week verses forty seemed like a pretty good deal.

Harry Jones, the landlord of the building which butted up against the dojo, approached me and offered to sell me his house at 20 Martin Street. We agreed on a price and I purchased the building for future expansion. I was now making plans to expand to the country and build another dojo surrounded by acres of land. One month later I purchased forty acres of land in Boone County, Kentucky.

Saturday, September 22nd, and Sunday, September 23rd, saw me driving to Toledo, Ohio, with some of my students to hold an AAU Official's Certification clinic at the University of Toledo. The clinic had been organized and scheduled by Doctor Don Small, a karate black belt and member of the faculty.

Photo taken in 1973. Standing are Barbara Dometrich and Hidemichi Kugizaki. Dr. Tsuyoshi Chitose is seated in the middle.

In October I drove to West Yellowstone, Montana, with my family and one of my black belt students, Charlie Hass, who assisted me with the driving. Upon our arrival on Sunday evening we checked into the Big Western Pine Motel. I was notified to relax and take it easy. The AAU meetings were not scheduled to start until Wednesday. On Tuesday afternoon, Don Buck notified me that the AAU Combative Sports Chairman (a full time position with the AAU which over-saw the sports of Judo, Boxing, Wrestling, and Karate), Mr. Jim Stevens, was going to hold a meeting at 9:00 PM at the Stage Coach Inn.

When I arrived at the Stage Coach Inn, I waited with a few others for Jim Stevens to show up. Finally, he came through the door and announced to us that he wanted to go somewhere else to talk. Don Buck, Caylor Adkins, Jon Evens, Ralph Castro, Don Small and I went with Jim Stevens to a bar to discuss the future of the American karate movement. We took some seats in a back room. After a couple of hours of small talk, Jim Stevens handed us each a piece of paper. He informed us that we were to write down the name of the person the group felt would make a good Chairman. The results were announced. Don Buck - 1 vote, Don Small - 2 votes, Dometrich - 3 votes. When Jim Stevens read these results I was surprised, but pleasantly so. I actually felt that I would have a chance to help American karate progress, to bring the major factions together and to make a contribution, just as I had wanted when I had first written the AAU ten years before. Almost as soon as the count was announced, Jim Stevens interrupted us. He informed those present: Buck, Adkins, Evans, Castro, myself and Dr. Don Small that the AAU thought that Dr. Small should be the nominee. At that time Don Buck asked Jim Stevens, "If you were going to hand pick your man, why did you have us meet with you and waste our time?" The group then got completely behind me, and the re-vote resulted in Dr. Small with 1 vote, while I now had 5. Jim Stevens still insisted that the AAU wanted Dr. Small and no one else. I saw the chance of a lifetime slipping away and did not know what to do. I showed a copy of my communications with the AAU ten years before to Jim Stevens but he was unmoved. Don Buck disgustedly shoved his chair back from the table and left the meeting and told everyone he was going to bed. I stayed, and to add insult to injury, Jim Stevens informed me that he would like for me to announce Dr. Small's nomination the next morning at the general meeting.

I arrived early the next morning for the general meeting. I was very tired, as I had spent most of the night walking the cold, windy, snowy streets of West Yellowstone licking my wounds. Soon everyone was present and the meeting was called to order. Like a good soldier I arose and placed Doctor Don Small's name in nomination and continued speaking. What I said was not pleasant as I admonished the hierarchy of the AAU for their back room dealings. I compared them with the problems going on in Washington D. C. with President Nixon. "Watergate has nothing on you," I told them. "You – yes all of you – speak to the youth of our country of fair play and sportsmanship, yet you conspire to rig our karate election. I have been told that what you are doing is legal under the AAU charter. It may be legal but it is highly suspect and immoral." The chairman rapped his gavel several times while I was speaking. I turned and looked at him coldly. "If you rap that gavel one more time while I am speaking I will come over there take it from you and shove it up a part of your body which has never seen sunshine," I said sternly. He put the gavel down. If you people wish to stay here and backstab each other, then go ahead and do so. Gichin Funakoshi did not need the AAU, my teacher Doctor Chitose did not need the AAU, and I don't need the AAU. I am going home and practice my kata. Goodbye." To my surprise I received a standing ovation as I left the room. Not everyone, however, was pleased. Dr. Don Small approached me as I was getting ready to leave.

"Bill! You have set the karate movement back twenty years," he stated.

"No, it is you and Jim Stevens who have set it back twenty years, and time will prove me correct."

After I returned to Covington, I continued to work at the Police Department and use my off time to work on the dojo. Because of all of the work we had to do at home and the dojo, 1973 seemed to fly by. Before I knew it, the Christmas season was here. Once again, because of long hours and lack of sleep, my weakened lungs failed me the day after Christmas. I passed out at home. I was taken to St. Elizabeth Hospital and put into intensive care. Some people thought that I had had a heart attack – I didn't. I had again developed walking pneumonia.

I was ordered by my doctor to report to Good Samaritan Hospital in Cincinnati for tests on the third day of January 1974. I was informed that I might have some serious problems and might have to stay in the hospital for two months of tests. Knowing that, I felt that hiring Charlie to a full-time position was a good decision. Some light snow fell as I gazed out of the hospital window. The snow began to build up as the temperature dropped.

I had several tests; various drugs were used in an attempt to overcome my lung condition. And yet, my lungs continued giving me trouble and I had a difficult time breathing. Toward the middle of January, I was informed by my doctor that I had developed chronic acute bronchial asthma. This was the good news. I also had a pseudomonas fungus in my lungs, which is incurable. Of the seventeen drugs the hospital tried on the disease, only two were partially successful in arresting it.

While I was in the hospital I received a telephone call from Chief Ralph Bosse. "Bill, how do you feel?"

"A little better," I answered.

"When you get out of the hospital, are you planning on returning to work?"

"Sure, Chief," I said. "I may be out earlier than expected."

"Well, I wanted you know that I am placing your name before the Board of Commissioners tonight for Lieutenant.

"Thanks, Chief," was all I could muster. Then as an after thought, "I will try to be back soon, Chief."

After one month I was released from the hospital and placed on special medication which, according to my doctor, might or might not help.

"The most important thing is to not overly tire yourself," the doctor told me. "I have also made arrangements for you to have your tonsils taken out."

I returned to the department as a patrol bureau shift commander. I had been on the department for ten years.

I was scheduled to have my tonsils removed during the last week of April. After they were removed I was given pain pills but I couldn't swallow them because my throat was so swollen. I could eat nothing except popsicles for a week. One day Barbara and I went to a movie in Cincinnati where she ordered some popcorn. It smelled so good that I couldn't resist. I ate one piece, no problem. Then another. Soon I had eaten most of the box. Thanks to the salt in the popcorn, two days later my throat was much better.

Barbara and I decided to take a vacation on June 1st and travel to Florida. I hooked our new travel trailer up to our new Plymouth for our trip. The night before we were to leave I worked all night on third shift. As we neared the Tennessee state line I was practically asleep at the wheel. Barbara told me to pull over and she would drive. Twenty-five miles later a flaw in the highway caused Barbara to lose control of the car on top of Jellico Mountain. Our car and the seventeen-foot trailer rolled over and slid down Interstate 75. The car and trailer came to a rest upside down, blocking all three lanes. Everyone was all right, but the trailer was totaled, and the car suffered extensive damage. My son, Billy, kicked the back door open. We crawled out and stood by the side of the road looking at the damage, thankful to be uninjured and alive.

I returned home, got the old jeep, bought a small camper, hitched it up and headed south. Nothing was going to interfere with my vacation. Billy decided to stay home with my mother. He had had enough vacation excitement to last

I am directing traffic after our wreck on Jellico Mountain in Tennessee during our first day of vacation, 1974.

him for the remainder of the year.

Shojiro Sugiyama Sensei invited our karate school to attend his A.A.K.F. (American Amateur Karate Federation) regional karate tournament in Chicago,

Illinois. Howard Fox, several other students from my school, and Debbie (who traveled from the Air Force Base in Columbus to meet us in Chicago) all entered the tournament. Howard broke his right hand during his final kumite match. However, he continued fighting and won the kumite Black Belt Championship. Debbie, in turn, won the Women's Black Belt Division for kata (there had been no Women's kumite at this tournament.)

Howard, Debbie, my wife and I drove to New Orleans five weeks later for the AAKF National Championships. Sensei Takayuki Mikami, a Shotokan stylist and member of the Japan Karate Association, was the tournament sponsor. Howard had a very bad cold, which gradually got worse as we headed south. Making matters worse, his broken hand had just started to heal.

Debbie Dometrich doing a fast snap kick at the Rickenbacker A.F.B. (1974).

Howard came in fifth nationally (which I felt was very good for a person with a broken hand and a 103 degree temperature). Debbie participated in the kata Division of the tournament and came in First, just as we expected. She was once again the National Kata Champion – it belonged to her.

Once the tournament was over I had the opportunity to go out and see New Orleans with Sensei Mikami in his Chevrolet Monte Carlo, along with Hidetaka Nishiyama, who sat in the right front seat, while Sensei's Richard Kim, Teruyuki Okazaki and I crowded into the small, cramped rear seat.

A few months after the tournament in New Orleans, Debbie received orders assigning her to the Kadena Air Force Base on Okinawa, Japan. A new chapter in her life was about to begin.

Chapter 24

1975-1979

The real hero is the man who fights, even though he is scared. Some get over their fright in a few minutes under fire, some take hours, for some it takes days. The real man never lets the fear of death overpower his sense of honor or his duty to his country.

General George S. Patton

A college professor, who was one of my older black belts, attended an educator's conference in Northern Ohio, at the University of Toledo. While he was at the conference, he was introduced to a professor at the university, Dr. Don Small. After engaging in small talk for a few minutes, their conversation turned to pastimes and hobbies. They were both surprised to learn that they had a mutual interest – karate. Dr. Small inquired as to who the visiting professor's teacher was.

"Bill Dometrich," my student answered.

"I know Bill," Dr. Small replied. "I haven't seen him since the AAU convention in Montana. Would you do me a favor? I would like to send him a short message, if you would be so kind as to deliver it for me?"

"I'll deliver it for you," my student said. "Sensei Dometrich will be glad to hear from you."

Taking one of his business cards from his shirt pocket, Dr. Small scribbled a short note on the back:

BILL, YOU WERE RIGHT, JIM STEVENS TOOK IT ALL.

Don S.

Upon receiving the business card a few days later, I read it with great interest. I thought that I understood the basic context of his short message, however, I was not one hundred percent positive. I wrote a letter to Dr. Small thanking him for his card and asking him to expound upon his statement on the back of it.

I received a detailed letter from Dr. Small dated March 3, 1975. In this letter he outlined many things which I had suspected about the AAU Convention of October 1973 but was not positive about. He told me that he had been introduced to members of the AAU hierarchy a full day before our meeting with Jim Stevens. Jim Stevens had introduced him to Olan Cassell, David Rivenes, Joseph Scalzo and other AAU officers as the "suitable" candidate to oppose Mr. Allen. In other words, he (Dr. Small) knew well in advance that he would be the chosen candidate. Dr. Small mentioned that he learned through pillow talks with his wife, Anne, that the reason Jim Stevens (the full-time AAU Combative Sports Chairman) chose Dr. Small for the Chairman's position was that he was controllable, unlike Allan, Don Buck or myself. Don also informed me in his letter that if Mr. Allan was elected, key AAU officials would arrange for his removal within a year – they accomplished their goal. A short time before the Washington, D.C. AAU Convention, Dr. Small (who by this time was totally disgruntled with the AAU hierarchy) learned that they were going to have Mr. Allan arrested if he showed up in Washington and refused to relinquish his chairmanship to Caylor Adkins. Dr. Small warned Mr. Allan about what was going to happen to him by telegram. This was the mysterious telegram that Mr. Allan showed to the AAU convention during October, 1975 meeting. As I read and reread the letter, I knew that I had made the right decision when I left the AAU. Dr. Small made short mention of the alleged relationship between his wife and Jim Stevens, except to state that it was a matter of public record. One of his last statements to the convention summed up the situation:

"As long as the AAU harbors Mr. Stevens, I cannot, for both personal and ethical reasons, participate in the organization."My doctor informed me I would have a better chance to overcome most of my lung problems if my family and I moved to Arizona. During the last part of February 1975, I took a three-week vacation from the department. I had purchased a two-year-old Lincoln Continental Town Car and Barbara and I packed it with our personal belongings and headed west to Phoenix. We were not positive if three weeks would be long enough to see a marked improvement in my breathing but we could at least look at the land and decide if it was a place where we would want to spend the rest of our lives.

When we arrived in Phoenix, we checked into a local motel and rested for a few hours. The short nap did us good; we arose, dressed in some sport clothes and drove across town to the karate school of a very good friend, Sensei Robert Trias, and visited with him. Trias received us with a smile and a hardy handshake. With Bob Trias, you got what you saw – a warm, hardheaded, blunt-speaking, Arizona hillbilly. People either liked Bob Trias a lot or they didn't like him at all. There was no middle ground with him. I really liked him and I considered him the true "Father of American Karate".

Sensei Trias made many contributions to American Karate: he was the first karate instructor in the United States, he was always frank and honest, and he was a true friend. Bob was never a phony – his word was his bond. If he told you something, that was it; he always kept his word. Bob's handshake was his seal. Barbara and I spent the remainder of the day talking with him about karate history and his most recent trips a few months earlier to Okinawa, Japan, and Europe.

I liked Arizona but Barbara was not impressed with the state or with the west in general. She felt, as the old cliché goes, "It's a nice place to visit, but I wouldn't want to live there."

After a couple of weeks of sightseeing, checking house prices, and visiting the local karate dojos, we started our long drive back to Kentucky. My breathing seemed like it had improved a little, but two weeks was too short of a time to be sure that the move would be beneficial to me. As we headed east, we decided to travel through Southern Texas where we would do some additional sightseeing. One of our stops was at Langtry, Texas, and the saloon of Judge Roy Beane.

Three weeks after Barbara and I returned to Covington from Texas, we adopted the cutest little brown and white dog – a wire-haired Jack Russell terrier named Moses. The owner had to move and was going to put him in the local dog pound if he couldn't find someone who would take him. Barbara took one look and fell in love with him. She nicknamed him "Mo Mo." Moses turned out to be a wonderful dog and one who would bring us many years of joy, love and entertainment. (Mo hated to take baths so if anyone asked him if he had to go to the bathroom, Mo would head for the hills. This was only one of Mo's idiosyncrasies.)

Shortly after Debbie arrived on Okinava I received a letter from her requesting any information I might have on Chito-ryu dojos on Okinawa, if any did in fact exist. I wrote Dr. Chitose and explained her problem to him, furnishing him with her military address at Kadena. Within a very short time I received a letter back from Chitose Sensei. He informed me that there were members of the Japanese Defence Force stationed on Okinawa who had studied Chito-ryu karate. One of them was a ranking Chito-ryu teacher, Sensei Masaru Inomoto. Sensei Inomoto contacted Debbie, she now had a Chito-ryu karate instructor, but even more importantly, she had also obtained a Japanese language teacher.

Shinken Taira pictured with O-Sensei Tsuyoshi Chitose.

A couple of weeks later I received a second letter from Debbie. Inomoto Sensei was also a student of Akamine Eisuke Sensei, a high-ranking Ryukyu kobudo teacher. After visiting Akamine Sensei's dojo, Debbie had sought admission but was refused membership by him. "Can you do anything to help me become a member of his dojo?" she implored me. "I feel that I must train in this art, it's so beautiful."

I wrote to Dr. Chitose explaining her problem and asked him if he could help her. Shortly thereafter, I received a letter from Debbie thanking me – she was now the first woman member of Akamine's dojo. Chitose Sensei had written to Akamine and informed him that I was like his son, and that Debbie, whom he had nicknamed Yoshiko, was like his grandaughter. Chitose was senior to Akamine's kobudo teacher, Shinken Taira. Out of respect for Chitose Sensei, Akamine accepted Debbie as his student.

The I.T.K.F. (International Traditional Karate Federation) World Tournament was scheduled to be held in Los Angeles, California. I flew there from my home in Kentucky and Debbie was flown there from Okinawa by the U. S. Air Force.

We were both on a small budget and secured lodging in the "Little Tokyo" area

Photo taken in the late 1970s of Akamine Sensei and Devorah (Dometrich) Herbst.

of L.A. Like everything else she had gotten involved in, Debbie had, in an amazingly short period of time, learned to speak fairly good Japanese.

After staying in Little Tokyo for one night, I telephoned my good friend Lt. Harvie Eubank to let him know we were in Los Angeles. A short time later, Harvie arrived and transported us to his home where he and his wife, Wanda, graciously put us up.

On my third day in L.A., I saw Takayoshi Nagamine who was in California to visit with Sensei Ota, an Okinawan sensei who had been a student of his father's.

Since Harvie and Wanda were working, Debbie and I caught a cab to attend an officials and contestants meeting at the Beverly Hills Hotel. By the time we arrived for the meeting, it had ended. The officials were crowding into the lobby. All of a sudden, Debbie was standing there eyeball to eyeball with Masatoshi Nakayama, Chief Instructor of the Japan Karate Association. She bowed very properly and spoke to him in Japanese. Surprised, he looked around and inquired as to who she was. Shojiro Sugiyama introduced me to Nakayama Sensei as her father and told him that we were friends of his.

It was over all too soon and Debbie and I parted at LAX; she returned to Okinawa and I headed east, back to Kentucky.

The next year flew by with the demands of the police department, teaching karate at the Yoseikan, Northern Kentucky University, Thomas More College, holding several clinics and hosting a U. S. Chito-kai tournament.

After the wreck on Jellico Mountain two years earlier, my son Bill decided that he would stay home with my mother while the rest of the family went on vacation in March, 1976. Bill, who was now almost twenty, had enrolled at Northern Kentucky University in Highland Heights. When not attending college classes or studying his lessons, he worked a part time job at a local pizza parlor. He never wanted to take time off from college or work. Barbara, Sherry and I packed our bright orange Volkswagen camper and with our dog Mo on board we headed west. We were going to visit the Mountain Home Air Force Base in Idaho. Barbara's brother, Sammy, was in the Air Force and was stationed there. As we drove toward the Rocky Mountains, we were thrilled by the majestic view. We were very fortunate during this trip; the only problem that we had to face was a flat tire. Luckily, I had a spare tire which, even though it had not been checked for a long time, had enough air to hold up until I was able to buy a replacement at a Chevron station in the next town. If it were not for the flat tire, our trip west would have been perfect.

We spent four days visiting and sightseeing with Sam, his wife Brenda, and their two daughters, Julie and Katie. Then Barb and I then headed south to Arizona and New Mexico. Our drive through New Mexico took us through Albuquerque where we learned of a little Zen Buddhist temple approximately forty miles north of Albuquerque. I aimed the Volkswagen camper north and drove into the mountains for a visit to the temple. The priest, whose name was

Early Jan/Feb 1973 at Columbus, OH. A classic "shotokan" head instructor Yuguchi Sensei, the author is to the right of Yuguchi. By Debbie is one of the Wilder brothers. Over my left shoulder is William "Bill" Swift. Over Yuguchi's left shoulder is Greer Golden. On the right are Senseis Milviski & Noveski of the Chicago area.

Gentei, and his wife both welcomed us with open arms. We spent the entire day at the temple. We meditated, chanted sutras, had lunch and talked at length with the head priest. Barbara and I offered to pay for our meal but the priests would never dream of taking our money in exchange for their hospitality.

"What can I do to repay you for your kindness?" I asked.

Gentei and his wife smiled. "Our cat, Troubles, just had several kittens and if you took just one of them off of our hands that would be a great help to us."

There were three kittens remaining in the litter and Gentei had already named them. One cat was named Daisy; she was white and yellow. Picasso was white, yellow, brown and black, and looked as if she had stepped out of a Picasso painting. The last kitten, a male, was named Sherlock. He was black and white. Sherlock, it seemed, was always in trouble. He loved to investigate the inside of shoes. He would go in headfirst then invariably get stuck and have to be rescued. He brought to mind the cartoon character, "Sylvester the Cat", with the addition of a white skunk stripe down the center of his back. Being a law enforcement officer, I naturally choose Sherlock. Our dog Mo had been raised with a litter of kittens and he loved cats. He immediately took charge of Sherlock, who became 'his' kitten.

Upon returning home I started rebuilding the house next to the dojo. The time had come to start expanding the karate school and its facilities. The classes at Northern Kentucky University and Thomas More College were going well, although attempting to work a full time job and teach eleven karate classes a week was beginning to take its toll on my health again.

The road leading to the forty-acre farm I had purchased was a mile and a half of dirt, rock and gravel that could only be traversed by a four wheel drive vehicle. I hired a private contractor to widen the road and pack the worst parts with gravel. The construction project on the road depleted all of the funds that I had allocated to build a new dojo in the country. So I found an old, white Ford F-250 four-wheel drive truck which would get me into and out of the farm regardless of the weather. I sold our Lincoln, bought the truck, and spent the remaining money on the road construction.

Barbara always demonstrated a great amount of technical skill. Later, she would hold black belt rank in Karate, Kendo and Iaido.

We continued to work on the dojo on Martin Street as we worked on the farm. No sooner was one project completed than we would start on another one. Since I had started teaching karate on Vine Street in Cincinnati over a decade before, I had taken no money for myself. All of the money we made went for the mortgage, dojo repairs, expansion of facilities, and now, for a mile and a half of road construction. On many occasions Barbara would need to use a portion of my paycheck from the department to cover the cost of the construction at the farm or the honbu. She never complained – she understood what my priorities were and are.

Barbara, George VanHorne, and another student started studying Kendo and Iaido under Professor Sadao Kotaka, an associate professor of biochemistry at

Barbara Dometrich (Mother of American Chito-ryu) training in Iaido.

Ohio University in Columbus, Ohio; he held Go-dan rank in both arts. Before moving to Ohio, Professor Kotaka taught at the University of California - Berkeley from 1959 to 1973. Barbara's first class in kendo and iaido was on March 6, 1976. George began on March 20. Kotaka Sensei was an outstanding teacher and very dedicated – he would drive from Columbus twice a month to teach at the Yoseikan – an hour and a half drive each way.

Barbara progressed rapidly and within a few years both she and George VanHorne had received their black belts in both kendo and iaido. Barbara, who always demonstrated great technical skill, also had something much better than mere technique. She possessed a keen mind and a no-nonsense attitude towards her martial arts training. She also had that trait which every true martial artist must have – heart. She would never back down or quit when training, regardless of injuries or her own personal exhaustion. During the mid and late 1960's, while in her thirties, she competed in several karate tournaments in the mid-west. When she was in her late forties, she competed in the United States National Kendo Championships at the University of Michigan - Ann Arbor, losing only one match to a yon-dan from Japan who had been the captain of his college kendo team.

While doing all of this, Barbara still managed to raise two children, work a full time job, and function as the chief administrator of the United States Chito-ryu Karate Federation. She became the "Mother of United States Chito-ryu", in name, spirit and deed. Chitose Sensei was extremely fond of "Bobbar-ah-san", as he affectionately referred to her. "Bobbar-ah-san good girl," he said, as he con-

Barbara, facing the camera, participating in the United States Kendo Championships at Ann Arbor, Michigan.

stantly reminded me of my good fortune in getting her to marry me.

Many years would pass before Barbara would receive the recognition she so richly deserved. During these years she toiled unselfishly, working many hours each week to assist the U. S. Chito-kai.

Debbie was getting discharged from the Air Force in 1977. She was to be mustered out at Luke Air Force base in Phoenix, Arizona. Barbara and I had purchased a three-year-old Lincoln Town Car and informed her that we would take a vacation, do some sightseeing and drive out to pick her up.

On our return we quickly found that we had another dojo guest. His name was Ken Sakamoto a student of Dr Chitose who would be staying with us for a while. I became extremely fond of Ken and soon came to look upon him as an extension of our family. Ken was large and solidly built for a Japanese, yet he was very flexible. He was very good at kata and exceptional in kumite. Within a very short time Ken and Debbie were dating, and soon it was announced that they planned to get married, which they did a few weeks later.

In October of that year, I received a telephone call from my Aunt Carrie, my mother's older sister, who lived in Fairmont, West Virginia. Both she and my mother lived together in her home in Fairmont. She had called me to tell me that my mother had died of a heart attack the night before. The funeral would take place in three days.

"I will be there," I said as I hung up – shocked.

"What's wrong?" Barbara inquired. She could tell from my face that something was wrong. With both of my parents now gone, I felt much older and I began to face the limitations of my own existence. Barbara, Billy, Sherry and I left the next morning for Fairmont to attend Mom's funeral.

I was nominated for captain at the police department and officially promoted during December 1977. I was assigned to the detective bureau as the Chief of Detectives, now officially known as Commander of the Crime Bureau. Prior to 1970, all promotions within the police department were based upon favoritism, or worse. A great many promotions were "bought" by bar owners who filtered money indirectly to certain city commissioners to promote police officers who could be easily "controlled" (bribed). After these officers were promoted they were expected to protect their benefactors.

The new Chief of Police, Ralph A. Bosse, the former Traffic Bureau Chief, despite being a product of this system, did attempt to do away with it. He introduced civil service examinations and review boards for all promotions through the rank of captain. I was the third Sergeant, the first Lieutenant and the first Captain to be promoted under the new civil service system.

After being promoted to Captain my new work hours were 8 AM to 4 PM Monday through Friday. I had every Saturday and Sunday off unless there was an emergency. The new hours were great, but they hampered my ability to continue teaching karate at both Northern Kentucky University and Thomas More College, so I turned both clubs over to Charlie Williams.

I was the Chief of Detectives for only six weeks before being re-assigned as the Commander of Police Services on January 2, 1978. Immediately after the beginning of 1978, the new city commissioners who had been elected in November were sworn in. A majority of the new commissioners were on the side of the mob. Over Chief Lyle Schwartz's objections, the commissioners appointed an older captain to the rank of Assistant Chief of Police and granted him the brand new title, "Sole Chief of Detectives", for life. Rumors ran rampant that a large

The author & wife Barbara in front of Akamine, Eisuke's dojo in Okinawa (1986).

payoff had been made to three of the commissioners by the local mob, who wanted to take over the city. My re-assignment put me in charge of the crime lab, property and evidence rooms, the records section and the crime prevention section of the department.

The permanent assignment of the Lieutenant Colonel and Assistant Chief of Police by the commissioners had tied the hands of Chief Schwartz. He was now unable to make specific assignments within the department. It was also obvious that certain members of the Commission were interested in getting rid of Chief Schwartz so that they could place their own man (the new Sole Chief of Detectives) in the top position of Chief of Police and open the city up to organized crime.

Covington was classified as a Class Two city under Kentucky law. Class One, Three, Four and Five cities could have their Chiefs of Police replaced fairly easily. For some unknown reason, the Kentucky Legislature made it nearly impossible to fire the Chief of Police of a Class Two city without court action. The commissioners who wanted to get rid of Chief Schwartz did not have the courage to take him to court. They did, however, put tremendous pressure on him to resign.

Even though I had been the Chief of the Crime Bureau, I was unaware that the FBI (Federal Bureau of Investigation) and the Kentucky State Police were each running an investigation of organized crime in Covington's government. Both investigations focused on mob influence, payoffs, obstruction of justice, and violations of the RICO (racketeering and organized crime) statutes.

The Kentucky State Police (and everyone within our department) were uninformed that the F.B.I. had an undercover operative functioning within the local mob. Tape recordings that he made were taken before a federal grand jury, where indictments were forthcoming against the new Assistant Chief of Police/Sole Chief of Detectives. News of the indictments hit Covington and the department like a bombshell. Within a short time, other indictments were lodged against the Assistant Chief, the Mayor, the Assistant Mayor, the City Manager, an Assistant Fire Chief and others. The former mayor was indicted on twenty-seven separate counts.

A few months passed before the Sole Chief of Detectives decided to resign before the trial. This would save his rights to a pension. If he were convicted before he resigned, he would lose his pension. By resigning in advance, even if he was convicted, he could keep his pension. The Chief had a wife and a young son to think of – his pension was important to all of them.

I was re-appointed Chief of Detectives by Chief Schwartz on July 28, 1978. My vacation was scheduled for the first week of August and the Chief told me to go ahead and take it. Barbara and I loaded our Volkswagen camper and with Sherry, our daughter, her friend Kim, Mo Mo the dog and our new French poodle, Prince, we headed south on I-75. Stopping for lunch at a Bob Evan's restaurant, we returned to our Volkswagen camper only to discover that it would not start. The starter motor had failed. So we pushed the camper to get it started. All the way to Florida, Barb, Sherry, Kim, and I took turns pushing the camper to get it going. After arriving in Orlando, a new starter motor was installed and our problem was solved – at least we hoped it was.

Kim had never been to Disney World and both she and Sherry had a good time. One day, while waiting in a long line at the "Hall of Presidents", I heard a familiar, deep voice from behind me. Behind us in the line was one of the Statler Brothers and his family. Sherry wanted to ask for an autograph, but I threatened to leave her stranded in Florida if she did.

"The guy is on vacation with his family," I told her. "Give him a break."

On our trip back to Kentucky I stopped at Valdosta, Georgia, to visit with Sensei Richard P. Baillargeon, a Shito-ryu stylist. At one time, Sensei Baillargeon had been a ni-dan in Chito-ryu karate. We spent a couple of hours discussing the current state of karate in the U.S.

When I returned to my duties at the police department, one of the things I did was check on the statistics of the crime bureau. I discovered that only nine and a half percent of the crimes committed had been solved. Since I had never been a detective I had a lot to learn. I spoke to each detective and asked what I could do to make the bureau run better and more efficiently.

"If you were Chief of Detectives," I asked, "what would you do to make the bureau's operations better?"

Almost to a man, I got the same answer. "Reduce the amount of paperwork we have to fill out daily." I went to the Cincinnati Police Department to gain some insight and new ideas in criminal investigation. After spending a week studying their procedures, I simplified the daily paperwork that each detective was required to complete.

After trimming the paperwork, I reorganized the Detective Bureau. I assigned each detective to special investigative areas. This enabled the detectives to get faster results and to see the end of a case, feeling a sense of accomplishment when a job was well done. Also, I could now hold each person responsible for the job to which he had been assigned. The new detective bureau was composed of squads that were responsible for investigating major crimes, burglary, arson, white-collar crime and documents, abuse of adults and children, and a petty crimes unit. The narcotics unit was a regional unit and was already in place. It was called, RENU (Regional Enforcement Narcotics Unit).

After the re-organization and easing the amount of paperwork done by each detective, I called a meeting of all the detectives to issue their new work guidelines.

"In the past the Chief of Detectives required each of you to document your work; every minute of every day was to be accounted for on paper. He did this to assure that you were working cases and not screwing off," I said to them. "You were so busy filling out paper work to CYA, you had no time left for work. Starting today you are going to operate under new rules. In the past you have been working without getting results. Your case clearance rate was a lousy 9.5 percent. Hell, the national average is 20.5 percent!" I continued.

The detectives all nodded in agreement.

"Starting today we are no longer work oriented. We are going to be results oriented. In short, I don't give a damn if you spend the entire month on a beach in Hawaii, as long as you get results and do the job. On the fifth working day of each month, however, I will review your work sheets and clearance rate files. I want results. I expect results. I demand results. And you are going to get results.

Debbie Dometrich graduating from the Kentucky Police Academy at Eastern Kentucky University in 1977. She is 26 years old.

If you are unable to get the results I want, I will transfer you back into the Patrol Bureau."

"Some days you will be required to put in long hours and work your butts off. On other days things will be slow and you can take it easy. There will be days when you want to skip a day and take it easy. If you do, see me and I'll arrange it, as long as you've been getting me results."

Six months later the bureau's clearance rate had jumped from an average of 9.5 percent of cases solved to an average of 31 percent solved. I had proved to them that I trusted them. I had turned them loose, let them think for themselves, and they had produced results far beyond my wildest dreams.

The marriage between Debbie and Ken Sakamoto didn't work out as they thought it would. He was a strong-willed Japanese who wanted an American wife who acted like a Japanese. She on the other hand had fallen for a Japanese man who she thought should act like an American. Regardless, it didn't work. Ken returned to Japan and would later marry one of Doctor Chitose's daughters, Reiko. Debbie became a police officer with the Fort Mitchell Police Department. Upon the completion of her four months at the Police Academy at Eastern Kentucky University in Richmond, Kentucky, Barbara and I drove down and participated in her graduation exercises.

As the investigation into city corruption expanded, I received several phone calls that included death threats. I left home for work early one morning and, later on, some "gutless wonder" came to my home and left a headless, gutted rabbit between my front door and the storm door. Barbara found the carcass when she left home later that day. Things were definitely starting to get rough.

I was on good terms with most of the criminal element in Covington. I never screwed them over or lied to them, and because of this we had developed a professional relationship. A few weeks after the rabbit incident I was told by three different people that there were rumors that a contract had been taken out on me. I then did something that I had never done before – I started carrying a back-up gun strapped to my ankle.

The trial had just started when it was declared a mistrial. Charges of intimidating witnesses and jury tampering came to the attention of the federal authorities. The trial was moved a hundred and sixty miles south to London, Kentucky.

I had been subpoenaed as a witness for the Assistant Chief of Police (Sole Chief of Detectives). His attorney, Howell Vincent, wanted me at the trial. I was confused by the subpoena. Police records relating to the case were also subpoenaed by his attorneys. I was ordered to locate the records in question and bring them to the federal courthouse in London, Kentucky.

I arrived with the records and waited in the hall until I would be called to testify. During a recess a few minutes before I was to take the witness stand, the Assistant Chief and his attorney reviewed the records that they had requested. Within minutes the attorney realized that the records he had subpoenaed would only hurt his case. I was told to return to Covington before I had the opportunity to testify.

Before leaving, I walked to a restaurant across the street from the federal courthouse and ate lunch. FBI agent Vince Behan saw me leaving the courthouse and followed me there. He wanted to know why I was leaving.

"I was told I'm not needed," I said.

"May I have the package that you have with you?"

"No, I can't give it to you," I replied. "I have been subpoenaed here by the defendant's attorney, it wouldn't be proper."

"I'll have to subpoena you," he told me. "I am asking you not to destroy the packet in your possession."

"I won't," I replied. "You subpoena me and I'll belong to you – package and all."

I left London, pointed my car north on I-75 and drove the one hundred and sixty miles back to Covington. After arriving at Police Headquarters, I reported to Chief Schwartz's office where I was handed a subpoena.

"Don't feel bad," he told me as he held up a second subpoena, "I have one too."

I went home to pack some clean clothes. The Chief and I drove south on I-75 back to London. The defendants, witnesses for the prosecution, and police officers were all billeted at the same motel. The Chief and I slept with revolvers under our pillows, just in case.

Those indicted in the federal courts were all found guilty. Most of those who were later indicted by the local courts were found not guilty because the Kentucky Commonwealth Attorney's Office had not handled the cases properly.

Our karate school received an invitation to participate in a karate tournament in Detroit which was being sponsored by Sensei James V. Morrone, Jr. and sanctioned by the American Amateur Karate Federation of Hidetaka Nishiyama. During the team competition, two of my fighters were hurt and were taken to the hospital. I had only two men left and I had to field a three-man team. I decided to compete for the first time in a long time, even though I realized that after the past year's court trials, I had had little time to practice and was not in shape. Being forty-four years old didn't help, either.

I drew an excellent fighter from Chicago, the current United States AAKF champion, Joe Gonzalez. Joe was famous for his foot sweep. Being a gentleman, he attempted to forfeit the match to me since I outranked him.

"I request that you award the match to Sensei Dometrich," he said to Nishiyama Sensei, the referee.

"No!" came Nishiyama's reply. "You fight!"

Joe, as expected, foot swept me twice during our fight. I knew that he was taking it easy on me. After his second foot sweep, he followed up with a fast hand technique and I was finished. Even though he defeated me, I still hold Joe in highest regard as a great karate man and as a great gentleman.

I received a telephone call late one night from Sensei Yukinori Kugimiya of Los Angeles.

"Can you meet Delta flight number 734 tomorrow morning at 9:30?" he wanted to know.

"Sure," I replied. "Who's coming in?"

"Kuzahara Sensei," he informed me.

"Who is Kuzahara Sensei?"

"One of Chitose Sensei's san-dans."

The next morning I met Sensei Kuzahara of Kumamoto, Japan, at the Delta gate at the Greater Cincinnati airport.

He announced that he was going to visit us for a few days. The few days became a week, then two weeks. After six months, the U. S. immigrations department insisted that Kuzahara go home – he had worn out his welcome (with the US government), and his visa.

Another guest from Kumamoto arrived while Kuzahara was staying with us. Yasuhiro Chitose (Chitose Sensei's son), whom we referred to as "Waka" (Young One), came to visit. A clinic at Northern Kentucky University's Regents Hall was organized in his honor. Waka taught a very detailed class on basics. He also instructed us in a new method of doing certain movements in the Potsai kata. He emphasized hip snap at certain locations to increase the speed and kime of some series of movements. Yasuhiro also coached us in a new method of doing Seisan dachi to increase the strength of the stance. He told us to squeeze our knees together as if holding a ball between them.

Word of the Iranian hostage crisis was flashed on the television as Waka, Kuzahara, and I, were sitting in my living room. I felt so embarrassed that my country was letting them get away with this and not taking immediate military action. It did look, however, like military action might be a future option. A week after the hostage incident, I drove to the Army recruiting station to re-enlist in the army reserves. I completed the paperwork and took my physical. Three weeks later I was sworn in as a member of the 259th Military Intelligence Company. I was forty-four years old.

• •

Chapter 25

1980-1984

When I die, do not weep or care, for my end will be as pure as a snowflake, which dissolves into the air.

Buddhist Saying

In Japan, kangeiko (winter training) took place during January, the coldest month of the year, and was scheduled to run from 6:00 AM - 7:00 AM each morning. The students and instructors arrived at the frigid dojo (because the heat was turned off) early in the morning. They would endure the cold, hard training as a method of strengthening their spirit. Some of the dojos included a barefoot run through the cold, snowy streets, wearing only a thin, sweat-soaked karate uniform. No one expected to learn new techniques during this training, but each one expected to polish the techniques he (and, in some cases, she) had already learned.

I wanted to initiate a type of kangeiko training at the Covington dojo but I realized that the format used in Japan had to be changed. Many students from Chito-ryu branch dojos expressed a desire to attend. Because of the great distances involved for many American students to travel to the Yoseikan, I made the kangeiko a one-day affair.

The first kangeiko of the United States Chito-kai was held on January 25 - 26, 1980. The weather was ideal. Snow had fallen and was piled two feet deep in front of the dojo. The thermometer dropped to fifteen degrees above zero. I couldn't have asked for better conditions.

The students checked in between 6:00 PM and 10:00 PM on Friday evening. They were awakened at 2:45 AM Saturday. The heat was turned off and the dojo clocks were removed from the walls. I didn't want the students to know how long they had been training or, more importantly, how long they had to train before the class would be over.

Formal training started at 3:00 AM and continued for six hours. Kangeiko started with fifteen minutes of zazen (seated meditation) followed by one thousand punches and kicks from the shiko dachi stance. As with most buildings with flat roofs, our roof was in need of constant repair. The roof had two leaks and buckets were placed on the training area to catch the water. The bucket closest to the restroom area had water in it while the bucket closest to the rear of the dojo had ice in it. The temperature in the training area fluctuated somewhere between the mid-twenties and the mid-forties.

The author standing in front of the Yoseikan Dojo a few minutes after completing Kangeiko, 1980.

After the thousand kicks and punches, additional vigorous exercises were done. As the second hour of training started, there was not a dry karate uniform in the dojo. Small steam clouds formed around the heads of the students as their warm bodies moved through the chilled air. The steam vapor rose to the ceiling, condensed on the cold metal grid work, and fell onto the students and the floor. (We had not insulated the ceiling between the dropped ceiling and the roof and the metal grid was extremely cold.) I could not believe my eyes – it was actually raining inside the dojo! The effect was that of a spring rain falling indoors. Towels were constantly being used to wipe up the water as training continued. We worked at full speed, performing basic punches, blocks and kicks. At 8:30 AM the students started running in circles around the training area, then they followed me out the back door of the dojo. We ran barefooted around to the front of the dojo and up Martin Street to Madison Avenue. The temperature outside had dropped to eight degrees above zero. We ran north up Madison Avenue. What a sight! Over twenty karate-ka running barefoot through the snow at near zero degree weather. We looked like a little cloud of steam that had miraculously sprouted feet.

Standing at the bus stop in front of Robke Chevrolet was a lone figure bundled up against the cold. He heard our bare feet and glanced in our direction. I saw a look of fear in his eyes as he saw the cloud, filled with crazy, barefooted people advancing toward him.

"Good morning!" I said.

"Good morning!" he answered with a surprised look as we ran past on our way to 12th Street.

We turned right onto 12th Street and started chanting a cadence like soldiers do when they run.

"We'll run all day and run all night.

We'll build our spirit and make it right.

We'll complete the run or we will die,

We are the members of the Chito-kai."

As we turned and ran south on Scott Street, the cadence changed to yelling out letters each time our left foot struck the ground, almost like cheerleaders leading the crowd at a football game.

"K - A - R - A - T - E", then we yelled "Karate!"

After that we started in with: "Y - O - S - E - I - K - A - N", then we would shout "Yoseikan!"

We entered the dojo through the back door. A couple of towels had been placed on the floor so we could wipe the snow and water from our frozen, discolored feet.

We bowed out of the Kangeiko, said the SHOWA and prepared to eat breakfast. Barbara and some of the women, plus a few moms had prepared a large breakfast for the participants. Our first kangeiko was a huge success – it has never been equaled in difficulty.

Two months after kangeiko, in March 1980, Barbara informed me that the karate dojo was in financial trouble with the Kenton County Sheriff's Department and the Internal Revenue Service. We did not have enough money to pay two mortgages, the gas and electric, water and sanitation bills, or the taxes. Since we were short on funds, Barbara had opted to pay the daily expenses and had neglected the taxes, hoping to catch up later, but the money never appeared and she never did catch up. Now we were in real trouble.

A few months earlier, Barbara had mentioned that we were having financial problems, but I had not given the matter my full attention. A few of the city's corruption investigations and trials had been going on at that time; I was busy with the trials and paid little attention to her. She never elaborated and I never fully appreciated the extent of the problem; I should have paid more attention.

Once she explained everything in detail, I realized for the first time the true extent of our financial problems. We owed taxes to the county for property tax, and the federal government for FICA and social security taxes. One of my black belts, Steve Crowley, a sho-dan, was a deputy sheriff. He agreed to pull the sheriff's paperwork, giving me an extra week to raise the money. I borrowed money from the police credit union and paid the sheriff, but I would need more time to be able to satisfy the IRS.

On Tuesday I drove to the IRS office in Elsmere, Kentucky for an appointment. I was unsure of the actual amount I would have to raise, but that didn't last long. The dojo, meaning Barbara and I, was over three thousand dollars behind in federal taxes.

Both pieces of property had originally been purchased on land contracts. Within three weeks Barbara and I secured a loan from a local bank, which allowed us to pay off both owners and have enough cash left over to pay off all of the federal taxes we owed. Fortunately, the dojo had been saved. Barbara and I learned a valuable lesson. We would need to budget better in the future.

The thought of losing the dojo put a fire in my spirit and I tightened up the classes. The tempo of the classes increased and towels were needed because we were constantly wiping sweat off the training floor. One of my black belts, Dave Steenken, was always standing in a pool of sweat, his karate-gi soaking wet. Dave started his training when I was teaching at Northern Kentucky University. He was a ni-dan in Chito-ryu, and was very good. Dave traveled to Japan and while there met a beautiful Japanese girl named Mieko. He married Mieko and stayed in Japan for a few years. During that time he became a student of Masatoshi Nakayama Sensei, the Chief Instructor of the Japan Karate Association. Starting over as a white belt, Dave received his Sho-dan from Nakayama Sensei in a short time.

The second kangeiko had more participants than the first. The training, how-

1980-1984

ever, while intense was not as intense as the first. The first kangeiko had set the standards by which all others would be measured.

Election time finally came around in Covington. Many of the crooked politicians who had been in office left by way of the ballot box or were forced to resign because of the scandal. Chief Schwartz was still in charge at the police department. He announced his plans to retire in the fall, as soon as a major project he had been working on was completed. He had gotten approval from the recently elected Board of Commissioners to build a new police headquarters building. The new headquarters would be built from the ground up and would be located at the corner of 20th Street and Madison Avenue. We were scheduled to move in by May 1981.

Debbie married an acquaintance she had met while doing police work and this time I knew that she had made the right decision. His name was Paul Herbst, an excellent young man. Paul was a state trooper with the Kentucky State Police at the State's Dry Ridge post in Northern Kentucky. Later he would move on from the K.S.P. and become Chief of Police of Lakeside Park in Northern Kentucky.

Debbie trained at the dojo as much as her work as a police officer allowed. She trained in karate but she spent more time on her Kobudo. It was obvious that

Debbie (Dometrich) Herbst demonstrating a bo kata to Chito-kai Hombu members in 1983.

she had fallen in love with this Okinawan art. Like everything she did, her police work soon became a life's love, as had her karate and her kobudo previously. She would save her vacation time and money, making it possible for her travel to Okinawa at least once a year and in some cases twice a year for two to three weeks of additional kobudo training. She also achieved black belt rank in iaido, achieving san-dan. By now, it was very obvious that her first love was Ryukyu kobudo.

The annual Chito-ryu tournament was scheduled to be held at the Ludlow High School gymnasium. (Ludlow is a small town which abuts Covington on its western border). The Mayor, Mr. Ronald (Lefty) Pegg, a former student, arranged for us to use the school gymnasium. We invited students from other styles and schools to attend.

Many excellent karate students participated in the tournament that day. One young, baby-faced, karate-ka from Chicago, who looked seventeen but was really 23, won the black belt division. He was quick and fearless. He attacked and backed up opponents twice his size. If the larger opponent stopped, the youngster would step up on his opponent's front leg and punch down on him. The young man was a Shotokan stylist and the Chito-kai students nicknamed him, "Billy the Kid."

The Chicago team was excellent; and won more than their share of trophies. Shojiro Sugiyama, their Sensei, would be very proud of them.

In 1981 we moved into the new police headquarters at 20th and Madison. It was a great facility. The new headquarters building included a weight room and racquetball court, which doubled as a basketball area. The evidence room and crime lab were fantastic when compared with what we had had in the past. Chief Schwartz had done more for the Covington Police Department than perhaps all of his predecessors combined. He had hung tough a few short years before when he had been persona-non-grata with many of the politicians who were later indicted. He would certainly be missed.

Chief Schwartz transferred me from the Criminal Investigation Bureau (formerly the Detective Bureau) to the position of Commander of the Patrol (uniformed) Bureau. He told me he wanted me to straighten out the Patrol Bureau. Discipline and morale both needed work. I was known as a stickler for clean, neat uniforms, shined shoes, neat, short haircuts, military bearing and being physically fit. I had my work cut out for me. The Chief believed that occasional in-house transfers kept everyone sharp and on their toes – I agreed. I needed to shape up a little myself; my uniforms had gotten a little tight since I had last worn them. Since I demanded that my officers be fit, I went on a diet and lost

Group with Inomoto (1997).

ten pounds. I was very strict when it came to uniforms. To my way of thinking, haircuts, weight control and cleanliness, were as much a part of the uniform as the blue suit. Roll call inspections were also getting slack. I informed my lieutenants that I expected proper, quick roll calls, with stand-up inspections.

One shift supervisor, Lieutenant Albert Bosse, a Vietnam veteran, was the half-brother of Chief Ralph Bosse, the man who had assigned me to motorcycle duty years earlier. Al had an uncanny way of knowing before anyone else that there was a problem. Whenever there was a problem on one of the beats, I would inform the three shift commanders. Lt. Bosse would often anticipate the problems and work out a solution before the other two shift commanders were even sure that there was a problem.

By the summer of 1982, many students were experiencing knee problems. The female students were having the greatest trouble. We re-evaluated our teaching program and located what we believed to be the cause. The new method of doing Seisan stance, introduced by Yasuhiro Chitose during the fall of 1979, seemed to be at the root of the problem. Squeezing the knees inward was causing undue strain on the inside of the knee. I modified the stance immediately, moving the stress point from the knee to the heels of both feet, while making sure that the tailbone was also tucked under. This modification solved the majority of the knee problems, and the strength of seisan stance improved dramatically.

On three previous occasions I had applied for admission to the Federal Bureau of Investigation's National Academy. Since I had submitted my first application 5 years earlier, several officers of lower rank had been selected to attend the academy. I had never been approached by any of my superiors about the fact that I wanted to attend, so I decided that it was time to have a talk with Chief Schwartz.

Chief Schwartz informed me that my name had been passed over because there was a question about my health. My lung problems were common knowledge in the department.

"Chief, if my health is so poor that I can't be considered as a candidate to the N.A., then it should have been too poor for me to remain a police officer."

"OK! I'll see that you are the next person to go," he promised me.

Chief Schwartz would be retired in a few weeks. Lieutenant Colonel Arthur Heeger, with whom I did not get along, was the front-runner to be Schwartz's replacement.

"How can you guarantee that I'll go to the N.A., Chief? You won't be here?"

"I'll still have some influence around here when I'm gone," Chief Schwartz assured me.

Chief Schwartz retired from the police department on the exact day he said he would. As expected, Art Heeger became the new Chief of Police. Albert Casson was named the Assistant Chief of Police. I was re-assigned, for the third time, to the Detective Bureau as its Commander.

Since the city corruption trials were almost over, I had more time to spend at the dojo. I trained harder and more often and became more active in daily dojo life. The membership of the honbu started growing again since I was taking a more active part in the classes. As has been the case with every dojo, many people join and few stay. A few, however, do stay for years and enter the higher ranks of the black belt division.

In December, we were invited to participate in a Shotokan tournament to be held in Chicago. The tournament was scheduled for March 1982. We accelerated our training so we would be ready for the event. We wanted to do well; especially after what the Chicago team and "Billy the Kid" had done to us the year before. The honbu team did much better than anticipated. Our kata team won a trophy for best team. We also won several other trophies in kumite and kata.

The author on right, bowing to Dr. Chitose in Canada (1982).

The United States Chito-ryu Karate Federation tournament was scheduled for May 23rd, 1982, at Ludlow High, four miles from the hombu. One of the male members of a honbu kata team failed to show up at the tournament. Sally Zeidler, a young brown belt, came to me and said that she had heard my missing student's name on her car radio as she was driving to the tournament. However, the young man in question had a common name, so we weren't positive that the radio report was about him. A fatal hit-skip car accident, in which a pedestrian was killed, had occurred in Mt. Carmel, Ohio. The accident happened early the morning of the tournament. I wondered if my missing student was involved. Later that day, before the tournament ended, it was verified that my missing student was the one who had been arrested. He had been driving his Datsun 280-Z, when he struck and killed a woman named Barbara Payne, the 22 year-old mother of a four-year old boy. The force of the impact had decapitated Ms. Payne. My student fled the scene after the accident. He was arrested later at his home. His trial was scheduled for the following year.

During October 1982, Chitose Sensei, now eighty-four years old, traveled to North America for the last time. He was going to visit Canada and the United States. The U. S. Chito-kai held a large clinic and banquet at Ludlow High School in Chitose Sensei's honor. Three hundred karate-ka and their families attended. Chitose Sensei's young son, Yasuhiro, traveled with him.

After the clinic and banquet – which were both very successful – Chitose Sensei and Waka (Yasuhiro) Sensei returned to Canada for a special Canadian Chito-kai tournament in O-Sensei's honor. Several carloads of students from the U.S. traveled to Canada to participate in the tournament. Many went simply because they wanted to stay with O-Sensei a little longer.

At the Canadian tournament my students received a big surprise when those who did the kata Potsai got low scores for mistakes they were said to be making in the performance of the kata. The movements we performed with hip snap were done differently by the Canadians.

"When did you learn this version of Potsai?" I inquired of one of the Canadian black belts.

"In 1979, when Waka was in Canada."

It seemed that Waka had taught one variation of Potsai to the U.S. students and another to the Canadians. Although I liked the hip snap method better, I modified our version of the Potsai kata to match the Canadian method and insure organizational uniformity.

When we arrived in Toronto, I had telephoned Sensei Masami Tsuruoka and asked him to attend the tournament and visit with Chitose Sensei. He came. It was quite evident that Chitose Sensei was very moved to see his early student from the late 1940s walking toward him to pay his respects.

A formal dinner was held at a local restaurant in Toronto's Chinatown. Chest pains had started plaguing Chitose Sensei, which concerned everyone. Chitose Sensei himself was also concerned about his chest pains and was prompted to prepare his will. Sensei Shane Higashi and I were greatly honored that Chitose Sensei asked the two of us to sign his will as witnesses. In his will, Chitose Sensei named his son Yasuhiro, as his successor.

The day after the banquet, I visited O-Sensei (Tsuyoshi Chitose) at Shane Higashi's home. I had the opportunity to talk with Chitose Sensei for the last time. As I left Higashi's home, Chitose Sensei and I both knew that we would never see each other again. Saying good-bye and driving away from my teacher – a man who had become my father – was one of the most difficult things I have ever done.

On November 22, 1982, Rebecca L. Berwanger, the girlfriend of the student who had been involved in the hit-skip accident, disappeared. She had borrowed one of his cars to go to work; the car was later located by the Cincinnati Police

The author (standing) shaking hands with his karate teacher, Doctor Tsuyoshi Chitose, for the last time. Photo taken in September 1982.

on the public landing downtown. Her body surfaced a few days later. She had drowned. My student showed up at my office in the Criminal Investigation Bureau insisting that he had to view the body, which was at the Hamilton County, Ohio morgue. I advised him not to go, but he insisted. We drove to the morgue where he identified Beth's remains. He was so emotional that I felt he might attempt suicide. I telephoned an old girlfriend of his, explained the situation and took him to her house for a visit. Afterwards, I drove him to my home so I could keep an eye on him. I didn't want him to hurt himself or do anything else foolish.

The year 1983 started with my student's trial for the vehicular homicide charge which had been lodged against him. Thanks to the diligent work of his attorney, he was acquitted of all charges.

In August I traveled to Canmore, Alberta, Canada, where I had been invited to teach a five-day clinic for the Canadian Chito-ryu Karate Federation. Ten of

The Canmore (Canada) 1983 Karate Clinic which was sponsored by Jack Kerr, a Canadian Mountie and black belt. The author was the chief instructor.

my students traveled to Canmore to participate. I drove my VW camper and pulled a smaller Coleman camper behind it. Barbara, Sherry Lynn, my daughter, and Sally Zeidler traveled with me, along with our dogs, Mo Mo and Prince.

The clinic had one hundred and ten participants. It was sponsored by the Canmore Chito-ryu karate club headed by Jack Kerr, a member of the Royal

Canadian Mounted Police. When I got there, I took one look at the training schedule and immediately decided to modify it. There were two thirty-minute breaks, one in the morning and one in the afternoon in the middle of the training schedule. Lunch was scheduled for one and a half hours. I increased the training time by eliminating the two breaks and cutting the lunch period to an hour. A voluntary evening training period was also established between 6:00 PM and 9:00 PM. The Canadians were very good. I felt that two areas of training needed emphasis: the development of better front kicks and the strengthening of the legs. I established the entire training regimen around these two primary areas of training.

A photograph of me taken by my wife on graduation day at the F.B.I. National Academy, March 23, 1984.

After Art Heeger became Chief of Police, he buried my application to the FBI Academy. He sent two other officers who were junior to me in both rank and time on the department. Art and I had never gotten along. This was Art's method of putting me in my place. I spoke to the new Assistant Chief of Police, Lt. Colonel Casson, about the problem.

"If I can help, I will," he assured me.

A few months later the Chief went on vacation. That's when Casson placed my name before the FBI Academy selection committee at Quantico, Virginia.

Other than my knee injury from the motorcycle accident thirteen years earlier, and my breathing problems, which my doctor had controlled with medication, I was in excellent shape for my age. My years of karate training had rewarded me with very good physical conditioning. However, I still felt that I needed an extra edge. The majority of the police officers attending the academy are in their mid-thirties. I would be forty-nine when I graduated from the academy.

The new police headquarters had a weight room in the basement, so I started training with weights three days a week. I increased my sit-ups to three hundred (four sets of seventy-five, on a 45 degree incline board). Nothing was going to keep me from being successful now that I finally had the chance to prove myself. The Assistant Chief had put his neck on the line for me; I had to prove I was worthy.

On Sunday, January 4, 1984, I reported to the FBI National Academy at Quantico, Virginia. The academy, situated West of I-95 on the United States Marine Corps Officers' School at Quantico, is approximately forty miles south of Washington, D. C.

While at the academy, we were required to study certain subjects, one of which was Constitutional Law. Firearms training and two hours of daily physical fitness training were also required courses. I did well in all of my classes, graduating with a 3.5 average. One subject which I elected to study was course #402 – The Theory and Practice of Terrorism. I 'maxed' the Terrorism course, making 100's on every paper as well as on the examination. I also signed up for Documentary Evidence, Criminal Psychology, and a police management course.

However, while at the academy I pulled one of the dumbest stunts in my life. Because Chief Heeger and I had never gotten along, I felt that the best way to get him not to attend my graduation was to invite him. If he thought I wanted him to attend, he would not attend in an attempt to puncture my ego. I was sure that he would send Assistant Chief Casson in his place. The Chief fooled me though, and showed up at my graduation. The Assistant Chief was very upset (he was fully justified) with me, and was in a rage. He had planned on attending my graduation with his family and making a vacation out of it. I felt terribly since, without his help, I would never have gotten into the academy in the first place.

I graduated on March 23rd, 1984. Barbara came to the graduation, so did Chief Heeger. I only wish that my mother could have lived long enough to have attended.

It felt good getting back to Covington, the department, and the dojo. I slammed my fist into the makiwara again and again as I switched from seisan dachi to zenkutsu dachi. I arrived at the dojo an hour early, so I could practice without any distractions. After I finished my makiwara training, I started practicing my favorite kata – Seisan. I told my students quite often that if Chito-ryu students were going to be restricted to doing only one kata, that kata would be Seisan.

I slid my left foot forward into seisan dachi. With my left arm I performed an outside chest block. I locked in my stance as I applied counter-tension between my hips, ankles, and feet. My tanden compressed, my hips vibrated, and my right fist shot forward in a chest punch. I felt my whole body "lock-up" as I converted kinetic energy into "kime" (the force which maximizes the effect of the kinetic energy on the opponent's body). The kime lasted only a fraction of a second, then my arm muscles released as my inner thigh muscles contracted then relaxed. My right foot slid forward as I repeated the entire sequence with my opposite side. I flowed through the kata almost unconsciously. After thirty-one years of karate practice, my body no longer controlled the kata – the kata controlled my body.

Dr. Tsuyoshi Chitose at home in Japan working on karate paperwork, which he personally handled for the entire organization.

Sherry Dometrich Kembre and Harold "Dusty" Kembre the day they were married (1984).

When I re-enlisted in the Army Reserves in 1979, I was assigned to the 259th Military Intelligence Company in Sharonville, Ohio, where I served as a counter intelligence agent. During May 1984, a good friend of mine, Chief Warrant Officer (CWO) Paul Beane, talked me into requesting a transfer to the 389th MI Company located at Bowman Field in Louisville, Kentucky. One month later I was re-assigned to the 389th, which was a sub-unit of the 11th Special Forces Group, headquartered at Fort Meade, Maryland. As a member of the 11th Special Forces Group, I would have to start parachuting again. I looked forward to becoming a member of my new unit. It had been thirty years since I had jumped out of an airplane.

1980-1984

I was finally promoted to Lieutenant Colonel (Assistant Chief of Police) in November 1984.

The author With Miyagi and Davenport

Barbara and I were sleeping soundly when the telephone rang at 10:00 PM on June 6, 1984. The call was from Sensei Shane Higashi.

"Chitose Sensei died on June 5, in a hospital in Kumamoto," he informed me with an emotion-choked voice.

An era had ended. What would the future hold for Chito-ryu now that O-Sensei was gone? I could only hope for the best. Chitose Sensei had been a second father to me – I would miss him dearly.

My daughter Sherry Lynn's wedding was scheduled for June 21, 1984. She was engaged to one of my former karate students, Harold "Dusty" Kembre. Dusty, a brown belt, was a Vietnam veteran and ex-paratrooper. He had been a member of a LRRP (Long Range Reconnaissance Patrol) team. Later he had flown missions (over nine hundred) as the gunner on a Huey helicopter. Considering that the average life of a helicopter crew was approximately three hundred missions, he was lucky to be alive.

The wedding had been scheduled for the same day that I was to leave for Fort Devens, Massachusetts, home of the 10th Special Forces Group, and the 11th SFG(A)'s two-week annual training at Fort Devens. My company commander granted me permission to arrive a day late (Sunday, July, 22) so I could participate in my daughter's wedding. The wedding was wonderful; my old friend, John

Nelson, attended, as did many karate students from around the U.S.

I arrived at the Boston airport at approximately 1:30 PM, Sunday. Chief Beane, accompanied by Sergeant First Class William Martin, met me at the gate.

"How did the wedding go?" the Chief inquired.

"It was a great wedding, it couldn't have gone better."

"Change into your BDU's (Battle Dress Utilities) in the rest room before we head for Fort Devens. We have a jeep parked outside."

After changing into my BDU's the three of us climbed into the jeep and drove north toward Fort Devens.

During my second night at Fort Devens I found myself in a Huey UH-1H helicopter getting ready to make a parachute jump. I had been given a very quick, ten-minute refresher course prior to climbing into the aircraft. We sat in the helicopter, four on each side, with our legs and feet hanging out. After reaching an altitude of 500 feet, the safety strap was unhooked. The Huey turned and banked as it prepared for its approach over the drop zone (DZ). I was afraid that I might fall out of the chopper prior to reaching the DZ. I was nearing fifty and realized too late that I was a little "mature" to be jumping out of a perfectly good aircraft. I had never ridden in a helicopter before, and I scared the living hell out of myself making my first parachute jump in thirty years – with a new type of parachute, an MC-1-B. Deep down inside, however, I really loved it.

Chief Heeger retired from the police department after serving as Chief for a little over two and a half years. The Assistant Chief, Casson, automatically took over as Acting Chief and held that position for several months before he was finally promoted to Chief of Police. In November 1984, I was promoted to Lieutenant Colonel and became the new Assistant Chief of Police.

I had not been Chief Casson's first choice; I was a compromise candidate. After my stupidity in not inviting the Chief and his family to my graduation at Quantico, I was surprised that he had agreed to accept me as his Assistant under any condition.

The morning class was over and the last student had left the dojo. As I walked through the small Japanese garden the sun was high in the sky, its brightness causing irregular rays of light to break through the trees and highlight various areas of the garden.

Standing on the small bridge was a very cute, little black boy approximately eight to ten years of age.

"You practice karate?" he inquired.

"Yes, I train in karate."

"You good? Bruce Lee's good."

"Yes, Bruce Lee is very good," I agreed.

"See that fence?" he said as he motioned toward the six-foot wooden fence which surrounded the garden. "Bruce Lee can jump that fence."

"I'm sure that he can," I agreed.

"Can you jump that fence?"

"I don't think so," I said.

"Then you ain't shit," he said with a deadly serious look on his face. He turned sharply and left the garden.

I lost it. I started laughing and couldn't quit. I was laughing so hard that I could barely walk back into the dojo. Barbara looked at me as if I had taken leave of my senses. I explained what had taken place in the garden a few seconds earlier, and she too had a good laugh.

● ●

Chapter 26

1985-1989

My thought is thought. It is never myself. I had thought that my thought was myself. But now I am aware - I made a terrible mistake.

Yoseiji Buddhist Temple service booklet

As the new Assistant Chief of Police, I had difficulty performing the job as I felt it should be performed. My relationship with Chief Casson, while very professional, was not conducive to a good working partnership. My job, as I saw it, was to handle the many small daily problems which always occur in the police department's operations. By doing this I would allow the Chief to concentrate on more important tasks, such as long-range planning and dealing with the Mayor and City Commissioners. My boss, Chief Casson, was doing a good job. He was a very honest person; the Chief was as straight as the white line on a Texas highway. After I had screwed up by not inviting "The Chief" to my FBI Academy graduation I was no longer in his good graces and I soon began to feel that I never would be again.

Nevertheless, as the Assistant Chief I had many young officers come to my office with complaints, problems, or ideas that might never reach the Chief. One Tuesday afternoon a young patrol officer brought in a friend who was working as a guard at the state reformatory in La Grange, Kentucky. Both of the young man's hands had been deformed since birth. His mother had used a drug – prescribed by her doctor – which had caused the damage. He wanted to become a police officer. The city of Covington, like all cities, had a city code and ordinances which governed its operations. One of the city ordinances defined physical standards for people making application to become a member of the police and fire departments. A person with one finger or thumb missing was considered "disabled" and was not allowed to apply for a position with either the police of the fire department.

I thought, "What if this same young man had had his hands damaged in combat?" This ordinance would keep him from being able to provide for himself and his family. If he had been a soldier we would be saying: "Gee, thanks for risking your life and limbs for your country. Congratulations on your purple heart and two silver stars, but please go somewhere else, you don't qualify." There was no doubt in my mind that this ordinance was not only unfair but probably unconstitutional. Although I had no authorization, I set about to rewrite the ordinance.

After researching several ordinances from other cities, I finally completed my revised city ordinance concerning handicapped applicants. The City Manager and department heads, including the Police and Fire Chiefs, were out of town. I took my revised ordinance to the Assistant City Manager, Arnold Simpson, a handsome young black man who had grown up in Covington and had a degree in law. (Many years later Arnold would become a Kentucky State Senator.) Arnold agreed with me. Everyone should at least be able to complete an application and take the various tests. If an applicant passed the test and performed all job requirements he or she should be hired. If applicants did not pass at least they have had an opportunity to take the test. Arnold got the ordinance passed.

Once the City Manager and the department heads returned to Covington, the Fire Chief was the first to review the new ordinance. He telephoned the Chief of Police, the City Manager and the other department heads immediately. I attempted to explain my reasons for rewriting the ordinance, however no one wanted to listen. The old ordinance was reinstated.

I was in trouble with the Chief again, but I was not sorry about the ordinance mishap. I felt my decision was fair, that it was in the best interests of future applicants and the city of Covington, and that what I had done needed to be done.

I injured my right knee while making a parachute jump during a weekend drill with the army reserve in Sellersburg, Indiana. The local ROTC was holding a membership drive and our unit performed a parachute jump as part of the show. We parachuted from Huey choppers at four thousand feet. The winds were gusting and we should not have made the jump. However, the Captain in charge, in all of his wisdom, decided that we should "go for it," so we jumped. The jump master yelled, "Go!" I shoved off from the chopper and plummeted earthward. As I looked down I could see Interstate 65 (which connected Louisville, Kentucky with Indianapolis, Indiana) four thousand feet below me; I was directly over it. The high winds immediately caused us problems but the really big surprise came when our parachutes opened. After exiting the aircraft we discovered that we were not wearing MC1-Bravo parachutes, which had steering toggles, but we were wearing the older T-10's that had no toggles. We more or less went where the wind blew us. Five soldiers hit trees, two hit high-tension electrical lines, one hit a fence, another hit a house, and a few others hit a barbed wire fence. So many were hurt that day, nineteen in all, that the jump became known as "The Sellersburg Massacre". I did not emerge from the "Massacre" unscathed; my "skillful" landing set me down none too softly on top of my weapon. I landed so hard, that the barrel of my weapon was bent to match the profile of my body. The left side of my body was black and blue and my left arm looked as if it were broken; it wasn't, it was just swollen. I also seriously injured my right leg and knee.

Over the next few months I attempted to strengthen my leg at the dojo during karate practice but regardless of how much I exercised my knee, it kept collapsing on me. After several months of exercising, it still had not improved. I went to see a doctor and that is where I got the bad news. The doctor told me I would have to have reconstructive knee surgery; he scheduled the surgery for the first week of April 1986. When I left the hospital on crutches, I had two large horseshoe staples, a cadaver ligament and a three-inch bolt holding my right leg together.

Lt. Harvie Eubank and my wife, Barbara. This photo was taken by me while we vacationed in Los Angeles during 1987.

I returned to work at the police department on crutches and resumed my responsibilities as Assistant Chief two weeks after the operation. I was still at odds with the Chief and had no plan to redeem myself to him. I felt badly about this because I really liked the Chief.

In the middle of May, I told the Chief that I was going to hang it up, that I had finally decided to retire.

"You aren't really leaving?" he asked in disbelief. "Why not think about it? Give yourself a couple of weeks before making a decision."

I accepted his advice as a friend. I knew that he was concerned and really didn't want me to leave. I knew in my heart, however, that it was time for me to leave the department. After a couple of weeks, and a lot of soul-searching, I submitted my resignation, effective June 2, 1986.

After retiring from the police department, I spent a great deal of my time rehabilitating my injured right knee by doing exercises at the dojo. Slowly my leg regained its strength and flexibility.

Barbara and I traveled to Florida during the latter part of June with one of my karate students, who also assisted us with the driving. A clinic had been scheduled in Orlando to help drum-up support for the International Chito-ryu Soke Cup tournament, which was scheduled to be held in Kumamoto, Japan, on November 2, 1986 at the Kumamoto Provincial Gymnasium.

Yasuhiro Chitose and Tsutomu Tashiro had come to Florida to teach some new techniques to the "Americans" and to encourage people to attend the tournament in Japan. Yasuhiro Chitose, whom everyone now referred to as "Soke", was now head of not only the Japanese Chito-kai but also the Chito-ryu World Organization which was called the International Chito-kai as O-Sensei Chitose had specified in his will. Tashiro Sensei, an older gentleman, had been appointed by Soke to the position of "President of the International Organization".

The clinic was held in the new Yoseikan Dojo of Orlando, Florida, which had been constructed by Sensei Art Rott and some of his students. The dojo looked like an old Okinawan dojo as it sat alone surrounded by woods. Karate instruction at the dojo was free. Sensei Art had several students who would love to travel to Japan, but they couldn't afford the airline tickets.

My wife, twenty-five students from throughout the United States, and I flew to Japan to participate. Upon arriving at the Kumamoto airport, one of my black belts ran past me and several other high-ranking members of the delegation and went through the doors of the terminal to greet Soke (Yasuhiro Chitose). It was the same student who had had the hit-skip accident and whose girlfriend had drowned herself. I did not realize it at that time, but this was a portent of things to come.

The tournament was well organized. During kumite, the participants sparred in bogu (armor). Several different generations of bogu were used, although the majority was of a newer, lighter design. While the bogu may have prevented some injuries, it caused many more: broken teeth when a chin-piece slipped causing the face bars to crash into a contestant's mouth; a broken nose when the face bars recoiled into a contestant's nose; a broken leg occurred when a contestant threw a round-house kick (mawashi geri) to his opponent's head and his leg struck the bars of the facemask. It was obvious that the competitors had not trained with the bogu before the tournament; otherwise, they would have had safer habits.

Japan had changed enormously since my last trip there in 1971. In 1986, it was an ultra-modern country that had become the economic powerhouse of Asia. Japan had almost every convenience found in the United States and a few that weren't. The country was clean, the people, as usual, very polite, and many of their buses, trains, and buildings were light years ahead of those seen in the U. S.

The majority of my students had never been to Japan. After the tournament ended they traveled to various cities including Kyoto, sightseeing and enjoying the culture. With most of my students remaining in Japan, Barbara, seven students and I flew to Okinawa to visit with Sensei Takayoshi Nagamine and his father. Upon our arrival we found lodging at a small ryokan (Japanese style hotel or inn) a block from Nagamine Sensei's dojo.

I asked Takayoshi about Chitose Sensei's oldest son, who lived in Okinawa. Chitose Sensei's oldest son had retained the family's original name of Chinen. Takayoshi arranged to take me to meet him. The next morning everyone climbed into several small automobiles and after a short drive we arrived on a hilly street where he had his home. In his youth he had been a karate man of great skill. Twenty-five years earlier (1961) he had been a police officer. As I was introduced to him, he lay on a couch, paralyzed from the neck down. He had been hit by a drunken taxicab driver in Naha city. He was a very handsome man condemned to spend the remainder of his life immobile and dependent on others to satisfy his most basic needs. I felt a kinship with this courageous man – I had to fight back tears. (Tears would have embarrassed him and I didn't want to do that.) I realized that, but for the grace of God, I might have been killed or paralyzed in my motorcycle accident fifteen years earlier. He, his wife and family were very kind to us. I now had some insight into Chitose Sensei's reason for wanting me to change my name during my visit to Japan in October 1971.

Upon returning to our hotel room, Barbara and I found a large beautiful Japanese doll awaiting us; it had been delivered while we were gone. It served as a "thank you" from the Chinen family for visiting and paying our respects to them.

During our brief trip to Okinawa, we visited Shuri Castle. We were transported northward up a winding road by bus. After leaving the bus, we walked up a road off to our right which led us to the "Shuri No Mon" (Okinawa's Gate of Courtesy) near the castle. As we walked up the hill the sights, sounds, and smells brought back memories of when I had first walked the streets of Beppu some thirty years before.

Before leaving Okinawa for our return trip to Tokyo, we had an opportunity to demonstrate Chito-ryu karate-do to Shoshin Nagamine Sensei's students. We demonstrated two kata; one was "Niseishi". Afterwards my students also performed the "Niseishi Kaisetsu" to illustrate the self-defense aspects of the kata.

When I returned to the United States, I made some teaching changes. I attempted to bring our standards more in line with the Honbu in Japan. The four Kihon Dosa kata and the three Kihon Kata replaced the three Taikyoku Kata. Replacing three basic kata with seven created some problems. The first two Kihon Dosa kata were so basic they offered no challenge, even to the new students. The third and fourth Kihon Dosa kata were, in reality, speed drills that were better suited for sparring training. In these katas, the student performs quick one-armed blocks and does not utilize a check hand, which is a key element of good, balanced basics.

The Kihon Kata, of which there were three, were overly challenging to new students. With their front, side, round and back kick combinations and three hundred sixty degree spinning turns, they were a little too difficult for beginning

The new Yoseikan Dojo in Orlando, Florida.

students. In my opinion, new students needed to learn a few basics well – front snap kick, reverse punch, lunge punch – and then build on these. They also needed to have the power to stop an opponent if attacked. Combinations such as those found in the Kihon Katas were better suited for advanced students. During the next three kyu tests, over a period of nine months, my students' body motion and overall skill level decreased.

Barbara and I drove over to a car dealer's lot to check out a used Itasca "Phaser," a diesel-powered motor home that had been advertised in the local paper. It was a small motor home and we both liked it. We bought it, took it home and packed it full. One week later we were headed west to Las Vegas and California. Our plans were to visit various karate schools and my friend, Lieutenant Harvie Eubank, who was now a senior karate student of Takayuki Kubota Sensei. We also wanted to visit with Yukinori Kugimiya's family in San Bernardino, California. Kugimiya Sensei had started two Chito-ryu karate schools in the Los Angeles area. His main dojo was located at the Nichiren Buddhist Temple in Los Angeles. He also had a branch dojo at the Pasadena Cultural Center. After teaching classes at both locations, I visited a good friend in Santa Ana, Sensei Fumio Demura. Demura Sensei invited Barbara and me to go to lunch with him. Upon arriving at the restaurant, Demura Sensei introduced us to Sensei Morio Higaonna (the grandson of Kanryo (Higashionna) Higaonna) who was going to have lunch with us.

I received orders during the spring of 1987 to attend the Intelligence Analyst (96B) School for four weeks at Fort McCoy, Wisconsin. I had requested a change of MOS (Military Occupation Specially). I thought the analyst's job would be more interesting. I had worked as a CI (Counter Intelligence) agent in the reserves for the past seven years it was very similar to police work – I wanted a change.

After returning to my unit at Bowman Air Field in Louisville, Chief Paul Beane asked me if I would be interested in re-enlisting in the army for a three-year tour of active duty under the army's AGR (Active Guard-Reserve) policy on a full time basis. "I'll give the idea some consideration," I answered.

I spoke with Barbara about the idea of my becoming an active duty soldier. She was supportive of my desire to return to active military service and gave me the OK, but just for three years.

"You know, if I'm in the army I won't be able to build your log cabin in the country as I planned," I told her. I looked for a new home in various sub-divisions, but Barbara wouldn't agree to any of them.

"You promised me a log cabin and I want a log cabin," she reminded me.

"Find one already built and if I can afford it I'll buy it for you," I told her.

Within two days Barbara had located a log home in Boone County, Kentucky. I paid some money down on the house on July 23, 1987, pending approval of my loan.

The papers ordering me to active duty arrived and I arrived at Fort McCoy on August 2, 1987, to take the AGR active duty indoctrination course. I was fifty-two years old.

As it turned out, the move to Boone County proved to be a good idea. Our log home was approximately thirty miles closer to my job with the 11th Special Forces Group assignment at Bowman Field in Louisville. Chief Beane lived in Pendelton County, Kentucky, several miles from my new home. We would meet at the Walton, Kentucky, National Guard Armory each morning and ride together to Bowman Field seventy-five miles away. The Chief drove his automobile and I paid him a weekly gasoline fee for the trip.

The local 389th MI unit's AGR contingent was headed by Major D. Alan Youngman. Second in command was CWO (Chief) Paul Beane. Several full-time time enlisted personnel were also assigned to the unit. In addition to our MOS skills, every member of the unit had one major additional duty and several other minor duties they were required to perform. SFC William Martin was in charge of training and operations. Sgt. Metro Fox (a former marine) handled the personnel and medical files. Sgt. Jeffery Payne (the clown of the unit who we fondly referred to as "Brain Damage") handled the payroll files. SSG Tom Lasch was in charge of supply. It was a good mix of men who not only worked well together but also liked each other and had a profound respect for each other's abilities.

It was only a few months after I signed up for active duty tour that the Beikoku Heitei Yoseikan Dojo (United States Soldier) karate club was organized at Bowman Field. Seven soldiers joined. Everyone had trouble with the movements at first, but within a few weeks they started making rapid improvement.

In December, after an episode of freezing rain and light snow, I was in my small Chevy LUV pickup truck headed to the Walton National Guard Center to meet Chief Beane. A large Ford truck in front of me slid on the ice-covered road; it went backward off the road and down a slope into some trees. Before I had time to react, I hit the ice and lost control as my truck turned sideways and proceeded to roll over. It was dark and my truck lights went off as I slid down Route 338 upside down – sparks shot by on both sides of the truck. Everything inside the truck was thrown out of the passenger's side of the vehicle. I was fortunate that I was wearing my seat belt and only received a small cut on my head. The truck was totaled.

The unit returned to Fort Devens for our annual training during January 1988.

In a C-130 a few minutes before making a parachute jump. CWO Paul Beane gives the 'thumbs up' sign with me.

I was asked if I could drive my diesel camper and be paid mileage. This would ensure that we would have wheels to travel off post once we arrived at the fort. I accepted the offer and loaded the camper with my equipment and that of Sergeant Major Mike Gobel, who was riding with me. One of the training plans of the 11th SFG(A) while at Fort Devens was to parachute six-man teams into the White Mountains of New Hampshire at night. These jumps were done in the snow with the soldiers wearing full combat gear – including MOPP (Military Oriented Protective Posture) – chemical protective gear. Numerous injuries were incurred.

The rucksacks had metal frames attached to them. Before hitting the ground, each soldier was to drop his rucksack to the ground using the attached lowering line. If you were going to hit a tree, procedures called for you to ride your ruck into the tree. Snow, darkness, and fog shrouded the valleys, making the paratroopers unable to distinguish a six-foot pine tree from a one hundred foot pine tree. This proved disastrous. Four Green Berets from one six-man team earned broken legs during the exercise.

Even with all of the injuries, however, almost every team completed its assigned mission. During winter training at Fort Devens, our unit learned a great deal about what we could and could not do in the future.

Sergeant Major Gobel decided to return to Kentucky in one of the C-130s and parachute in to Fort Knox. I returned home in the camper with Staff Sergeant Jim Botkin as my passenger.

When I arrived home I found my wife Barbara very upset. Jim Botkin had no sooner left for his home in Lexington when she broke down crying. Sobbing, she told me she thought she might have cancer. A few days later a series of tests proved that she was, thankfully, cancer free. A great weight was lifted off both of our shoulders.

Sergeant Fox and I received orders to travel to the 11th SFG (A) Headquarters at Fort Meade, Maryland, for two weeks. We were to report to the Major in charge of a specific area of special operations. Sergeant Fox and I were then ordered to report to the ITAC (International Threat Analysis Center) on M Street in Washington, D.C. where we were to conduct research for a special project. "Foxie," as Sgt. Fox was commonly known in the unit, was at the ITAC for

Pictured here are: Sgt. Metro Fox (extreme left), myself (fifth from right, front row), Chief Warrant Officer Paul Beane (to my right), Sergeant Major Gobel (to my left), Major Burd, the detachment commander (over my left shoulder). This photo was taken in Louisville, Kentucky, in 1993.

the entire two weeks; I was there only during the last week. I had been ordered to remain at Fort Meade to update some top-secret files at the group headquarters. As I reviewed the files, it became obvious that they were a total mess. One week later, after working six 12 to 15 hour days, the files had been updated and filed in individual boxes. While the files still needed a lot of work, they were at least usable in an emergency situation if the need arose.

Metro and I left Washington early on Friday morning and headed west toward Louisville. It was a drill weekend. The reservists were filing into the reserve center when we arrived at 5:30 PM that evening. First formation was scheduled for 6:00 PM and a parachute jump was scheduled for Saturday. Sgt. Fox's name and mine were added to the jump manifest. After first formation the Jump Masters held a safety briefing and the mandatory refresher training which is held before each and every jump. The jump was scheduled for noon Saturday on the Corregidor drop zone at Fort Campbell, Kentucky. It was dark Saturday morning when we boarded the two and a half ton trucks that transported us to Standiford Field at the Louisville Airport. Parachutes were issued, put on, and checked by the jumpmasters, whose job it was to assure that no malfunctions occurred. The sun had been up for over an hour before we boarded the two C-130s flown by the Kentucky Air National Guard. Wearing full combat gear, we struggled as we walked up the rear ramp into the aircraft and waddled to the canvas seats. The two C-130s, each of their four large engines roaring, taxied down the runway in preparation for takeoff. The aircraft flew NOE (Nap-of-the-earth) – flying low using natural cover such as hills, trees, and folds in the earth for cover. NOE requires the pilots to keep the aircraft a few hundred feet above the ground to avoid radar and missiles. The flight gave the passengers the impression that they were on a very long roller-coaster ride. Barf bags were always in great demand and the Air Force seemed to have an endless supply of them. We flew for over an hour as the plane wound its way toward Fort Campbell and the drop zone (DZ).

That summer had been very hot. We were told that it was 108 degrees on the DZ. I was flying in the lead plane with General Mike Davidson, who had been a member of the Louisville special forces unit when he was a junior officer, and two U. S. Marine Lieutenant Colonels – LTC Henderson, a USMC Reserve officer, and LTC Gipe, an active duty Marine who was stationed in Louisville. Gipe commanded the MEPS (Military Enlistment Processing) Station in Louisville.

Sitting across from me was a young Green Beret in his early twenties.

"Sergeant Dometrich, have you jumped the Corregidor DZ before?"

"Sure have."

"How long ago?"

"Thirty-five years ago this month," I answered. He did a bad job of disguising his amazement that a man as old as me could still walk, much less jump out of an airplane and walk away.

The jump went well. SFC Martin, who had driven a deuce and a half (a two and a half ton army truck) from Louisville to Fort Campbell, was waiting for us at the drop zone.

"Sergeant Dometrich, you'll be taking the truck back," SFC Martin told me. "I intend to fly back and parachute into Fort Knox."

"No problem," I replied.

On his jump into Fort Knox, SFC Martin broke his back. He would never jump again and had to leave the unit. I was assigned his duties as the Operations and Training NCO.

I was sitting at my desk attempting to get the training operation file updated and pondering the up-coming IG (Inspector General) inspection when the telephone rang.

"389th MI Company, Sergeant Dometrich. Sir, this is not a secure line," I answered.

"Sergeant Dometrich, this is Major Donaldson of the Air Guard at Standiford Field. Is Major Youngman or Chief Beane in?"

"Hold on sir, I'll get one of them for you."

"Chief, I have a telephone call for you!" I yelled across the room.

Major Donaldson had called to request some personnel from the 389th to assist with an airborne operation scheduled for Wednesday. Our unit and the Air Guard had developed a friendly relationship; we constantly supported each other. We were scheduled to jump from a C-130 at Fort Knox. General Mike Davidson, the Commander of the Kentucky National Guard and a former Green Beret, was to be the jumpmaster for the operation. The jump was to be filmed. There were cameramen in the C-130, on the DZ, and in a helicopter which was to fly alongside the C-130. If the filming was successful, a recruiting film for the Air Guard would be the result.

Both units arrived at Standiford Field Wednesday morning dressed in full combat gear. The day was almost cloud-free and a cool, crisp wind blew across the airport runway toward us.

"I'll need someone to jump on the first pass over the DZ to test the wing direction," General Davidson said.

"I'll be the Test Dummy," I blurted out.

"Sergeant Dometrich," General Davidson corrected me with a slight smile forming on his lips. "The proper term is 'turbulence tester.'"

Lieutenant Colonel William "Bill" Whitney, a former Green Beret who now worked for the Kentucky National Guard, told the General that he too wished to be a "turbulence tester".

"I'll use you both," the General told us.

"Start onloading!" a Loadmaster yelled.

We walked single file up the ramp as we entered the C-130 transport and made our way to the ever so comfortable canvas seats.

Whitney and I took the two seats nearest to the left door on the plane – he was the first person to jump, I was second. After the "turbulence testers" exited the aircraft, the "pathfinder" (person who sets up the drop zone and is responsible for DZ safety) would notify the plane's pilot to make in-flight adjustments as he observed the direction the winds carried us.

During the jump I made a very poor exit from the aircraft, which almost cost me my life. After viewing the film of the jump several days later, LTC Whitney brought a copy to the 389th and asked me what I was doing still alive.

I had just completed the next month's training schedule and was putting the finishing touches on the old training records in anticipation of the I.G.'s inspection tour when I was informed that two men in suits were waiting in the hall to see me. They introduced themselves as the lawyers of the young man who had not been allowed to apply at the police department and for whom I had rewritten the Covington city ordinance. The city was facing a large lawsuit. The old city ordinance, which had been reinstated, was now being challenged as unconstitutional. Substantial monetary damages were being asked for and I was requested to give a sworn statement concerning the incident which had taken place several years before. The old city ordinance was overturned and the city of Covington paid dearly for its shortsightedness. The young man was hired and became an excellent police officer. My faith in him was proven when I met him several years later at the public library. He had risen to the rank of Lieutenant and was preparing to take the Captain's examination.

Barbara scheduled a karate picnic to be held at Big Bone Park in Boone County, Kentucky. The park was located approximately four miles from our home. We invited Shane Higashi of the Canadian Chito-kai to attend as our guest instructor. Shane came with one of his students, Sensei Mike Delaney of Halifax, Nova Scotia. The picnic was a huge success. Approximately one hundred people participated. In addition to three hours of training on basics and kata, with great detail given to Seisan, Potsai and Chinto, a children's tournament was also held.

In August 1989, the 389th MI was ordered to Quantico, Virginia, the United States Marine Corps officers' school. Our mission was to support the 11th Special Forces Group's needs for real time, real world intelligence services. We were assigned to an isolated area, a small island away from the main post that was surrounded by a river. This same area was used by the Marine's secret "Blue Light" mission. "Blue Light" had been the U. S. Marine Corp's counter to the Army's "Delta Force", but was never adopted. We moved our personal gear and working gear into the huts, which were to serve as both our barracks and secured work areas. Our work at Quantico was classified as "Top Secret" and concerned real world missions. Personal vehicles were not allowed in the area since it was restricted. We were briefed about enemy satellite overflights and were required to remain inside the barracks during the time the satellites were over the Eastern United States.

Provisions for an airborne operation were made while we were at Quantico and the Marines were nice enough to supply us with Sea Stallion Helicopters to jump out of. We had the opportunity to ramp jump from a little over four thousand feet as the Stallion flew over the lush green hills and fields of Virginia.

Upon my return to Louisville, I telephoned Barbara to ask about how the karate school was doing and to inform her that I was back in Kentucky and would be home for supper.

"What do you want for supper?" she asked.

"How about some spaghetti?" I answered.

"What a surprise!" she replied.

Spaghetti is one of my favorite foods. If it weren't for ham, bologna, spaghetti, Twinkies, and Coca Cola, I would have died from starvation years ago.

Chapter 27

1990-1994

Life moves on, whether we act as cowards or heroes. Life has no other discipline to impose, if we would but realize it, than to accept life unquestioningly. Everything we shut our eyes to, everything we run away from, everything we deny, denigrate or despise, serves to defeat us in the end. What seems nasty, painful, or evil, can become a source of beauty, joy and strength, if faced with an open mind. Every moment is a golden one for him who has the vision to recognize it as such.

Henry Miller

My army SF unit was reorganized into four detachments. Major Wayne L. Burd was the Commanding Officer of Detachment 2, Support Company, 1st Battalion, 11th Special Forces Group. The Major was a reservist, but he was a hands-on type of officer. As an AGR active duty type, I was the unit NCOIC (Non-commissioned Officer in Charge). It was my job to handle the paperwork, orders, pay, operations and training schedule for the unit on a daily basis. Our battalion's headquarters was located at Newburgh, New York, a short drive north of the United States Military Academy at West Point. Shortly after the newly formed L-TO&E (Table of Organizations and Equipment) reorganization, the detachment received orders to go overseas.

One evening after supper, I told Barbara that I had to go overseas for a few weeks. I was allowed to furnish her with some limited information but was forbidden by military regulations to give her any detailed information.

"What are you going to do overseas?" she inquired.

"If I tell you, I will have to cut your head off and put it in a safe," I replied with a smile. Special Forces wives were used to hearing this; it was a stock answer. When the wives heard this, they knew that we could not and would not provide them with any details.

We were going to Europe to do some work with NATO (The North Atlantic Treaty Organization). Part of the unit was stationed in England while several other detachments were sent elsewhere. I was stationed in England at a base known as RAF Watton. After accomplishing our mission, we boarded a Lockheed C-141 Starlifter, a military jet transport approximately the same size as

The author by an abondoned bunker. I am tired, hot, dirty, hungry and thirsty (not necessarily in that order).

a Boeing 707, for the trip home.

True to my word, I returned home five weeks and two days from the time I had told Barbara I was going overseas. I telephoned her from Bowman Field.

"I'm ba-a-a-a-ck," I said when she answered the phone.

"Well I'm glad," she answered. "Will you be home for supper tonight?"

"I'll be home within two hours," I assured her.

"What do you want to eat?"

"Spaghetti!" I replied.

After coming home I returned to training at the little dojo in Covington with a vengeance. It felt good to be back at the dojo and to be able to teach my karate students again. During the classes I taught, I pushed myself to my physical limits. The students, as always, followed along and kept up to the best of their ability. When I did this, however, I was not the good instructor that I should have been. I lost a few students due to the physical and emotional strain they had to endure. I was positive that they left because of the accelerated pace of the training. Occasionally, my asthma gave me trouble but as long as I took my medicine it stayed under control. My knees were not as kind to me. I wore knee braces during the majority of my practice sessions and always when I taught classes. Other than an occasional breathing problem and the pain in my knees, I did not feel fifty-five. Hell, I did not feel thirty-five. I felt great! I attributed this to my many years of karate training and my military lifestyle, both of which allowed me to remain in peak physical condition.

I stood before the makiwara gazing at it. How often had I stood like this since my first training session in Beppu thirty-seven years before? I couldn't even hazard a guess. I stepped forward into seisan dachi and placed my right fist against the straw to measure the distance. The makiwara snapped backward as I slammed my fist into its straw-covered top again and again.

Barbara videotaped me doing the kata "Chinto" at the dojo one day after class. Upon reviewing the videotape I began to realize how much my technical skill had deteriorated, mainly due to a lack of practice while being on active duty with the army. Looking at the videotapes I saw many mistakes which, if made by one of my advanced students, would have brought sharp criticism from me. I practiced "Chinto" for over an hour as Barbara videotaped each performance. Whenever I spotted a mistake, however slight, I would modify my technique to the accepted pattern. An hour later I felt that, while my performance of the kata was still unacceptable, I had made a remarkable improvement. My most pressing problem was "rust". I didn't move like a black belt; my techniques lacked snap and kime. My three-year enlistment was almost up; I would be getting out on August 2, 1990. After that I could practice as much as I wanted.

Many of the older karate students continued to practice hard and make improvement. As in every karate school, there were many newer students who joined the karate school only to sample karate. Many left, but a few did stay and eventually became an integral part of the dojo.

I was still attempting to find a satisfactory method to integrate the techniques required by Japan into the training regimen at the dojo. I had no problems with Shihohai kata and the requirements for the higher ranks. My concerns lay with the lower ranking kata – Zenshin Kotai, the Kihon Dosas and Kihon Kata I through IV. These lower-ranking kata did not seem to work well for us. I objected to Zenshin Kotai on the grounds that it wasn't appropriately challenging; I felt very strongly that new students should learn how to do a front kick before they were taught a side kick. The Kihon Katas were still, in my opinion, too complicated for the vast majority of new students. The early use of side, round and back kicks plus the 360-degree spinning turns, an integral part of the Kihon Katas, did nothing to enhance a new student's ability to defend him/herself after a short period of training.

During this time, I was my own worst enemy. I wanted to teach the kata that O-Sensei had established, not as Soke directed. Yet, I also wanted to do what I knew was in the best interest of my students. I attempted to do both and that caused me a great deal of anguish. I flip-flopped back and forth several times, causing a great deal of confusion among both my newer students and my older students, many of whom had been with me for several years. This was a troubling time for all the members of the U. S. Chito-kai and I accept total blame for it. I should have had the fortitude to teach the Taikyoku katas, which I knew were better, but I didn't.

I was convinced that lower stances were better suited for beginning students. Funakoshi Sensei listed this as number seventeen of his Twenty Precepts. "Kamae wa shoshinsha ni, ato wa shinzentai." – Low stance for beginners, natural stance for advanced students. My belief in the lower stances for beginners was also reinforced by a Master of Tai Chi, Sifu Mok Lau, of Cincinnati, Ohio. The lower stances stretch new students' muscles and at the same time teach them to properly utilize their entire body mass when performing a technique. After students advance, they are taught to utilize a higher stance; the ability developed during their basic training period never leaves them, and they will retain the feeling and awareness of total body connection.

During the decade since Soke had taken over (1984-1994) I was in a quandary about doing what Japan wanted and what I knew without any doubt was best for my students. Chitose Sensei (O-Sensei) recognized my problem in 1973 during his visit to the United States Chito-kai Honbu. He told me then, "Dometrichi, you are in charge of the United States and know what is best for your students, so you must make your best decision as to training." I will always remember O-Sensei's words, even though I had ignored them after his son, Yasuhiro, took charge.

I had planned for years to build a karate dojo near my home in Boone County. Chitose Sensei told me that if I ever got it built he would like for me to name it the "Chito-kai Kan", which means, "Chito-kai School".

My next-door neighbor, Mike Helme, was employed in the construction indus-

The author with Inomoto and Debbie (1997).

try. I hired him and his brother to bulldoze a small flat area on the hillside behind my log cabin. My army buddies, headed by Chief Warrant Officer Paul Beane, came to my aid and helped me dig the holes for the pylons on which I planned to construct my small karate dojo. We worked on the project during our time off from the army (June and July, 1990). Everyone hoped that the pylon bases would be strong enough – since they were a 50-50 mix of concrete and Budweiser cans. With this new dojo I would soon have the convenience of training with some of my advanced students at my home. This was especially nice since the U. S. Chito-kai Honbu is in Covington – 30 miles from my home. I planned to start on the dojo's construction during September 1990.

Fate, however, was going to have its say and I was unable to start construction on the dojo during September. The Iraqi army invaded Kuwait, their small neighbor to the south on orders of Saddam Hussein on August 2, 1990. That night at midnight was to mark the last day of my three-year active duty tour. Like all U. S. military units the world over, we received a teletype message extending all enlistments of active duty personnel. My enlistment was extended until May 1991. After the bombing campaign started on January 17, 1991, I was extended until November 1992. Everyone on active duty at the unit could have cared less about having their enlistments extended. We were professionals and we all loved military life. We would get out when we got out. No big deal.

With the advent of Desert Shield, we started putting in longer hours at Bowman Field and our training took on a more serious character. All of the active duty personnel in the detachment volunteered to go to the Middle East. I request assignment to the Middle East and forwarded my request to 1st Battalion. I waited and waited, but heard nothing from 1st Battalion concerning my request. After my third attempt to volunteer, I received a telephone call from Captain Miller, 1st Battalion's Executive Officer.

"Sergeant Dometrich, how many of your detachment volunteered to go to Saudi Arabia?"

"Almost everyone, sir, isn't that great!" I answered.

The other end of the telephone was silent for a long time.

"Wrong answer," Captain Miller said. "I'm going to ask you again. Now! How many men of your detachment have volunteered for Saudi Arabia?"

"Almost everyone, Captain," I repeated.

"Again, wrong answer," Captain Miller reiterated. "Now, listen to me very carefully. Colonel Bergquist does not want anyone from your unit volunteering, am I making myself perfectly clear?"

"Loud and clear sir!" I said loudly into the phone.

But, being a hardhead, I submitted requests for duty in Saudi Arabia two more times. After the fifth request, I received another telephone call from Captain Miller.

"Sergeant Dometrich, it appears that I can't stop you from trying to go to Saudi Arabia. I do want to make it clear, however, I can't save your slot in Detachment 2 and you will have to find another position, if and when you return. Do I make myself perfectly clear?"

"Yes sir, perfectly clear, sir," I answered.

A special karate clinic was scheduled for November 1990 at Higashi Sensei's new karate

Sherry Dometrich Kembre performs Ni-Sei-Shi Kata.

dojo in Toronto, Canada. Soke was going to attend and teach a clinic on new techniques. I wanted very much to attend. Since my five requests for duty in the Gulf had been rejected, I decided to attend the clinic and see Higashi's new school. I filled out the required paperwork and forwarded it through military channels to obtain a special pass that would enable me to travel to Canada for the clinic. Orders were cut which would allow me to legally enter Canada without being declared AWOL or a deserter. I left Higashi Sensei's telephone number with Chief Bean in the event I would be required to make a hasty return to the Special Operations unit.

Barbara, several students and I drove the five hundred and fifty miles to Toronto. At the clinic, a new Chito-kai patch, very similar to the old design, was shown to us. Also, techniques which consisted of two concepts and included rapid 180 degree and 360-degree turns and spins were introduced.

Higashi and I practiced side by side in his crowded dojo. During a short break, he looked at me and said, "Isn't this great? We are the only style to do these techniques."

"They're OK," I replied, "but will they work in a self-defense situation?"

Sensei David Akutagawa acted as Soke's translator for the clinic. It was a good clinic, but even as I tried to focus on training, my mind was thousands of miles away in Saudi Arabia.

A few of my detachment members and karate students were there with a Special Operations unit. Sergeant Robert Shaffer, an S.F. (Special Forces) type and a Chito-ryu brown belt assigned to the Kentucky National Guard, asked me to write a letter stating that he had worked as a reporter for the Karate-Do News Bulletin. I wrote the letter which, with help from General Mike Davidson, got Bob to Saudi Arabia as an army news correspondent. After he arrived in Saudi Arabia, Bob, in all of the confusion, wrangled an assignment to the 5th Special Forces Group.

The air offensive against Iraq started on January 17, 1991. I moved a television set into the Army Reserve Center and every time there was a special bulletin or a Pentagon briefing we would stop what we were working on to watch it.

While we were eating lunch one day, a civilian stopped by our table and asked us how long we thought the war was going to last.

"It will be a short one or a long one," I said. "I don't think it will be the usual run-of-the-mill war."

After I left the restaurant I thought about what I had said and considered it a stupid statement. What was a "usual run-of-the-mill war" anyway? I didn't know and neither did anyone else.

We thought that there was a chance that the war would get bogged down and with so many U.S. Chito-kai members in the reserves, we were worried that the organization would be unable to properly host the Soke Cup. The Soke Cup is the International Chito-ryu Championship tournament held every three years and during the last tournament in Canada I had agreed to host the next one. I returned the "Soke Cup – 92" flag which I had accepted from Soke at the tournament in Vancouver, Canada, in 1989. I sent a letter to Soke and explained that many members of the U. S. Chito-kai were either members of the regular Army or the reserves and had been called to active duty. I didn't want the Soke Cup to fail because of our inability to staff it as a result of the war. If I waited until the last minute to send the flag back, Soke wouldn't have enough time to make other arrangements. But by sending it back early and not waiting until the last minute, Soke would have eighteen months to make other arrangements. I apologized for having to return the flag.

Saddam Hussein had made a great many terrorist threats against the United States. Everyone at the Army Reserve Center started carrying side arms. I carried a Sig Sauer P-226 in a shoulder holster with an extra magazine attached to it under my BDU's (Battle Dress Utilities) where it could not be seen. We couldn't stop a car bomb, but if someone came in shooting, he or she would be in for a big surprise. No major incidents occurred, but we all thought, "better safe than sorry." One thing was for sure; whoever attacked a member of my unit had better be ready for a fight.

The ground war started on the February 24. That night several members of my unit and I made a night training jump onto an airfield. Once again, I injured my left knee; I was three weeks shy of my fifty-sixth birthday. Four days later on the 28th of February, the "100 hour war" ended. I realized once the war was over that the U. S. Chito-kai could have hosted the Soke Cup, but on January 17 we had no way of knowing that. I had already sent the flag back and had no intention of asking for it to be returned.

One nice thing that occurred as a result of Desert Shield and Desert Storm was the way we, as soldiers, were treated by the civilian population. People took time to stop and talk to us and wish us well, even though we were not being sent overseas, and they would smile and wave at us. It was a good time to be an American soldier and, for a change, it felt good.

I attended karate classes at the Yoseikan in Covington approximately twice a week after Operation Desert Storm ended. My recent knee injury was giving me a great deal of trouble. I wore a brace when practicing so it wouldn't collapse.

I had introduced once again, the kata and techniques that Soke wanted taught, but I still felt that these techniques were inferior to what the students at the hombu in Covington were learning. The students practiced the Kihon Dosas and the Kihon Katas and other required techniques and kata as established by Soke in Japan. It was still my opinion that the techniques were not well thought out for beginning students. The constant changing back and forth was still causing confusion among the students, for which I must take complete blame. I was trying to comply with the International Chito-kai requirements and to please Soke. I blamed myself for the confusion. Once again, I felt that my students' basic techniques were starting to deteriorate. So, in trying to follow my heart and what I felt was best for my students, I again started teaching my beginning students the Taikyoku series of basic kata. I felt that this change was necessary to create stronger stances and basic techniques.

I took a week's leave during September 1991. Barbara and I went camping at Audra State Park in West Virginia. During our third night of camping we were awakened at 2:30 AM by a park ranger who had a telephone number we were to call immediately. It was an emergency. I made the call and was told that our son, Billy, whom we called Bill or B.J. (his initials) now that he was older, had been admitted to Saint Elizabeth Hospital with pneumonia and was not expected to live. Hurriedly, we packed the camper and rushed back to Covington immediately. It was 9:45 AM when we arrived; we drove straight to the hospital. B.J.'s doctor, Dr. Cohen, took us aside and told us the bad news. Our son had full-blown AIDS. This news hit my wife and me like a ton of bricks.

The author at a tournament in early 1970s, with an injured right hand.

"Your son has told the nurses that he wants to die and to leave him alone," Dr. Cohen informed us. "Perhaps you can talk him out of this attitude," the doctor said, looking at me.

Upon entering the room, it was obvious that Bill was having great difficulty breathing. I could relate to his suffering because of my asthma.

"Hi kid, I hope that you're feeling better," I said.

"I'm sorry dad. Please don't let me die," he pleaded.

"I'll try to not let you die," I answered, knowing full well that this was one promise I couldn't keep.

Bill stayed in the hospital for three weeks for tests and evaluations while I returned to work at the unit in Louisville. At the end of each workday I would drive to the hospital to be with Bill. I slept in a chair in his hospital room and tried to comfort him. He slept very little and in the early morning hours when he was awake, I would bid him goodbye as I left for Louisville at 4:00 AM for another day's work at Bowman Field.

Finally, Bill was released to go home. He had many pills and other medicines which he had to take on a daily basis. He also had to make regularly scheduled visits to Dr. Cohen.

"I don't know how long he'll live," the doctor informed us. "It will help if he has a good, positive outlook, doesn't tire himself and doesn't worry. He may live for two years or more – it's impossible to say."

At the end of November 1991, I was scheduled to report to the hospital at Fort Knox and have my left knee (the one that I had injured in February) operated on. The operation seemed successful and my knee was fine for a while. Approximately eight weeks after the operation my left knee started to give me trouble again. I put my leg brace back on and decided to wait until my knee gave out before having another operation. Nine years and two months later, I had my left knee totally replaced with a mechanical, artificial knee.

During all of 1992, my son Bill was in and out of hospitals with various symptoms which I have since learned are related to AIDS. I was still driving between Louisville and Covington daily, a round trip of approximately 200 miles a day. On a few occasions I had to travel on business for the unit. When I was away I phoned Barbara to checked on Bill's condition.

Kathy Webster, a registered nurse and one of the best friends my wife and I have, assisted us greatly with our son during this trying time. She would take her own spare time and stop by his apartment to check on him, see that he was taking his medication and comfort him to the best of her ability. She was and still is a very close friend.

In August 1992, the Soke Cup was held in Sydney, Australia. The United States sent a team to the Soke Cup which didn't do well. (The U.S. team had the highest average age of any team at the Soke Cup.) Brian Hayes, the Chief Instructor of the Australian Chito-kai, did an excellent job of hosting the tournament.

Several American students were taken aside to receive private instruction by Masaru Inomoto, the head of the International Chito-kai Technical Committee, on the direct orders of Soke while at the Soke Cup in Australia. Upon their return to the United States I was put under pressure by a few of them to switch the U. S. Honbu's requirements back to the Japanese beginner's technical requirements – again – those same techniques that had caused massive confusion earlier.

Two black belts approached me with the idea of holding an annual United States Chito-kai summer camp. I agreed to give it a try and sent a letter to Soke to run the idea by him. I told him that if we did have a summer camp, I would like for him to attend as the Chief Instructor. He said that he would attend and we set the date of the camp – the last weekend of August 1993. Everyone was very excited about the prospect of a local summer camp (Up to this point, my students and I had been attending a camp in Banff in the western part of Canada.).

Sergeant Fox and I again received orders to report to Washington D. C. for temporary assignment to the ITAC. We reported in on Monday morning. On Tuesday morning we left for Fort Meade and spent half a day at 11th SF Group Headquarters getting detailed instructions about our next assignment. After returning to Washington, we were kept very busy performing our assigned tasks; we were successful.

Soke Chitose advised me that I was to travel to Canmore, Alberta, Canada, to take a test for Hachi-dan. I had never heard of a technical test for any rank above Go-dan – this was a first. I was also required to present two short papers. One paper was titled "What Chito-ryu Means To Me", and the second was, "How Can We Improve Chito-ryu".

In August I attended the Canmore clinic with Sensei George VanHorne and four students from the U. S. Chito-kai. Soke Yasuhiro Chitose headed the clinic. He was assisted by Senseis Tashiro, Inomoto, Kugizaki, Tanaka, Higashi, and Akutagawa.

Upon arriving at Canmore, I presented Soke with the two papers which he had requested some months earlier. My, "How to Improve Chito-ryu" paper said we should adopt sound business practices, start answering our mail in a timely manner, and start acting like an organization that was democratic and international in scope. It wasn't long before I knew that Soke was not happy with my paper. I also knew that few, if any, of my suggestions would be heeded.

I attempted to take every class while in Canmore but I missed three. I missed one because of a scheduled sight-seeing tour north to the glacier, although when we arrived at the glacier it was so foggy we couldn't see. I missed the other two classes because of a two-hour meeting that was scheduled for the next day.

Tsutomu Tashiro, a true warrior, a true heart, and a true dedication to budo.

On Wednesday afternoon both Higashi Sensei and I were informed that we were to test for the rank of Hachi-dan. We were escorted away from the others into a kitchen and cafeteria area. After shoving the tables and chairs aside so we would have room to demonstrate the required techniques, Higashi Sensei and I stretched and warmed up. Seated at one of the cafeteria tables were Soke, Kugizaki and Inomoto, who were to be the test board. Kuzahara Sensei acted as the translator and board secretary. I was requested to do one kata of my choice. I did Ryushan and, in truth, I didn't do it well. I could not blame my knees, because, for once, they weren't bothering me. The problem was rust; I hadn't been training the way I should have because of my military duties. When I finished, Higashi Sensei performed his kata which, while not perfect, was better than the one I had done. We were never told the results of the test. I would have been satisfied to have a "You flunked!" but nothing was said and we were left hanging.

The next afternoon the meeting started at 2:00 PM. Present at the meeting were Soke Chitose, Tashiro Sensei, Inomoto Sensei, Kuzahara Sensei, Kimura Sensei, Higashi Sensei, Akutagawa Sensei, VanHorne Sensei, Ingabritsen Sensei and several others.

Kimura Sensei, the International Chito-kai general secretary, chaired the meeting. Tashiro Sensei, who was in his seventies, tendered his resignation as the President of the International Chito-kai. I nominated Higashi Sensei of Canada as a candidate for President. I thought that my nomination would be seconded and voted on by those present. The room suddenly became very quiet. After a brief conference in Japanese at the head table I was politely informed that Soke would choose another President. I reminded everyone present that the name of the organization was the INTERNATIONAL Chito-kai and that many countries other than Japan made up the 'International'. However, Soke had made his decision. He would choose HIS new President at his leisure after returning to Japan.

"The only thing 'international' about this organization is the name," I told them. "If this was truly a democratic organization each country should have one vote – including Japan." My comments, as expected, did not go over well with Soke. I was not trying to be a maverick. I said what I thought needed to be said. However, in doing what I had thought was in the best interest of the organization, I had unwittingly committed seppuku.

Kimura Sensei then stood up, took the floor and proceeded to present the organization's budget report and financial statement. After seventy-five minutes of listening to this one report, I made a motion that we vote to accept the financial report as is, so we could move to other, more important business. Soke informed me and the others present that Kimura-san had spent a lot of time preparing the report and we owed him the respect of hearing it in its entirety. Three and a half hours later the meeting was recessed for supper. We were to be back in our seats at 6:30 PM and the meeting would continue. By 11:30 that night I was doing a slow burn, much to the amusement of Sensei George VanHorne. Here were the key personnel of the International Chito-kai, trying to build a large organization and they couldn't even keep a business meeting on schedule. Someone who really cared about the advancement of Chito-ryu at an international level and about the legacy of Dr. Chitose had to tell these men the truth, even if it hurt. All of those present had dreamed of building a large international organization, but the entire process was managed worse than a "mom and pop" grocery store. The "two-hour meeting", which had begun at 2:00 PM, adjourned at 2:00 AM – only ten hours late.

The 1993 U. S. Chito-kai Summer Camp was scheduled to be held at Camp Ernst, a YMCA camp, approximately fifteen miles from downtown Cincinnati. Soke had agreed to the date and everything was going according to plan. Then the bombshell hit.

A short time before camp was to take place, I was notified that Soke could not attend the camp. I was given a choice for a new date, but could not re-schedule Camp Ernst, which had other activities scheduled at that time. We lost our deposit for the camp and had to scurry to locate a facility which would rent to us on such short notice. What was to be a summer camp did not happen, and the result was a disaster. In the end, we finally located a small grade school gymnasium with an old gym floor that was desperately in need of repair and rougher than the concrete outside. On this small, overcrowded gym floor, Soke worked the students in tsuki-kaeshi (two quick 180 degree turns with punches), rinten-hanten (one or two 360 degree turns while lunge punching), and countless other techniques which wore out my student's feet and knees. Later I heard, but could not substantiate, that Soke knew well in advance that he would not attend the summer camp as scheduled, but he still waited until the last moment to notify me.

After training at Ludlow Elementary School, Soke told me that he wanted to go to my home to rest. He said he would appreciate it if I did not invite any students to my home. While Soke and I were alone in my living room, I asked him to look at my Chito-ryu kata and make comments as to how I could improve them. He made very few suggestions, which I felt meant that he approved of the way I performed the kata.

The next day Soke, Barbara and I drove to Camp Ernst so I could show him the great facilities that we had lost because of his last minute date change. I agreed to hold another summer camp at Camp Ernst in 1994 and he promised that he would attend the camp without fail. Time would tell.

I said my farewells to the army in October. No longer would I have to get up at 4:00 AM to get to work on time. No longer would I be working ten and twelve hour days or thirteen to fourteen days without a day off. I would no longer have to sleep in the snow, jump out of perfectly good airplanes in mid-flight or put up with the bull-throwing of the guys in the unit. Only God knew how much I was going to miss the army. On October 27, 1993, I was handed an Honorable Discharge – it was my fourth.

During January and February of 1994, my son Bill gradually got worse as the AIDS consumed him. Barbara and I were attempting to take care of Bill while managing the dojo and preparing for the upcoming summer camp at the same time.

1990-1994

Barbara and Debbie flew with Bill to Boston, to see an eye specialist. By this time Bill was in a wheelchair and almost blind. Bill's sight had been slowly deteriorating since the final days of last year and it had now faded to the point where he was almost totally blind. With his mother and Debbie, he flew out of the Cincinnati area with very little of his sight remaining. He returned home from Boston totally blind. The operation was a complete failure.

Along with everything that was happening, I had the added stress of two of my students going to Japan; they wanted to visit the International Chito-kai Honbu in Kumamoto to train.

"I have no problems with that," I informed them. "However, if you learn of any modifications to the kata or new techniques, I want you to show them to me and the other ranking black belts first. Nothing is to be taught to any of my students without my permission." Both men agreed to my conditions and assured me that they would comply. They both went to Japan and returned with no news of changes or modifications.

As I was teaching a class at the Yoseikan Dojo on Tuesday, July 26, I noticed that several students were doing certain techniques differently than I had taught them. When I inquired about what was going on, the student who had run in front of his ranking sensei to see Soke when we were in Japan in 1986 informed me (from the second row), "This is the way it's being taught in Japan."

I realized then that the students who had gone to Japan had broken their word to me. I was deeply irritated by this breach of trust on their part. Both men had started as white belts under my direction and both had reached their current rank of Yon-dan because I had taught them. After the long hours of teaching karate at the dojo, working with my wife to set up a successful summer camp, and staying up nights with my dying son, the strain finally got to me and I lost it.

I was teaching an average class, not too easy not too difficult. After I became aware of their treachery, the class immediately became much harder and very demanding. Their betrayal hurt me very much. After the class, several students told me that the class was one of the best I had taught in years. Martin McKamey, who was leaving for Italy the next day, came to me after the class and thanked me for such a wonderful class. He thought that I had taught this demanding class as a going away salute to him. A student who had been with me for twenty-five years also approached me after the class.

"Shihan, do you think it would be OK if a few black belts and I come out to your house tomorrow night to talk to you?"

"Sure thing," I said. "How about 7:00 PM?"

I told Barbara about the students coming out on Wednesday night.

"What is it about?" she inquired.

"I don't know," I replied. "They know that B.J. is very sick. I guess they want to see what they can do to help us with summer camp and the school."

On Wednesday, July 27, four students arrived at my home shortly after 7:00 PM. The student who had approached me at the dojo, the same one that I had made the President of the U.S. Chito-kai, presented me with a letter requiring me to do the following things:

1. I was to resign as the head of U. S. Chito-ryu;

2. I was not to practice karate for one year;

3. I was not to come near the dojo on class days for one year;

4. I was to have absolutely no contact with any of my students;

5. After one year, if I complied with the above, I might be allowed to return to train in my dojo, but I would not be allowed to teach.

They also told me that the organization had not grown fast enough and they held me responsible for that lack of growth. I reminded them, that I had placed them in positions of authority so they could manage the organization during my tenure in the army. The President was the chief of operations for the organization. Two of those present (the two who had traveled to Japan) had been appointed by me to head the U. S. Chito-kai technical committee.

I asked what had they done to help the organization grow while I was away on active duty. Not one of them had ever made an attempt to open his own dojo. On several occasions I had requested that these students consider opening branch dojos in several surrounding areas: Dayton, Ohio; Eastgate (an area in Cincinnati); Florence, Kentucky. Not one of them had ever tried to open a dojo, yet, here they were demanding that I give them my dojo, the dojo that my wife and I had built at the request of Doctor Tsuyoshi Chitose and which we had financed with our own money.

Barbara became very upset. I thought that she might strike one of them. I sat there stunned. I was exhausted physically, mentally and now, spiritually. Perhaps my son's illness, my lack of sleep and working to get ready for our first summer camp had taken its toll. I did not get upset, which surprised them, and in truth, it surprised me even more than it did them.

I informed them that I would think over their proposal and I would let them have my decision within three days on Saturday, July 30, at the monthly Executive Committee Meeting scheduled to be held at the Hombu. The next two days (Thursday and Friday) were hectic to say the very least. The instructors of all the branch dojos, except the one dojo in New Jersey, voted to keep me as head of the organization. Under the U. S. Chito-kai Constitution the head instructors and dojo owners were the ones with voting power, not the bureaucrats that had darkened my door on that fateful day.

The members of the Board of Directors informed me that if I resigned and turned the organization over to the "palace guard" (as the students who had come to my home came to be known), they would resign from the organization, quit teaching Chito-ryu, and seek admission to other organizations or styles. Twenty-seven years earlier when Dr. Chitose had put me in charge, he had made me promise that I would build a good organization and honbu. He understood that as a young police officer it would be impossible for me to travel and build a large organization. Dr. Chitose had made me the chairman of the U.S. Chito-kai for life. Now, twenty-seven years later, if I resigned, Doctor Chitose's dreams, as well as Barbara's and mine, would be destroyed.

Saturday morning at the Yoseikan Honbu, the Executive Committee meeting was convened. The instructor from New Jersey flew in to attend. He was the only member of the Board of Directors to vote against my remaining in charge. He had come to me ten years earlier asking me to accept him as a student and now here he was trying to throw me out of the organization that my wife and I had founded.

When I refused their demands to resign, they stood up from the conference table and threw down their pre-dated resignation letters. The resignations were dated four days earlier, the Wednesday night that they had come to my home.

I chose to talk to the five of them alone. The meeting had been very tense and I felt that I could relieve some of the tension by speaking with these students alone. I dismissed my supporters, making them feel slighted; they didn't understand why I had sent them away and they were very upset by the lack of loyalty exhibited by the "palace guard". I then attempted to talk to "the guard" not as an instructor, but as a friend. Except for the instructor from New Jersey, each of them had started their karate training as white belts under me.

"My son is dying of AIDS, don't you think this is a bad time to do this to me?" I asked them.

"Any time is bad," the Japanese (who had started with me as a white belt) said coldly. "When he does die, that will be a bad time, too."

As they stood up to leave, the student I had looked upon almost as a son (the student involved in the hit-skip and who's girlfriend drowned in the Ohio River) stared at me and said coldly, "You are a disgrace to Chito-ryu Karate. In a couple of weeks you will find out who the real boss is."

I couldn't believe my ears. I couldn't believe that this student, whom I had stuck with through thick and thin, could say this to me.

I informed Yasuhiro (Soke) Chitose that "the guard" had resigned after attempting to illegally take over the United States Chito-ryu Karate Federation and in doing so had violated both the U. S. Chito-kai and the International Chito-kai Constitutions. In fact, I sent a fax to Soke and informed him that they had violated the International Chito-ryu Constitution as approved by him. They were in violation of Article 3, Membership Section 9, sub-section 1, and were to be expelled from the International organization immediately. Article 3, Section 9, sub-section 1 stated that:

The author, at 64 years old with a black eye from sparring, and Arthur Rott, founder of Florida Dojos. He also sold us the honbu.

"Those members who withdraw from the member country's association are regarded as having withdrawn from the International Chito-kai organization."

I received a fax back from Soke. He demanded that I contact the students and negotiate with them. I informed him that I would not contact them or negotiate with them. I had asked them at the meeting to reconsider, and they insulted me and threw their resignations at me. I felt that if they wanted to negotiate, they should contact me.

The next fax that I received from Soke (Yasuhiro Chitose) informed me that he wanted me to give him permission to negotiate with the students who had tried to depose me. My answer was, "No."

His next fax stated that unless I authorized him to negotiate with them, he would not attend the 1994 U. S. Summer Camp. By this time it was obvious that he, Soke, was refusing to enforce his own International Chito-kai Constitution for some unknown reason. I did not feel like continuing the "Fax War" with him. He had fouled up my summer camp in 1993, and he had given me his word that he would, without fail, participate in the 1994 camp. I notified him that I was withdrawing his invitation. He was no longer expected to participate in our summer camp – we would do it without him. In his final fax, Soke informed me that I was to close my dojo immediately. My immediate reaction was, "Who died and made him king of the United States?" On August 12, 1994, I sent a final fax to Japan announcing that at one second after midnight, the 13th day of August 1994, the United States Chito-ryu Karate Federation would become an independent organization.

Within a few years others would also leave the International Chito-kai. Akutagawa Sensei of Canada, and Inomoto Sensei, who had been the co-chairs of the International Chito-kai Technical Board with Kugizaki Sensei, would leave as would Ikeda Sensei, a member of the Board. Ken Sakamoto, Yasuhiro's brother-in-law, who had replaced Kimura Sensei as the International Secretary, also left, as did Nagata Sensei, the International Chito-kai President. I was but the first of many. The Chito-kai organization which had been so successfully run by Chitose (O-Sensei) Sensei, the founder of the Chito-ryu style, was starting to disintegrate under the direction of his son, Yasuhiro.

The United States Chito-ryu Karate Federation, now an independent organization, held its first summer camp at Camp Ernst, as scheduled, using the talent of the senior black belts of our own organization. That first summer camp was successful beyond our wildest dreams. A hidden blessing was that we had proven to ourselves that we could function as well, if not better, without the international organization. Months later I was informed by a Japanese friend that Yasuhiro Chitose had been behind my attempted ouster. He had instructed a couple of those students who had tried to oust me, that they should present their demands to me at the worst possible time in my life and I would most likely give in to them because of the pressures I was experiencing.

They had picked the right time, my son B.J. died at home from AIDS on September 20, 1994 at 2:25 PM. Less than a month after the end of our first successful U. S. Summer Camp, my son was gone. He was thirty-eight years three months and eleven days old, however he would forever remain my little boy.

At B.J.'s funeral, five of the people who less than seven weeks before told me that I was a disgrace to Chito-ryu, that my son had to die sometime, and who had attempted to evict me from my own karate school, showed up outside the funeral home in which my son's body lay. They were ordered to leave the area immediately by some of my very irate students. The next few months were hectic. A new Constitution was created, a new patch was designed and Shihan Lawrence Hawkins, Jr. became the new President of the U.S. Chito-kai.

William J. Dometrich II, who died of AIDS during September 1994.

As the sun rose on January 1, 1995 and marked the start of the new year, it also rose upon a newly independent United States Chito-ryu Karate Federation. On New Year's Day, a new plaque was placed just inside the entrance of the United States Chito-ryu Karate Federation's Honbu, the Yoseikan Dojo on Martin Street. I read the first part of the Mission Statement that was on the plaque:

> "All members of the United States Chito-ryu Karate Federation shall be guided by the insight of Doctor Tsuyoshi Chitose (O-Sensei), whose dedication established our past, whose genius determines our present, and whose vision shapes our future. We will preserve his place in karate history."

Standing at the dojo entrance, I felt a renewed sense of pride in those students who had remained loyal to me during the recent upheaval, and who would assist me as, together, we would take Chito-ryu karate-do into the next millennium.

• •

Chapter 28

1995-1999

This is the place where we must sever...You go thousands of miles my friend. Once forever, like the floating clouds we drift apart... The sunset lingers like the feelings of my heart.

By the poet, Li Pai

January 1995 saw a National Test Board established by the United States Chito-ryu Karate Federation. All of the students throughout the United States testing for the rank of ik-kyu (1st degree brown belt) and higher would now be required to appear before the National Test Board. In order to be promoted, applicants must complete the national test form, take a written test and have their thesis mailed in to the National Test Board at least one month prior to the test. The test for ik-kyu through san-dan was scheduled for Saturday at the Yoseikan Honbu in Covington. Anyone who failed his or her test would be allowed to retest every six months until they were able to pass the required test. The test for yon-dan (4th degree black belt) and higher was set for Friday night at the Chito-kai Kan, (my home dojo in Boone County). The higher-ranking students were required to meet different standards than those applied to the lower-ranking students. Candidates for 4th and 5th dan had to be sponsored by a ranking member of the Shihan-kai. If these candidates failed the test they were not allowed to automatically return to be retested. If the sponsored candidate did fail their test, two things happened: first – the sponsoring shihan would get in trouble because he had assured the test board that the candidate was ready to test; second – the candidate who failed the test would not be allowed to retest until re-invited and re-sponsored, by another (different) Shihan, which could take years. The retest was not an automatically assigned privilege or right.

The first National Test Board was scheduled for March 1995. All applications, theses, photographs and fees were required to be at the U. S. Honbu at least thirty days prior to the test day. Those applications which were received late were rejected. The National Test Board was to be convened biannually (every March, my birth month, and October, Chitose Sensei's birth month). In conjunction with the test, a national technical clinic was also scheduled for Saturday afternoon.

The first nationally scheduled test was flawless. It could not have been better. Everyone testing was well prepared and passed easily. Hanshi Masami Tsuruoka, my sempai, was the guest instructor at the clinic.

Tsuruoka Sensei also attended the second summer camp at Camp Ernst in August where he introduced a new concept of relaxation training. These new training ideas were well received by the U. S. students and the results could be seen immediately in their improved performance.

In October 1995, the second United States Chito-ryu Karate Federation's National Test Board was again convened at the Honbu. Much to our dismay the second national test board was the exact opposite of the first test. Several students were unprepared and failed their test. Stricter rules were established for appearing before the Test Board. The joke throughout the organization soon became that the motto of the National Test Board was: "We don't like anybody."

An instructors' course was introduced at the 1996 summer camp. It was designed to assist the teachers at the various Chito-ryu dojos. Earlier that year, members of the organization had traveled to Puerto Rico to help establish a viable Chito-kai on the island. The U.S. Chito-kai had also spread into India and Canada; we even had students in England. We were invited to travel to Egypt, Pakistan, Nepal, Africa, Russia, and Soviet-Georgia to demonstrate Chito-ryu with the possibility of starting Chito-ryu schools there.

From 1977 through the year 2000 the U.S. Chito-kai hosted several clinics at the Yoseikan honbu. These clinics were taught by a "Who's Who" of distinguished karate and martial arts instructors. Among them are: Dr. Hiroyuki Tesshin Hamada, Hanshi, Chair of the International Division of the famed Dai Nippon Butoku Kai of Kyoto, Japan; Masami Tsuruoka, "Father of Canadian Karate"; David Akutagawa, Chief Instructor of Chito-ryu in western Canada; Fumio Demura of Shito-Ryu; John Sells, the noted karate historian and author of the best-seller, "Unante"; Patrick McCarthy, well-known martial arts historical researcher, and member of the prestigious Dai Nippon Butoku Kai of Kyoto, Takayuki Mikami 1959 Japanese karate champion; Masaru Inomoto and Tatsunori Ikeda, both former members of the International Chito-kai Technical Committee. Also visiting were Masukazu Kawakita, the 1997 All Japan full contact karate champion and his father Kazunori Kawakita who once was five-time

Sensei John Sells demonstrates kata at the U.S. Chito-kai Hombu. He is the author of the historical book on karate: Unante.

All Southern Japan kumite champion for 1963 through 1967.

I was invited by Shihan Joe Mirza, President of the United States Amateur Athletic Union Karate Committee to accompany him to the World Karate Tournament in Aritzo, Italy in May 1997. During one of the breaks in the tournament Joe, Sensei Chuzo Kotaka, the women's team coach, and I went downtown sightseeing. Stopping at a very old Catholic church we went inside. Once inside the church both Joe and I entered a pew for a few minutes of personal prayer. As we started to leave Joe and I knelt and made the sign of the cross. As we were walking toward the door, Sensei Chuzo Kotaka walked along beside me.

"Dometrich Sensei, I did not know that you were Catholic?" he inquired.

"Oh, yes, Sensei," I replied. "I am Catholic, Buddhist, Muslim, Hindu, Jewish – a little bit of everything."

Shihan George VanHorne, Sensei James Davenport and I traveled to Okinawa in August for the fiftieth anniversary tournament celebrating the founding of the Okinawan Karate Federation. George had left Kentucky a few days before Jim and I and he was waiting for us when we arrived.

Naha in August is extremely hot. The temperature rose to ninety-nine degrees every day. I told George and Jim that I didn't care how hot it was, we were going to wear our Chito-kai dress suits and ties. I felt that since we were on Okinawa where my Sensei was born, we were his representatives and should dress in a manner to demonstrate our respect for O-Sensei.

Immediately upon entering the new Okinawan Budokan, a young Japanese girl, who was a greeter, spotted us and said, "Oh! Special Guests." She proceeded to pin a corsage on us, then escorted us to the VIP section in the balcony. We had only been in our seats for a short time when word was sent to Takayoshi

Nagamine, who was teaching a clinic on the main floor, that I was present in the audience. Upon learning that I was in the building, Takayoshi had his assistant take over the teaching and came upstairs to greet me. It was like seeing a long lost brother again.

"You must come downstairs with me so I can introduce you to my students," he told me.

After we were introduced to his many students, the three of us paid our respects to Takayoshi's ninety-year-old father Hanshi Shoshin Nagamine, who was kind enough to allow us to take a photograph with him. Over the next few days we found the tournament, clinics and demonstrations very inspiring.

George VanHorne left Okinawa early, leaving Jim and me behind. He had to pick up his son Edgar, who had been staying with the Kawakita family on Kyushu Island, before returning to the United States.

Jim Davenport received permission to train at Eiichi Miyazato's Goju-ryu dojo (the Jundokan). For several days he ran to the dojo twice a day (in 90 degree heat) from our hotel – the Naha Higashi Hotel (Naha East Hotel). The run covered about four miles round-trip.

At twilight one evening, while Jim and I were walking north on Kokusaidori Street, two Japanese walking in the opposite direction noticed our polo shirts, which were adorned with the U. S. Chito-kai crest.

"Chito-ryu!" the older Japanese said loudly.

It took me a couple of seconds to recognize the gentleman. It was Shihan Toshikatsu Okamoto, a Chito-ryu Hachidan who lived in Okayama City. He had lost a great deal of weight – I had last seen him at the International Chito-ryu Soke Cup in 1989. We communicated to the best of our ability for a few minutes, bowed, and then continued on our way.

Several days later, after Jim and I had visited various dojos around the island, we boarded an All Nippon Airlines plane for our short hop to Kumamoto City, located on the island of Kyushu. We planned to visit with several of the Japanese friends we had made over the years.

The first person we saw was Masaru Inomoto Sensei, former Chairman of the International Chito-kai Technical Committee. Inomoto Sensei took me to the gravesite of our teacher, Chitose Sensei.

I walked to the front of O-Sensei's grave and bowed. Looking at the grave, I felt very sad and lonely, almost as if O-Sensei had deserted me.

Standing in front of Dr. Chitose's grave brought back decades of fond memories. He was one of the greatest karate sensei in Japan and he would be greatly missed.

"Osu, Sensei," I said as I bowed a second time.

I stood there in silence for several minutes as I contemplated the years gone by: my first meeting with O-Sensei, his refusal to accept me as a student, then his change of mind and my final acceptance. Without this man and his wonderful karate teachings, my life would have been incomplete.

"Domo arigato gozaimasu, Sensei," I said softly as I bowed again. Slowly, I walked from his grave back to Inomoto's car.

On Wednesday afternoon Inomoto Sensei invited a few former members of the International Chito-kai to stop by his dojo and visit with us. Some of those who came to visit were: Ikeda Sensei – a former member of the International Technical Committee; Ken Sakamoto Sensei – the former International Chito-kai Secretary; and Nagata Sensei – the former International Chairman. The topic of discussion among all these men was the current state of affairs of the International Chito-kai. I gained a new insight into why most of the present problems existed. Before parting company, all of those present agreed to strive for the advancement of Chito-ryu in our own areas, and to always keep our beloved teacher's lessons present in our classes and our hearts.

Two days later Kazunori Kawakita and his son, Masukazu, arrived at Inomoto's home in their Lexus 400 to take Jim and me to their house and dojo in Nogata. Our visits with Inomoto and Kawakita couldn't have been better. But it was now time to return home and continue our mission on O-Sensei's behalf.

Jim and I flew to Tokyo to begin our return trip to the U. S. We changed our flight plans to include a three day layover in Hawaii. During our short stay, we visited with Sensei Charles Goodin, the editor of "Furyu Magazine", Chuzo

Kotaka, the United States A.A.U.'s National Coach, Sensei Lee Donohue, the current Chief of Police of Hawaii, and Sensei James Miyagi, a former Chito-ryu stylist under Sensei Tommy Morita several decades before.

Mike Awad, a sensei of the United States Karate Association, who had a karate dojo on the east side of Cincinnati, notified me that on June 20, 1997 he was hosting a clinic at his dojo. The guest instructor was Kyoshi Patrick McCarthy, a world-renowned martial arts historian and member and certified instructor at the famous Dai Nippon Butoku Kai in Kyoto, Japan.

The Dai Nippon Butoku Kai – Greater Japanese Martial Arts Virtue Society – was founded by the Japanese Imperial Family in 1895 for the preservation of the principles upon which the traditional Japanese martial arts were founded. The Dai Nippon Butoku Kai has its headquarters in Kyoto, Japan. A martial arts college, the Bujutsu Senmon Gakko – Dai Nippon Butoku Kai Martial Arts Specialty Academy, was founded in 1911 to train teachers.

The clinic was very informative and Kyoshi McCarthy's presentation was excellent. It was obvious to everyone present that he was very familiar with the subject matter and that he enjoyed teaching. Before we knew it, the clinic was over – it was 10:30 PM. Patrick, three of my students and I drove to the Yoseikan in Covington and continued training until 5:30 the next morning.

Pictured here are, from left to right: Ken Sakamoto, former International Chito-kai Secretary and Treasurer; the author; James Davenport, Deputy U.S. Chief Instructor; Masaru Inomoto, former Head of the International Chito-kai Technical Committee and Minoru Nagata, former International Chito-kai President.

Sherry Dometrich Kembre, Sei-San Kata.

Earlier, Shihan George VanHorne and Sensei Jim Davenport had approached Patrick McCarthy concerning the possibility of my becoming a member of the Dai Nippon Butoku Kai.

We left the Yoseikan at about 5:30 and I drove Kyoshi McCarthy back to Sensei Awad's home in Ohio. It was during the drive back that Kyoshi McCarthy brought up the subject of the Dai Nippon Butoku Kai and his conversation with George and Jim.

Shortly after Kyoshi McCarthy had returned home, he wrote and told me that he had nominated me for membership. Within a very short time I received a letter of inquiry from Doctor Hiroyuki Tesshin Hamada, Hanshi, Chairman of the International Division of the Dai Nippon Butoku Kai requesting that I complete the enclosed application. A couple of months after I had mailed my application I was notified that I was to be interviewed by Hamada Hanshi in Norfolk, Virginia. My wife and I drove to Virginia where I met another candidate, Shihan Ken Tallack from Canada. After an excellent dinner with Hamada Hanshi on the night of our arrival, Ken Tallack, several of Hamada Hanshi's students, my wife, and I eagerly anticipated the next day's training. I was inducted into the Dai Nippon Butoku Kai in May 1998 by Hamada Hanshi. A few months after becoming a general member, I was accepted as a regular member.

I had received two diplomas from Dr. Hiroyuki Tesshin Hamada. One diploma recognized my 7th Dan, the second diploma acknowledged my title of Kyoshi. Both diplomas were signed and sealed by His Majesty, Higashi Fushimi Jigo, a member of the Japanese Imperial Family (the Emperor's cousin) and the Chairman of the Dai Nippon Butoku Kai.

Now approaching my mid-sixties, I have redirected my life, not only to Chito-ryu karate, but also to the preservation of all traditional forms of Japanese budo.

On Sunday, October 4, 1998, five U. S. Chito-ryu students and I stood in the center of the gymnasium at the Old Dominion University in Norfolk, Virginia. Seated before us were twenty-two ranking members of the Dai Nippon Butoku-kai. Seated at the center of the row of tables were two members of the Japanese Imperial Family. I gave the honor of performing the first kata to my daughter, Sherry Lynn Kembre. She was to demonstrate the kata, Seisan. I performed the second kata, Kusanku Dai, followed by three self-defense techniques from the kata. The kata team consisted of five students with Sherry in the center position. Jim Davenport, Dr. Jerry Wellbrock, Alec MacKenzie, and Daniel Davenport were the four corners of a box – Sherry was the center. Sherry performed the kata Potsai (Bassai) empty-handed as the other four students demonstrated the kata utilizing weapons (bo, sai, tonfa and nunchaku – actually Okinawan farm tools). The kata was synchronized which made it more difficult. The weapons, along with Sherry Lynn, moved and twirled in unison. Also there to lend their support to the United States team were my wife, Barbara, Shihan George VanHorne, David Tollis, and Cindy Webster. As far as I know, our demonstration was the first time that Chito-ryu karate-do had been demonstrated before members of the Dai Nippon Butoku Kai and of the Imperial Family.

Sensei Patrick McCarthy, noted research historian and author of several books, demonstrating the meaning of a kata movement at a clinic in Northern Kentucky.

The United States Chito-ryu family, which I had founded along with my wife, was our family. I had been most fortunate to have attracted many excellent students over the years. Some came into the dojo and stayed, while others came for a short time and then left, never to return.

Little Debbie was by now ranked Shichi-dan by her kobudo sensei, Eisuke Akamine, head sensei of the Ryukyu Kobujutsu Hozon Shinko-kai. She had also achieved Go-dan in Chito-ryu karate and San-dan in Iaido. She retired from police work, and now taught kobudo clinics throughout the United States and Canada.

My youngest daughter, Sherry Lynn, was a schoolteacher and had garnered two Masters degrees. She had achieved a Yon-dan in karate and was the best kata person I had ever trained. Her husband, Dusty, had tragically died of a stroke at a young age but I was a proud Grandfather of two wonderful, beautiful grandchildren, Kira and Dylan, which she and Dusty had given me.

Barbara, my wife, was the main stay who had in truth put it all together. She had put up with me over the many years of our marriage. Barbara was a serious student of the martial arts, having achieved black belt status in both Kendo and

Pictured here are, left to right: Daniel Davenport; James Davenport; His Excellency Higashi Fushimi, Jigo (a Buddhist monk, Chairman of the Dai Nippon Butoku-kai and cousin of the Emperor) and his wife; the author.

Iaido, in addition to her high rank in Chito-ryu karate-do. I had indeed been a very blessed individual. Even with the heartbreak of my son Bill's death and my betrayal by a few of my trusted students, life was still great and had been good to me, if for no other reason than I had married one hell of a woman.

On October 9, 1999, the Yoseikan Honbu Dojo, also the Chito-kai headquarters, in Covington, had the honor of hosting a clinic for Dai Nippon Butoku Kai members from several eastern states and Canada. Hamada Hanshi was the principal guest instructor; Ken Tallack and I assisted. After the clinic, Shihan Tallack was promoted to Shichidan and granted the title of Kyoshi. I was promoted to Hachidan and granted the title of Hanshi. I had been a Shichidan and Kyoshi for twenty-seven years, three hundred sixty-four days. One day shy of twenty-eight years, I had at last been promoted. I felt that if Dr. Chitose had still been alive, he would have approved.

I had switched my stance and hand positions many times during my makiwara practice, as I reminisced about the past. I had used my elbows, my knees, and performed back fist strikes against the makiwara. My fist flashed forward striking the makiwara for the last time. My thoughts returned to the present – the eternal now. I stepped back from the makiwara and bowed to the post in front of me. Through the years, this post had become an important and unique part of my life. I turned and faced the picture of Dr. Tsuyoshi Chitose, which hung at the Kamiza of my dojo.

Pictured here in October 1999 are the author and Dr. Hiroyuki Tesshin Hamada, Hanshi - Chairman of the International Section of the famous Dai Nippon Butoku-kai.

After bowing slowly, I turned to leave. The familiar creak arose from the floor. "I am going to have to fix that someday," I thought as I strode across the floor. My mind once again drifted to years past and to Junko Arakawa's little Buddhist priest, Roshi Naganuma, who had told me almost fifty years ago:

"The way of seeking the truth, be it religion, or budo, is a way without end. Do not dwell upon the goal, but enjoy the path for true seeking is a travel to infinity, an endless quest."

As I left the training area, I thought, "He certainly was right."

Chapter 29

Looking into the Future

Never try to teach a pig to sing. It waste your time and annoys the pig

Paul Dixon

My endless quest continued into the twenty-first century with the arrival of the year 2000.

Our organization was growing slowly. Some problems arose but I didn't feel that it would become serious.

My left knee was starting to give some difficulty than it had here-to-fore in the past. It was totally weakened to a point it would collapse on me occasionally when I least expected it. I had a visitor at the dojo one afternoon, we were demonstrating various kicks. As I demonstrated a mawashi-geri with my right leg my left collapsed sending me crashing to the floor. Later that week I went to the Veterans Hospital on Vine St in Cincinnati, Ohio to have it examined. The Doctor informed me that both knees were worn out, that my left had to be replaced as soon as possible. January 3rd 2001, I checked into the hospital to have the knee replaced with a mechanical one. One week later my wife drove me home from the hospital. I had spoken to people who had this same operation, most said it was no big deal. I usually get well quickly, but my leg operation proved the exception. I expected to be laid up for approximately one month, however I was laid up for over four months. Three months were spent living and sleeping in a chair in my living room. As May arrived I once again was back in my bed and was able to get around with a cane. One month later I didn't need the cane and was back to work at the Boone County Sheriff's office and was able to return to the dojo to practice once again.

Left to Right: Fumio Demura, the author, George Anderson, Osama Ozawa, Julius Theiry in the mid-1980s.

The September 11th terrorist attacked in New York and the Pentagon shocked not only the nation but the majority of the world with its total disregard for civilian life. My first reaction was to cancel the United States Chito-kai national banquet and seminar that we had scheduled a year in advance for October, but after much thought we decided to go ahead with our plans. After all it was Dr. Chitose birthday party.

Our October 2001 national banquet and seminar, was also to celebrate my 50 years anniversary in martial arts. We held the event at the Drawbridge Motor Inn in Ft Mitchell Ky which is 10 minutes from the greater Cincinnati airport and 5 minutes from the

U.S. Chito-kai headquarters. We were required to guarantee them we would use 20 rooms. Both Barbara and decided to give it a try. If we came up short we would pay the difference. When the event was over we had used one hundred and twenty nine rooms, there were over 200 students who participated in the three hours of training. We broke them down into three divisions, white belt, green and Brown and Black. We assigned the participants to their training areas and rotated the instructors every hour. Hanshi Masami Tsuruoka was our guest Instructor. After the seminar we prepared for the banquet. At these banquets we discuss our future plans for the organization, award diplomas of Dan and have a guest speaker. During this event my wife Barbara introduced Sensei Christopher Johnston who is from Toronto Canada. They announced to the crowd of nearly three hundred that this book, my book, I had

Looking into the Future

Been working on for the past decade had been published. Sensei Johnston presented me the first copy for my 50 anniversary. After the banquet a group photo was taken of the ranking members of the United States Chito- kai and guests.

I had been informed by Hanshi Hamada, the director of the international division of the Dai Nippon Butoku-kai that I was expected to attend the World Butoku-sai which was scheduled to be held in Kyoto Japan during the end of April , early May 2002. My wife and I traveled to Japan with twenty one students and our two grandchildren.

The Butokuden, headquarters of the Dai Nippon Butoku Kai, was impressive. Just to enter into the building makes you stop and think of how many individuals have trained here, demonstrated, practiced and taught their arts. Doctor Jigoro Kano founder of Judo, professor Morihei Uyeshiba founder of Aikido, and Ginchin Funakoshi father of modern karate are just a few. The sword cuts in the many round columns attest to the vigor and seriousness of the training of previous years.

I was one of many who were given the opportunity to demonstrate before members of the Royal Family and members of the Hanshi board. The United States Chito-kai did various demonstrations before the board. International members from countries around the world demonstrated their techniques before the Hanshi board. . We were also treated to demonstrations by members of the Hanshi board and other top instructors from Japan. The size and success of the Butoku-sai can be attributed to one man, Dr. Hiroyuki Tesshin Hamada the director of the International division of the Dai Nippon Butoku -kai.

In 2003 the West Virginia shibu dojo of the U.S. Chito-kai once again held its annual seminar at Audra State Park, much like the seminars we held there in the eighties, The park is in the middle of no where, very rugged, with large rocks and trees. A beautiful stream flows rapidly as the water flows over small waterfall just above the swimming section. Thirty students attended the seminar which covered basics, kata and self defense. The first year back at Audra one of the ranking students stated, "Gee you know it has never rains when we train here".

The curse was cast, the hex was on and just as we started to train, a thunder storm settled above us and a very cold chilling rain descended upon us for the entire seminar, which lasted four hours, At times you could hardly see your hand in front of your face. Once the seminar was over the rain slackened to a slight on and off drizzle.

During the next few years, we continued to train, ask questions, seek additional knowledge, to improve ourselves. One thing became very apparent to me was that the method in which a person does karate is inherent upon several things. Most important among these are age, injuries, flexibility, and desire. but most important of all is their mental state. Some people are the aggressive type, other are more passive. The more aggressive are usually the same in kumite. The passive type on the other hand are usually counter punchers. Funakoshi once said " If you have a hundred students, you have a hundred styles in the dojo". As I grow older I felt closer to the Okinawan roots of Dr Chitose than the Japanese ones.

A pleasant surprise was when my daughter Sherry Kembre, Go-dan in Chito-ryu became more active in the U.S Chito-kai and the dojo. Her time is limited but she is always there when my wife and I need her. When she performs kata, its like watching Dr. Chitose's young son doing the technique.

In May 2003 I was once again invited to my hometown of Clarksburg West Virginia and giving the key to the city and a plaque was established at the city limits honoring me. This was arranged by three of my students form Clarksburg. Kevin Drummond, Michael Messinger and Jackie Cross.

In 2004 there were many memorable events that the U.S. Chito-kai participated in. We were visited by Masaru Inamoto, in which he taught various kata to some of our most senior students. Another outstanding event was our October

The author demonstrating a kata at The Dai Nippon Butoku-Kai in Kyoto, Japan (May 2002).

The author in Clarksburg WV, standing by one of the signs at the city limits. This location is one block from where he was born.

The author and Mark Chisenhall, 4th Dan, at Audra State Park (2003).

annual banquet and seminar. We had invited Hanshi Tsuruoka for our honored guest, however due to illness he was unable to attend. His son David Tsuruoka came in his place, It was very obvious he had the same passion for teaching as his father . His teachings was very clear and organized and was received very well by the students.

November 2004 we traveled to Norfolk, Virginia to participate in the Di-Nippon Butoku-sai. There were forty -four Chito-kai members participating. All Chito-kai members wore Hakayma's as did many others, Kendo, Iaido. Etc. They demonstrated precision as they strode before the Hanshi board. During the closing ceremony I was awarded a silver cup, "Sho" for outstanding demonstration. I was very happy for my students because in truth this was their trophy, not mine, they did the demonstrations, not me. In retrospect everyone there did great demonstrations and had good spirit. It is too bad all of them could have received the same cup. At the closing banquet I was inducted into the DI-Nippon International Hall of fame for Karate along with Hanshi George Stobbarts (Portugal) for Aikido, Hanshi o Baika (Taiwan/USA) for Kendo and Kyoshi Alan Tattersol (UK) for Jiujutsu.

As 2005 arrived we prepared for a new year of plans, travel, training and brotherhood. The United States Chito-kai suffered a minor setback. I had released one of my senior students due to attitude and a letter received from him which I fully accepted as a resignation letter. I also released another senior student for insubordination . With them four dojo's left our organization, they will be missed but in time they will be replaced. I do wish them well.

March 15th 2005, I celebrated my 70th birthday, A party was held at my honbu dojo by my family and students. Many senior students who have been with me thirty or forty years were in attendance. On June 6th, my wife and I celebrated our 50th wedding anniversery a party was hosted by our two daughters, Sherry Kembre and Devorah Herbst. At the age of seventy I can look back and see many mistakes I have made, not only in karate but in everyday life. As a karate teacher it is my duty to help my students make fewer mistakes than I did, not only in karate but in their everyday lives. Hirokazu Kanazawa a shotokan stylist, one of the leading teachers in the world once said, "I never realized there were two types of shuto blocks, the snapping one and the power block." Without a doubt Kanazawa sensei is one of the best teachers in the world. For every surprise he receives, I receive several. I am still learning.

What I have learned during the past fifty years of my Endless Quest?

a. Karate's biggest benefit isn't about fighting but how to improve your health, physically mentally and spiritually, and become a better human being.

b. That karate-do is always superior to Karate-dough.

c. That it is always easy to find imperfections in your teacher's technique if you look close enough.

d. That no karate teacher is perfect - but then no student is perfect either.

e. To speak politely and with courtesy to everyone regardless of their rank and position.

f. To be humble and to always keep a (shoshin) beginners mind throughout your life.

The author in 1967, when Chitose visited the U.S.

g. To be careful when selecting a karate teacher, then remain with him or her for life, regardless of events, or problems. This is loyalty and without it there is no Karate-do, only karate-jitsu.

h. Say nothing derogatory about anyone at any time, it belittles you, not them.

i. What is truth to one may be false to another. Each person sees life differently.

j. Never quit your training and seeking after the truth. This is the secret of the endless quest.

I have attempted to teach each of my students to the very best of my ability. The quest is never ending, There is no end to the "Endless Quest" until your final day.

Epilogue

Karate-do is not a means to an end. It is both the means and the end.

I hope that you have enjoyed "The Endless Quest." While the story of "The Endless Quest" is my story, there are many stories almost exactly like it. Countless Americans served in the Far East as servicemen. Many of them trained in various martial arts and brought these arts to the United States. Japanese martial arts such as Karate, Judo, Aikido and Kendo all became rooted here during the 1950s and 1960s.

The author during the summer of 2000.

All of these former servicemen have similar stories to tell of their own "Endless Quest." Many of these older American martial artists are now starting to pass away and are not leaving records or manuscripts of their training in Japan, Okinawa and America. I hope to encourage many of the remaining older martial artists to record their histories as pioneers of American budo. They, their training and their stories are bridges to the past. Many of these pioneers were taught by many old Oriental Senseis who were born in the 1800s, and who have become legends.

If any older Sensei is reading this book, I wish to remind you that you are responsible for the success of martial arts in America. You are the bridge between the traditional martial arts of the past and the present. My students and your students will remain to carry on the traditional martial arts legacy well into the twenty-first century and long after we are gone. We, as their sensei, should leave them with good techniques and an appreciation of their martial arts heritage. As our students continue spreading the traditional martial arts into the next millennium, let them do so with an appreciation of the history of their art. Give them this historical knowledge as they too continue on their own endless quests.

William J. Dometrich

About the Author

Originally from the state of West Virginia, William Dometrich has resided in Kentucky for the past forty-five years. He began his martial arts training as a young seventeen-year-old paratrooper, stationed with the Eleventh Airborne Division at Fort Campbell, Kentucky. He had his first karate lessons from a United States Marine who had been stationed on Okinawa. Volunteering for overseas duty in the Far East he arrived in Japan where he began to seek out a karate teacher. Luck with was with him as he eventually became a student of Doctor Tsuyoshi Chitose, the grandson of Sokon "Bushi" Matsumura, who is now recognized as one of the greatest twentieth century karate masters of the Japanese Empire. Dometrich remained with Chitose Sensei right up until the good Doctor's death in June of 1984. While stationed in Japan, Dometrich also became acquainted with the teachings of Zen Buddhism and returned home as a Buddhist.

He started college at Fairmont State Teachers' College in Fairmont, West Virginia during 1955 and was married one semester later. Moving to the greater Cincinnati, Ohio, area was an employment move, however after a few years in the business world he decided that it wasn't his cup of tea. He joined the Covington, Kentucky, Police Department during February 1964. While at the Department he served as a patrolman, motorcycle cop, patrol sergeant, patrol lieutenant, patrol bureau commander, services bureau commander, Chief of Detectives and, finally, as the Assistant Chief of Police. During this time he continued to study police science at both Eastern Kentucky University and the University of Kentucky. Eventually he attended and graduated from the prestigious F.B.I. Academy at Quantico, Virginia. While working as a police officer, he founded the United States Chito-ryu Karate Federation at the urging of his teacher, Doctor Tsuyoshi Chitose.

He re-enlisted into the United States Army reserves when he was forty-five years of age. He attended the U. S. Army's 4th ITAS (Intelligence Training Area School) at Fort McCoy, Wisconsin and became a counter intelligence agent. Upon his retirement from police service, he volunteered for active duty with the army and became a member of the 11th Special Forces Detachment, 389th Military Intelligence Detachment. Returning to the 4th ITAS he now trained as an intelligence analyst. Becoming a member of the 389th meant that he would have to start parachuting again, which he did (after 30 years) at the age of fifty. He has served in both Asia and Europe as a member of the Army. Certain areas of his duties were classified above Top Secret.

Upon retiring from the military he became a Deputy Sheriff in Boone County, Kentucky where he continues to work today. In his spare time he devotes his life to the U. S. Chito-ryu Karate Federation, and to traditional karate training and research. Now ranked a Hachidan, Hanshi, by the famed Dai Nippon Butoku-kai, Dometrich and his wife Barbara reside in a log Cabin in the woods of Northern Kentucky, approximately thirty miles south of Cincinnati, Ohio.

www.ingramcontent.com/pod-product-compliance
Lightning Source LLC
Chambersburg PA
CBHW071557080526
44588CB00010B/933